IMAGES
of America

AROUND SOUTH HILL

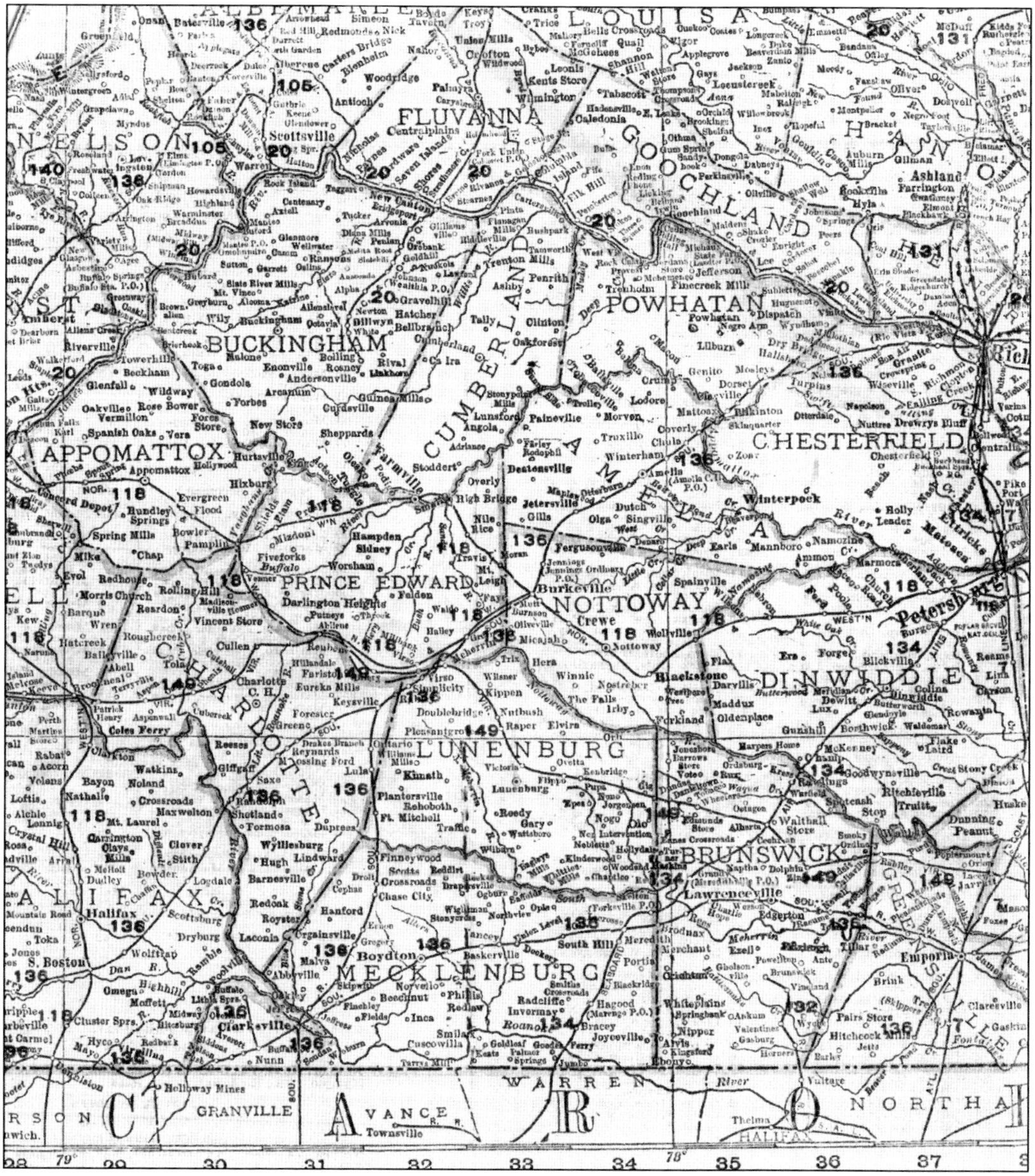

This is a 1916 railroad map cutout section of Mecklenburg County, Virginia. The broken line down the center illustrates the western boundary of the territory (right of the line) that is covered in this text. This imaginary line was established in the 1760s. Those living east of the line would serve in the coastal 22nd Virginia Militia, and those to the west would serve in the mountain 98th Virginia Militia. (William C. Gregory.)

On the Cover: In the 1930s, just north of South Hill in a curve on U.S. Route 1, the property in the curve became home to the Pine Tree Trailer Camp Drive-In. This general store also served bar-style beer on tap and had a slot machine. The billboard to the right advertises the Raleigh Hotel 85 miles away. Later, U.S. Route 1 went to the left side of the store. In 1940, the store was operated by Harvey J. Newton, who soon left to return to farming. (Virginia Newton Minnich.)

IMAGES
of America

AROUND SOUTH HILL

John Caknipe Jr.

ARCADIA
PUBLISHING

ISBN 978-0-7385-8713-4

Published by Arcadia Publishing
Charleston, South Carolina

Printed in the United States of America

Library of Congress Control Number: 2010933314

For all general information, please contact Arcadia Publishing:
Telephone 843-853-2070
Fax 843-853-0044
E-mail sales@arcadiapublishing.com
For customer service and orders:
Toll-Free 1-888-313-2665

Visit us on the Internet at www.arcadiapublishing.com

Contents

ACKNOWLEDGMENTS

A great many people have helped with the history, stories, and photograph collections for this book. Two years ago, William Gregory sent me his collection, and Frank Malone of the South Hill Chamber of Commerce and museums provided me a copy of their collection of photographs from the recent 100th anniversary celebration. The unique family collections of Beth Kinley Dunn, Roy and John Wootton, Waller Randolph Hite's great-grandfather Waller Taylor Bracey, Dwight L. Moody Jr., Larrie Matthews and Rick Hendrick of Hendrick Motorsports, Jimmy Thompson, and Tommy and Judy Stanley all added special dimensions to each chapter. Photographs by R. L. Harris Sr., Peter M. Axson Jr., Joe Noah of Lakeside Flight, Parker Oil Company, Inc., and the U.S. Army Corps of Engineers helped to put a unique perspective on the communities. Collections of Virginia Dare Wright, Jennifer Reamey, Ellen Thompson of Community Memorial Health Center, Ida Mae Callahan, Virginia Newton Minnich, John Edward Goode Taylor, and St. Andrews Church were invaluable for rounding out several of the stories. Many others provided photographs and are referenced in the text, but a special thank you goes to the Mecklenburg County Clerk's office and staff, Frank Nanny Jr., South Side Regional Libraries of Boydton and South Hill, Peeble's corporate office, and CWO3 (Ret., U.S. Army) Ronnie Bugg for their contributions, histories, and research.

I want to thank Nick Elmes of the *South Hill Enterprise* for his support and encouragement and to Mrs. Anne Brulatour Sr., along with other members of the Rose family and Rosemont farm (orchard), vineyard, and winery for their support, history, and encouragement.

To Arcadia Publishing for the support and opportunity to publish this volume, thank you. And lastly, to my unyielding supporter, encourager, photographer, scanner, printer, motivator, critic, and love of my life, my wife, Betty McKinney Caknipe, thanks!

The following are abbreviated in the courtesy lines:

Betty McKinney Caknipe (BMC)
U.S. Army Corps of Engineers (COE)
Memory of Clara and "Spot" Thompson (CST)
John Caknipe Jr. (JC)
Memory of Peter M. Axson Jr. (PMA)
South Hill Chamber of Commerce (SHC)
South Hill Museums: doll, railroad, tobacco farm life, and wildlife (SHM)
Tommy and Judy Stanley (TJS)
William C. Gregory (WCG)
Memory of Waller Taylor Bracey by great-grandson Waller Randolph Hite (WRH)

INTRODUCTION

In 1723, South Central Virginia was surveyed by Col. William Byrd, who patented several thousand acres surrounding the Bluestone Creek/Roanoke River area and built Bluestone Castle. In 1745, Lunenburg County was formed, and a survey crew arrived to establish a central location for a county courthouse. They pinpointed an area, the Piedmont Plateau, which extended from present-day Brunswick County to Charlotte County. This plateau serves as a natural watershed. The Meherrin River to the north is 225 feet, and the Roanoke River to the south is 200 feet lower than the ridge. Along the ridge were two high points; Walkers Mountain, the highest, (near present-day South Hill) was too close to Brunswick County for a courthouse. To the west was Burwell's Quarters (present-day Fairview). The latter site was selected, and a courthouse was built. By 1765, the county had grown, but it was such an expansive area that the governor ordered it be divided into three counties—Lunenburg, Mecklenburg, and Charlotte.

With land patents from the governor for the eastern half of the county and land grants from the King of England for the western part, settlements were encouraged, especially along the rivers to establish a ferry and navigation system. This system would provide furs and produce to the Commonwealth and to England. In the 1780s, there were three established communities in Mecklenburg County—St. Tammany on the Roanoke River, Burwells' Quarters on the Meherrin River, and Mecklenburg Courthouse, also near the Roanoke River. The low grounds along the waterways served as rich farmland with water for mills, stills, and irrigation. It was also discovered that along these creeks and rivers the former inhabitants had been mining gold, silver, and copper, and these resources were still abundant.

In 1792, St. Tammany (formerly Blanton's Ferry on the Roanoke River) was chartered by the Virginia General Assembly as the first town in Mecklenburg County. The ferry was sold many times, and prominent owners included Samuel Hopkins and William Hendrick. In 1793, a post office was established with the first postmaster in the county being John C. Courtney, who was not appointed until October 1795. In 1900, the Richmond-Petersburg and Carolina Railway established a station to include mail delivery about a mile shy of St. Tammany. They named the community Bracey in July 1900. Although a parcel of land was platted for Bracey, it was never incorporated.

In the southwest corner of eastern Mecklenburg County, below the Roanoke River on the North Carolina state line, was another early community—Palmer Springs. In the 1790s, Amasa Palmer was promoting the medicinal value of the springs, while at the same time Buffalo Springs in the western part of the county was being promoted. Without the resort development of Palmer Springs, little success was to be had. Following the Revolutionary War, Col. Samuel Hopkins (brother to Dr. John Hopkins of Maryland) received a tract of land in Palmer Springs. He was in a land venture surveying North Carolina and was offered an opportunity to survey the new territory of Kentucky, which he accepted. He became a major general in the U.S. Army and the namesake for Hopkins County and Hopkinsville, Kentucky. The Hopkins grant was next to a grant given to the family of Fields Jefferson around 1760.

Dr. John Drake became a surgeon in the North Carolina infantry during the Civil War. After the war, he returned to his farm in Palmer Springs. When his children went off to college, he and his wife moved to Clarksville in 1882 and began a pharmacy with the slogan "Dr. Drake—Shake and Take" on all his prescription bottles. Dr. Drake was also involved with the Palmer Springs Resort (lodge), which was attended by John Philip Sousa around 1905. Also of Palmer Springs fame was the previously mentioned William Hendrick. He was the father of numerous Hendrick descendants, including present-day Rick Hendrick (of Palmer Springs), member of the eight-time NASCAR Sprint Cup Series championship team.

On September 16, 1811, Daniel Nolley of Greenville County left his son Rev. James Nolley a 2-acre parcel in South Hill to establish a community center—South Hill Academy (the first in the county). Reverend Nolley was a noted East Coast thoroughbred racehorse breeder. He established a breeding farm near Walker's Mountain for his stud named Dragoon, foaled in 1802 of "Old Soldier" Lee's Mark Anthony. In April 1814, Reverend Nolley established a post office, and his petition was granted as postmaster. In 1817, the community center on his breeding farm became a meetinghouse and house of worship. On August 1, 1817, he and Elizabeth Moore were married there. The community was originally located just south of Walkers Mountain near the Meherrin River. With the completion of the Boydton to Petersburg Plank Toll Road in 1852, the community moved. Three miles put it closer to the commerce route at a point referred to as Ridgefork, or Binford's Fork, at the intersection of High Bridge Road (Chaptico Road) and the new toll road. After the Civil War, the old post office closed in 1866. It reopened in July 1867 in the new South Hill, which now consisted of a single building hosting a tavern, post office, and ordinary.

With the arrival of the Atlantic and Danville Railroad in 1889, South Hill moved again. Along the plank road, about a mile south (near the community of Flat Creek), a 55-acre parcel from the estate of W. W. Harris was platted and surveyed by William Adkins. It was laid out in a circular fashion modeled after Washington, D.C., but with two Main Streets, one on each side of the railroad. The Commonwealth of Virginia granted a charter on February 16, 1901, and South Hill became a town. That same year, two tobacco warehouses were built, along with the Bank of South Hill, and the nearby community of LaCrosse was also chartered. By 1903, South Hill was advertising 13 businesses. In 1904, South Hill had the first annexation, Flat Creek, to include the lands of S. J. Bugg, R. E. Yancey, and D. B. Bell (and their stores), which included the cemetery and the soon-to-be new public school.

Since its beginnings, South Hill has positioned itself as the town of highways. First were the rivers for the batteaux, then the Boydton Plank Toll Road for wagons and horses. This was followed by the railroad with numerous passenger trains. For the automobiles came the National Byway Route 31, U.S. Route 1, U.S. Route 58, and U.S. Interstate I-85. The following photographs are a compilation of almost two years of research and thousands of hours of interviews. This volume presents a photojournalistic overview of an era that is rapidly fading from the memories and graphic collections of our ancestors. Most of South Hill has been rebuilt numerous times, as history shows that throughout every decade the early frame buildings burned. Even after the arrival of U.S. Route 1 in 1927 and the construction of predominantly brick buildings, South Hill still had its trouble with fires, but continues to be rebuilt in its prosperity.

One

The Early Beginnings

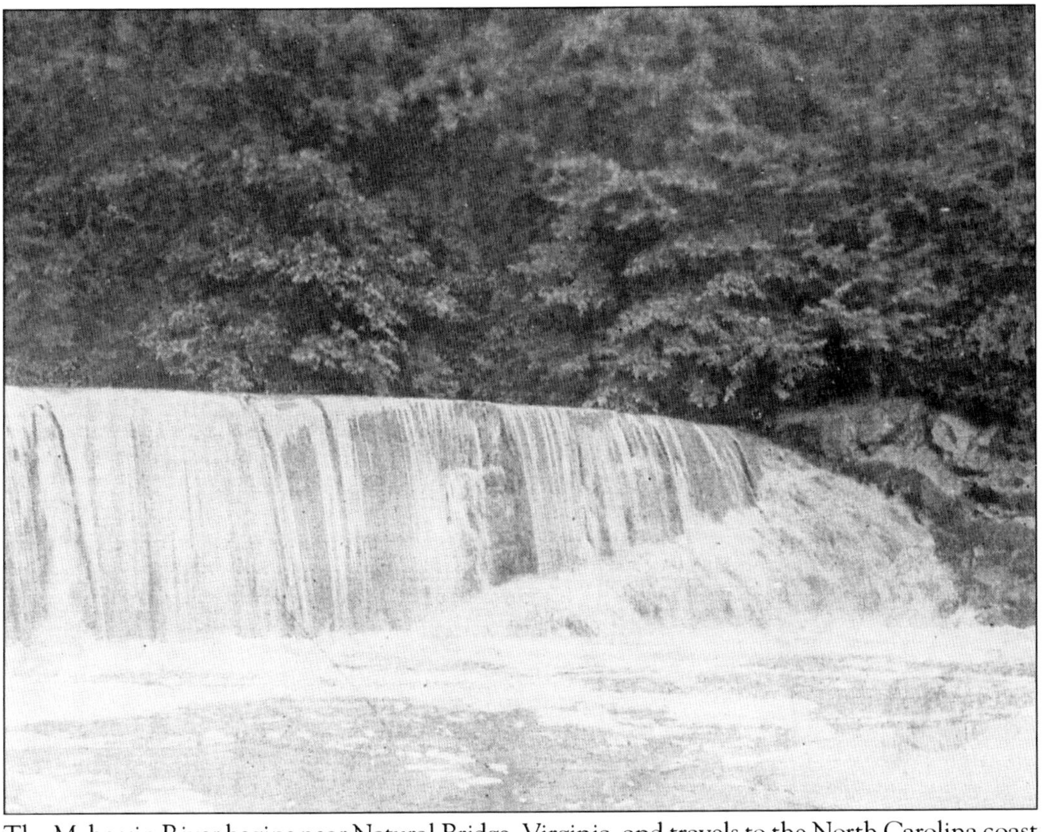

The Meherrin River begins near Natural Bridge, Virginia, and travels to the North Carolina coast at the northern tip of the Albemarle Sound—used for commerce of batteaux for trading goods, supplies, and slaves in exchange for furs, tobacco, cotton, peanuts, wheat, and corn in the 18th century. Much smaller than the Roanoke River, traveling the Meherrin was a short season, and it was used primarily for irrigation, fishing, and water supply for mills and stills. (WCG.)

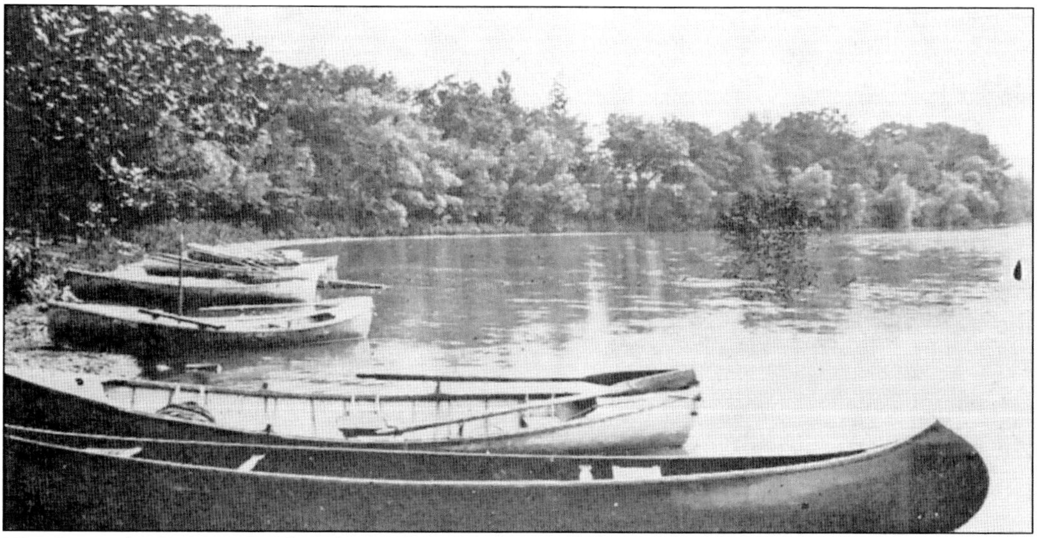

The Roanoke River stretches from the Roanoke Valley in Virginia to the southern tip of the Albemarle Sound. It was used beginning in the 17th century for trade and, by 1830, had a steamship line, moving seasonally, that traveled up and down the river. Ports were established to create trade centers all along the river from Roanoke Rapids, North Carolina, to Brookneal, Virginia, and at Clarksville, Virginia, the ships could cross over into the Dan River and proceed on to Danville, Virginia. (TJS.)

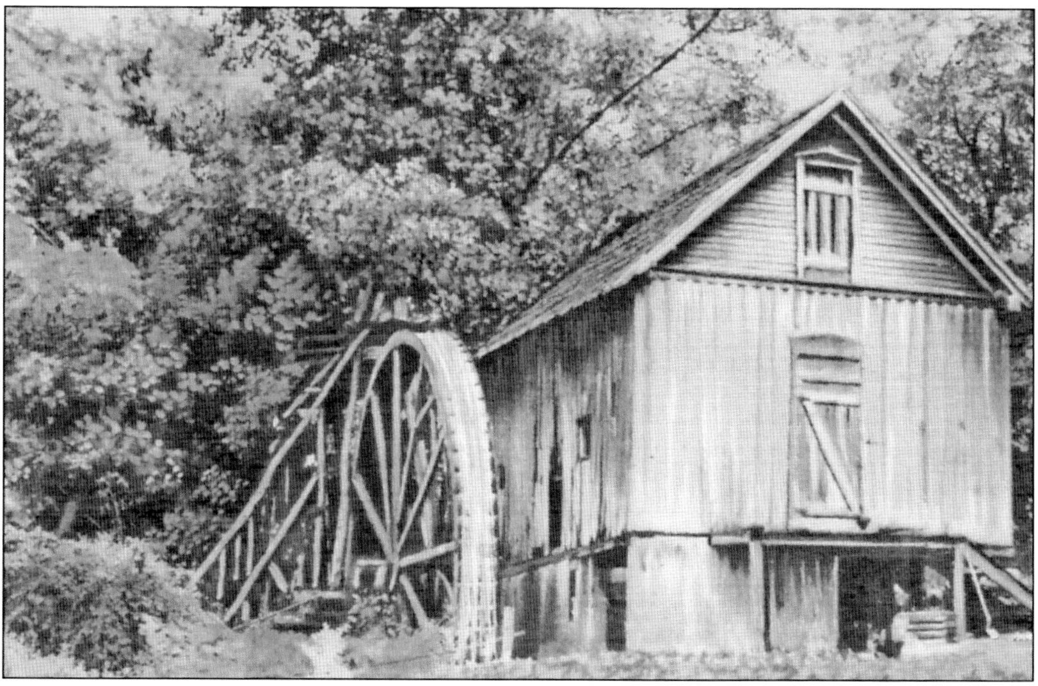

Gristmills dotted the county's waterways—rivers and creeks. A necessity for plantation and community, the mill was a major production plant of flour, feed, and sawmill operations. A miller always wanted a neighbor to be an apprenticed wheelwright or blacksmith for maintenance, repairs, and expansion. Payment was a percentage of the product produced, which would be used for barter. (TJS.)

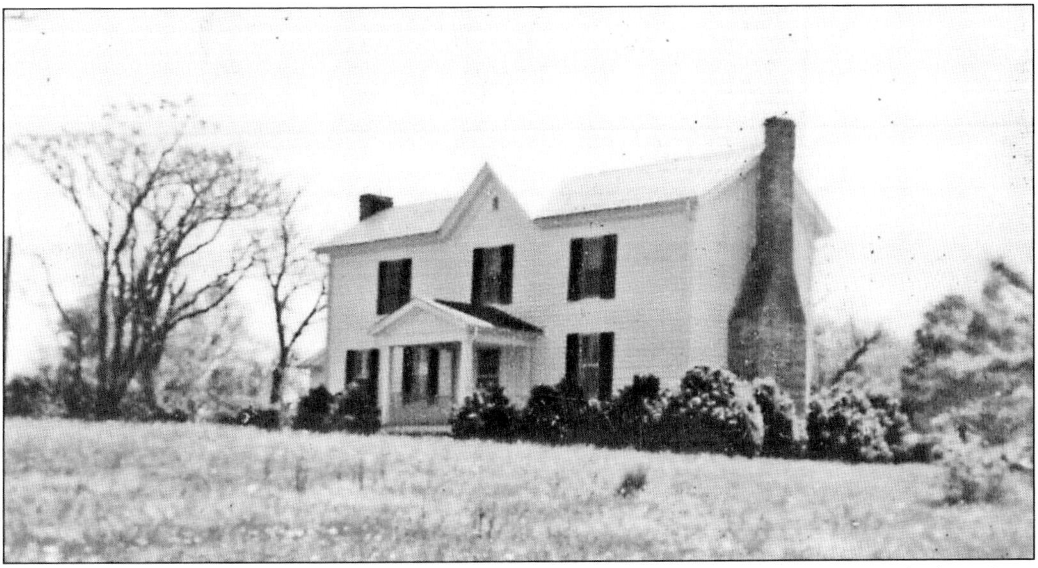

China Grove was the first known plantation established along the Roanoke River before 1700. With a new governor in office, Samuel Bugg of New Kent County began to patent lands along the Roanoke and even traded with the local Native Americans in the 1680s and 1690s. The central part of this structure is believed to have been completed before 1700 by Bugg. The home burned in 1975. (CWO3 Ronnie Bugg.)

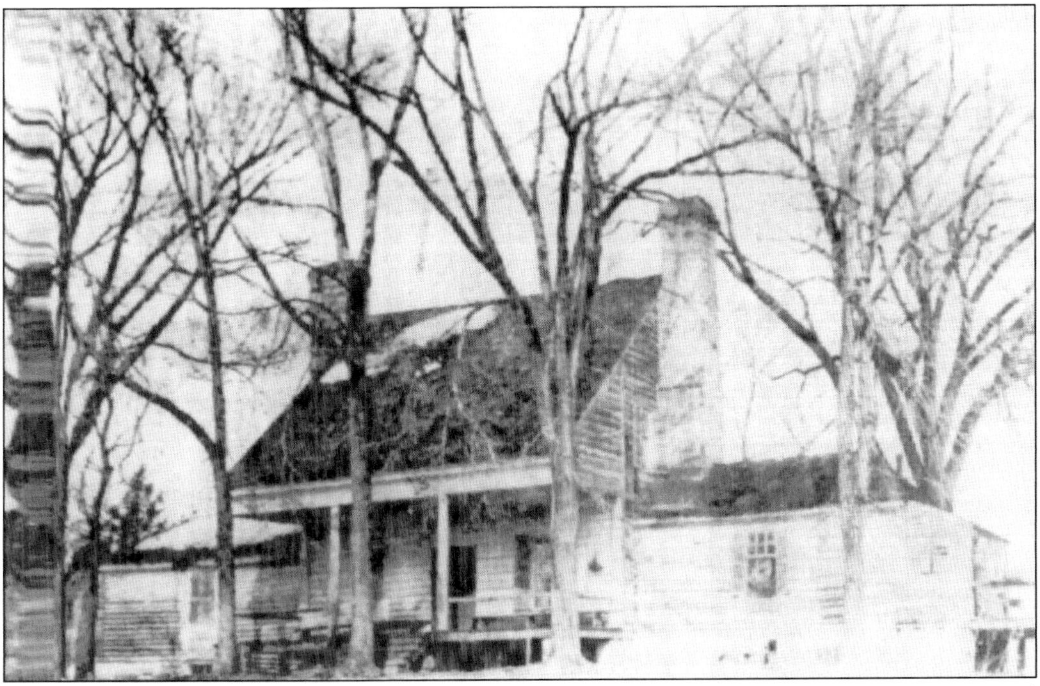

About a mile downstream, Samuel Bugg III built his home around 1771 on a 400-acre parcel named Elm Hill. In 1781, he was advertising the home for sale in a Williamsburg paper. In this ad, he included a lengthy description of the amenities and orchards, and described the house as "newly remodeled." It was purchased by Sir Peyton Skipwith. Archeologists have found ruins on the grounds of a 16th-century town being located along the river. (Clarksville Regional Museum.)

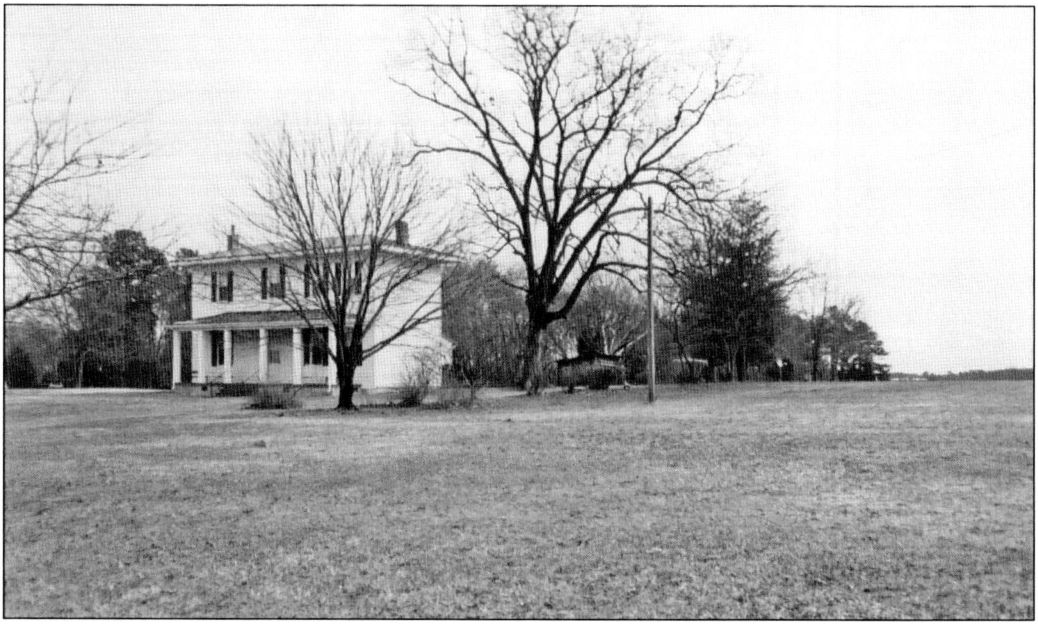

Dr. V. H. Hicks came to the area around 1810 and built this home between the Roanoke and Meherrin Rivers. In 1867, he became ill and was cared for by Dr. Latinius I. Rose in his home/hospital for 13 days before he died. The home and property had been purchased in 1844 by Walter Hite, who later divided it among his children. One daughter married a Butterworth who operated a thriving dairy for many years in this area, which became known as Flat Creek. (Patsy Boswell.)

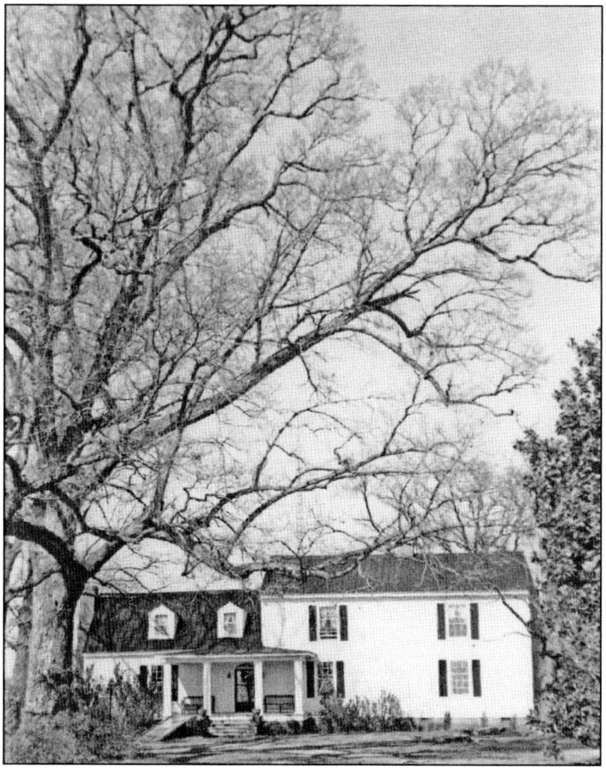

Around 1780, the Thomas family built their home near Black's Ferry, Joyceville. In 1850, the farm was purchased by Dr. William F. Pennington. Completing a new and larger home nearby on Poplar Creek, he sold the farm to Dr. Latinius Rose in 1858, and it is now known as Rosemont. It served as a hospital during the Civil War. The farm is still in operation and in the Rose family today and hosts Rosemont Winery. (Anne S. Brulatour, fifth mistress of Rosemont.)

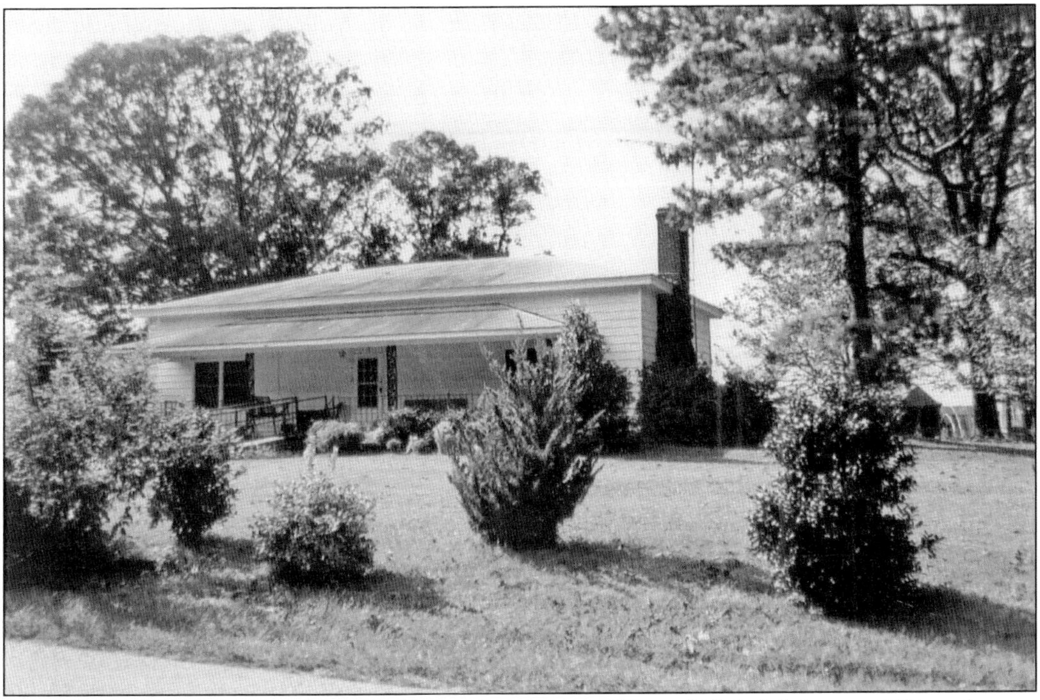

Dr. Latinius Rose graduated from Jefferson Medical College of Philadelphia in 1850 and came to Mecklenburg County as a school headmaster for the six Gale children in June. He moved on to North Carolina and began a medical practice and married his partner's sister, Portia McKoy, in 1853. With a malaria outbreak, he moved his family back to Mecklenburg County. A devout man of religion and education, he immediately began collecting funds for a church and school, completed in 1867. He was a leader of the Rehobeth Church and School for many years. (JC.)

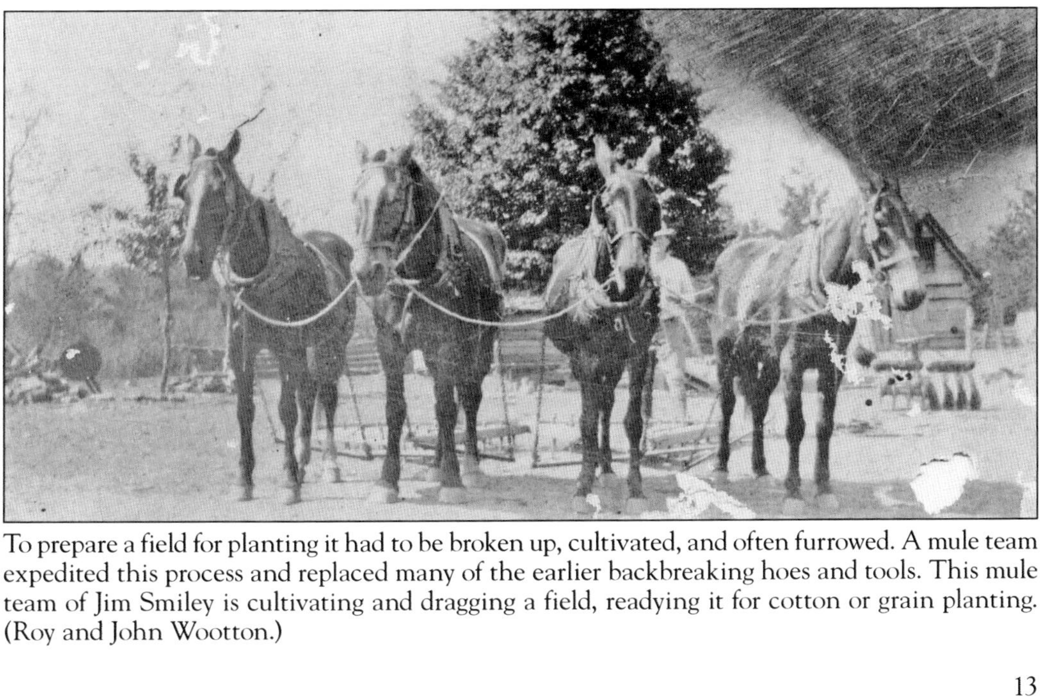

To prepare a field for planting it had to be broken up, cultivated, and often furrowed. A mule team expedited this process and replaced many of the earlier backbreaking hoes and tools. This mule team of Jim Smiley is cultivating and dragging a field, readying it for cotton or grain planting. (Roy and John Wootton.)

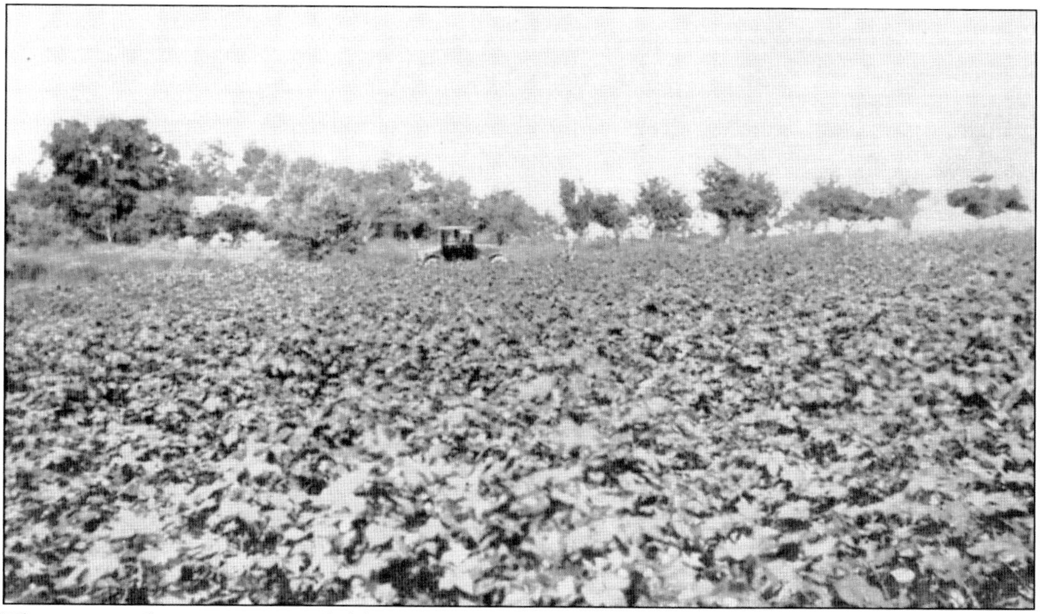

This is a good mature cotton field readying to blossom. Once the blooms dry, a cotton ball will form, surrounded by a hard, crusted, jagged shell with a seed in the center. The ball must be removed from the shell (picking) and the seed removed (ginning) before being processed into thread. Note the Model A in the distance. (TJS.)

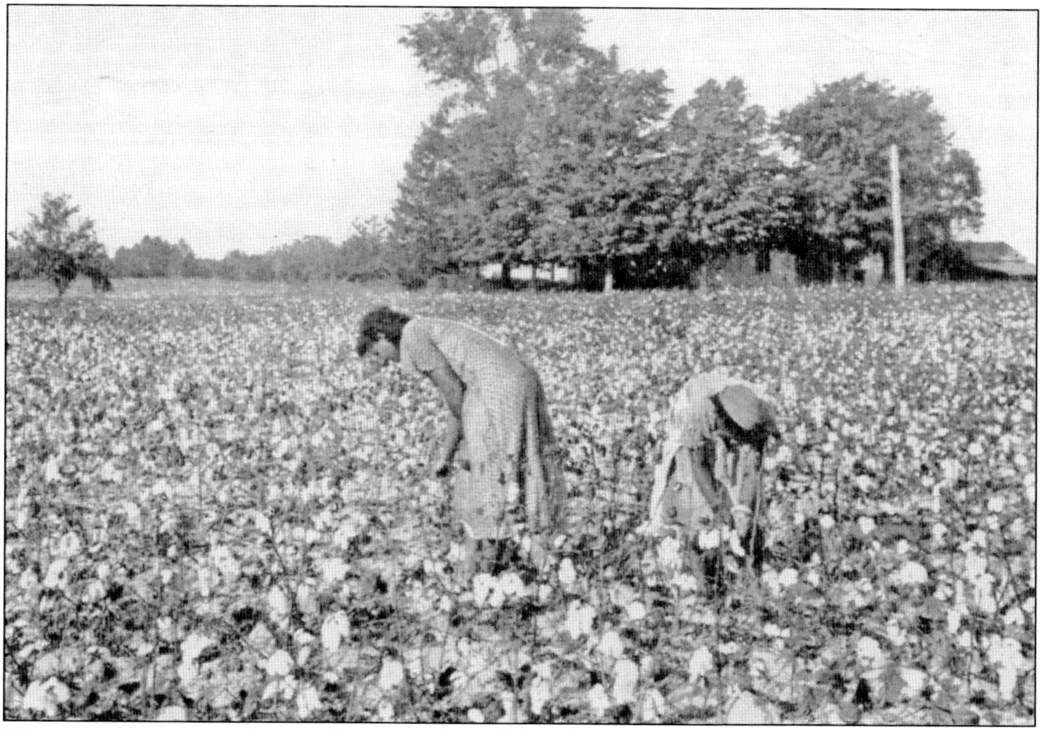

Harvesting cotton is a long, arduous, and painful task, but it was necessary as a staple crop. The fiber was used to make most clothing, fabric, bedding, and linens. It was highly prized in all of Europe and usually sold for a high price. (TJS.)

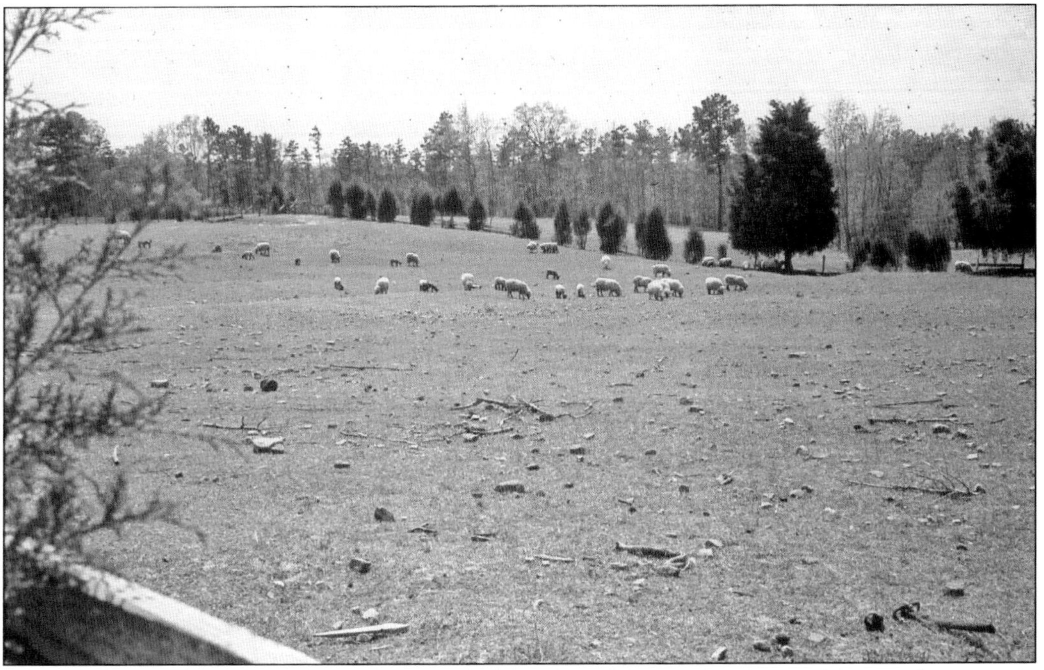

The second-most-prized material was that of sheep's wool for cooler-climate fabric and extremely durable clothing. Many farms had animals for food, toil, and recreation. Sheep provided all three, plus the wool for thread and export. An easy animal to maintain, even small farms would have a flock to provide for the families' needs and as a complement to other operations. (PMA.)

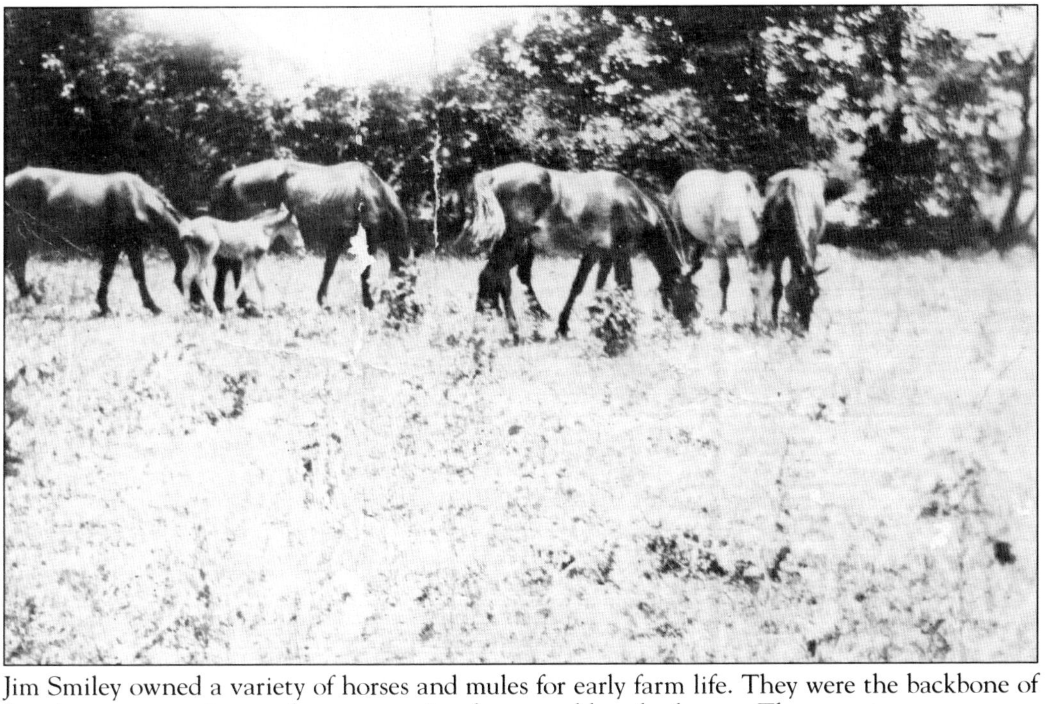

Jim Smiley owned a variety of horses and mules for early farm life. They were the backbone of farming, construction, and transportation for several hundred years. They continue to serve as animals for recreation, leisure, therapy, and gaming. (Roy and John Wootton.)

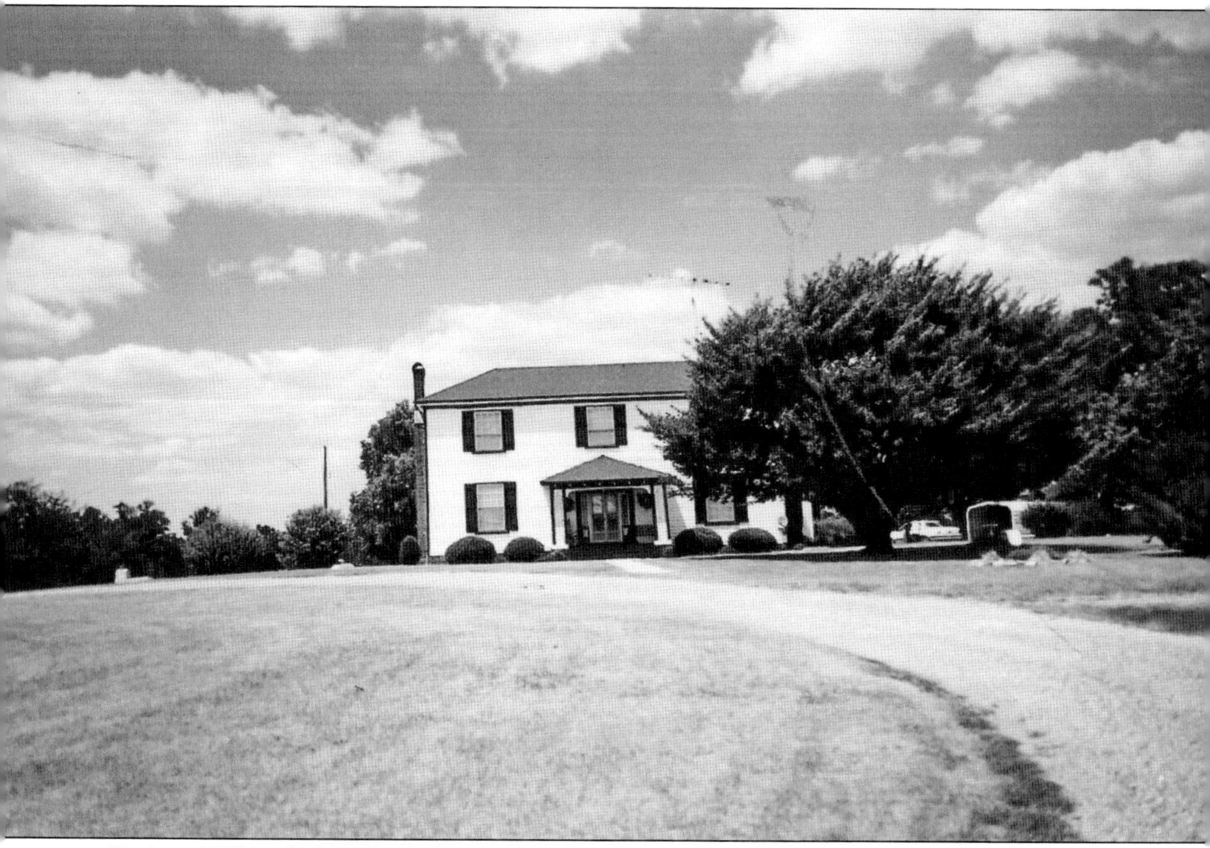

Built in 1787 by Col. William Green, there was a chamber (bedroom) built on all four sides of the house, which was situated on a tract of 1,447 acres. Each chamber had two beds and a fireplace. It served as an ordinary, tavern, stage wayside, and in 1815, a post office was established. Colonel Green continued adding parcels to a point where, by 1820, he owned nearly 6,000 acres. (Mildred A. Callahan Jones.)

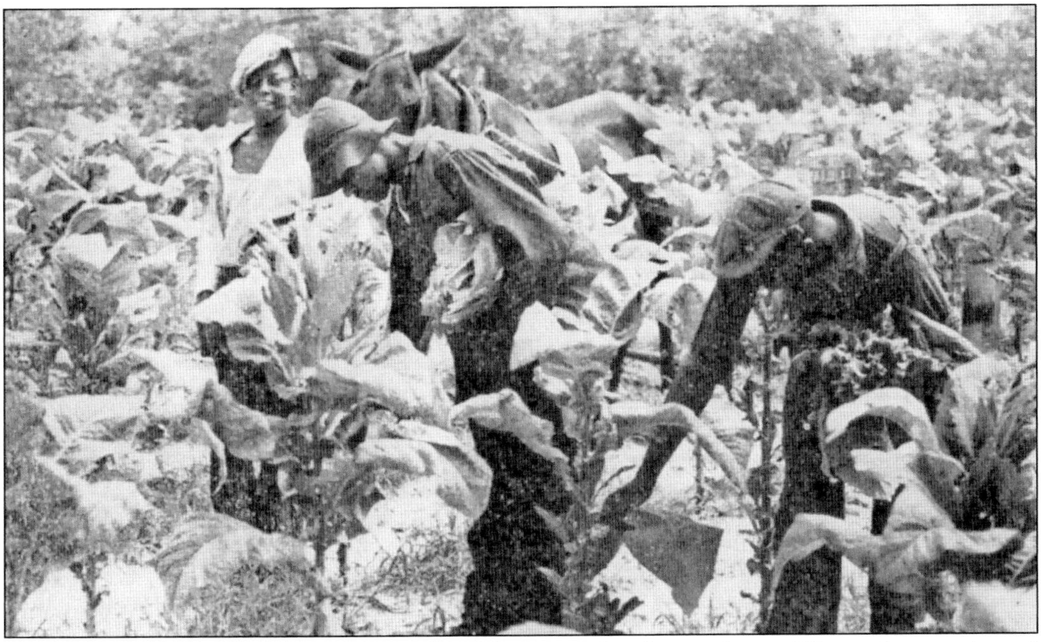

The primary Virginia crop/export since the 17th century has been tobacco. The seeds were planted in covered plant beds to protect them from the frost. About 6 inches tall, they were transplanted into a furrowed field. At maturity, the leaves turned from green to yellow and were harvested (picked) three or four at a time, requiring six to seven pickings per stalk. The leaves were loaded into a sled, taken to a barn, and strung onto a stick. (TJS.)

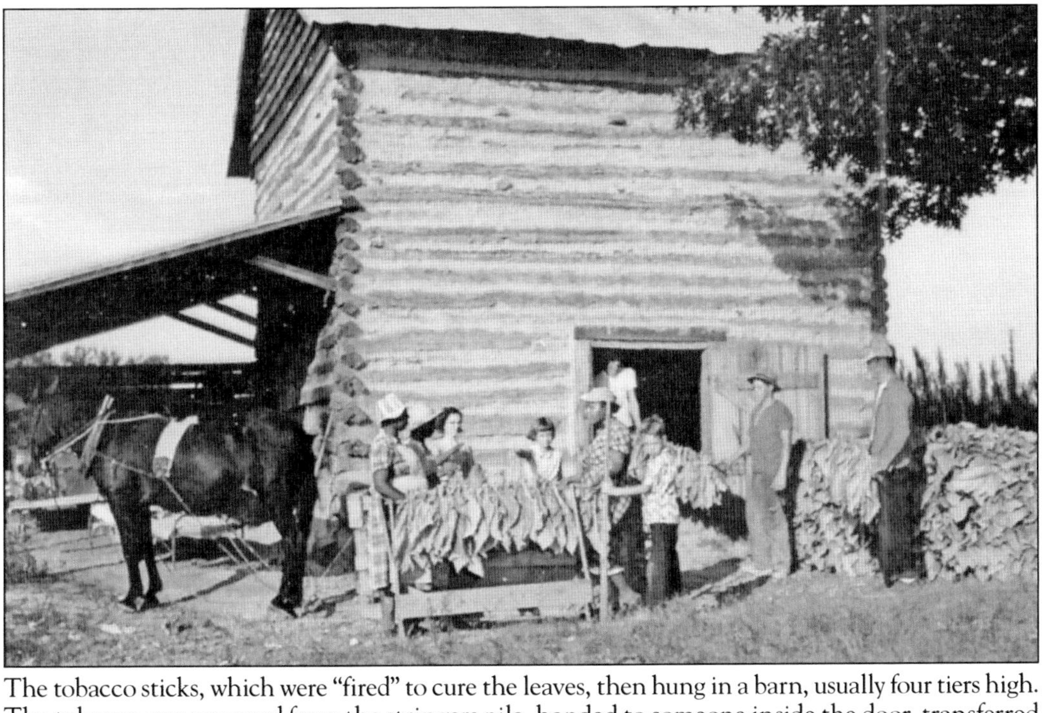

The tobacco sticks, which were "fired" to cure the leaves, then hung in a barn, usually four tiers high. The tobacco was removed from the stringers pile, handed to someone inside the door, transferred up to a catcher, and then passed farther up to a hanger. It was a labor-intensive process. (TJS.)

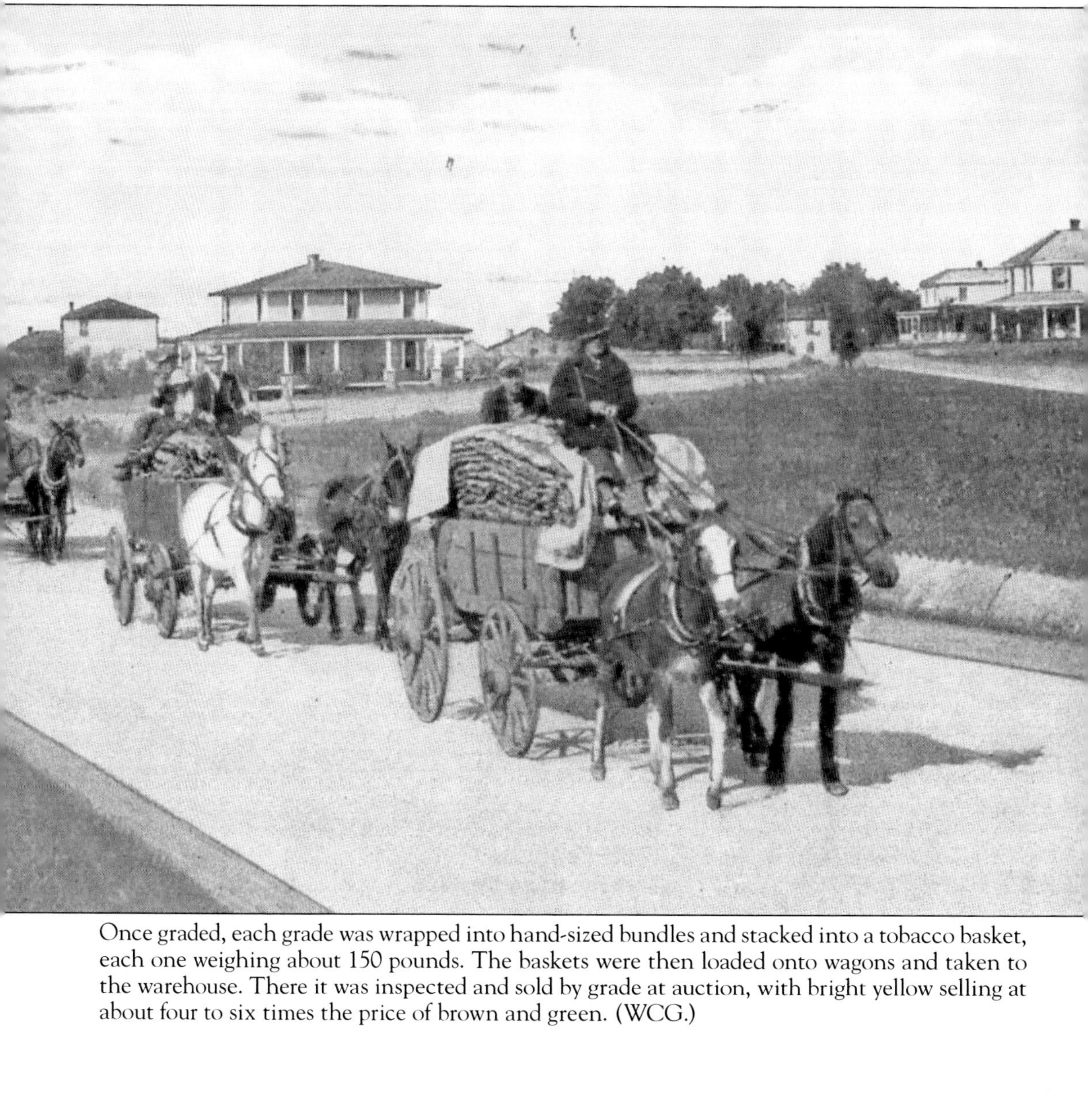

Once graded, each grade was wrapped into hand-sized bundles and stacked into a tobacco basket, each one weighing about 150 pounds. The baskets were then loaded onto wagons and taken to the warehouse. There it was inspected and sold by grade at auction, with bright yellow selling at about four to six times the price of brown and green. (WCG.)

Stills for processing corn, grains, and fruits were found on most farms for preserving and for a cash crop. Following the Civil War, the United States imposed a $1-per-gallon tax on distilled products. By 1900, most towns and some counties required a license, but in 1916, Virginia began Prohibition (four years before the United States). Moonshining, though illegal, became a new form of employment. In this 1930s photograph, Sheriff Will Callahan, Aubrey Pentecrest, and Tom B. Nelson are seizing a bootleg still from Walter Redd. (Michael Harris.)

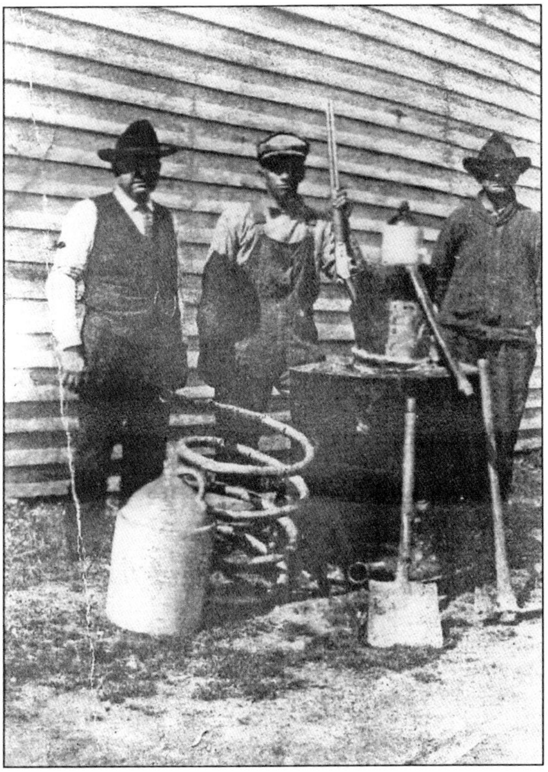

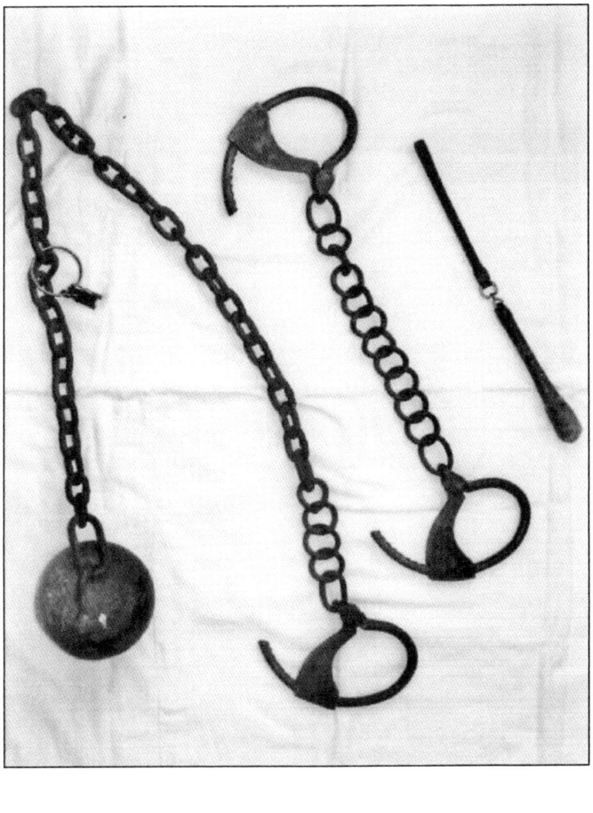

Incorporated in 1901, South Hill did not have a jail until 1952. If a prisoner had to spend the night, he would be attached to a ball and chain, placed in handcuffs, and locked inside the police station. This gear was also used for years in transporting prisoners for trial and lockup at the county courthouse by local sheriffs and other law enforcement officers. (Henry H. Gregory Jr.)

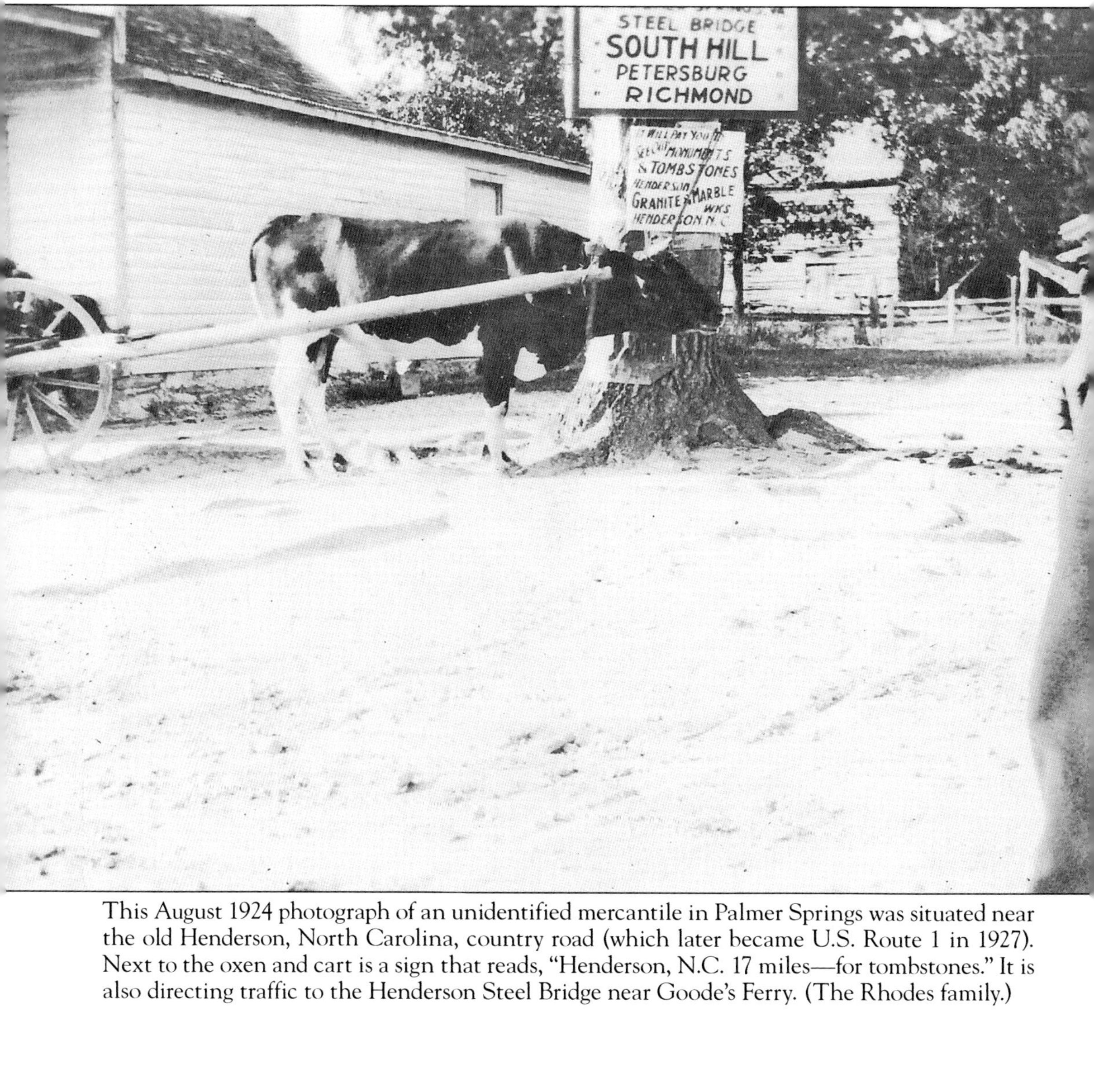

This August 1924 photograph of an unidentified mercantile in Palmer Springs was situated near the old Henderson, North Carolina, country road (which later became U.S. Route 1 in 1927). Next to the oxen and cart is a sign that reads, "Henderson, N.C. 17 miles—for tombstones." It is also directing traffic to the Henderson Steel Bridge near Goode's Ferry. (The Rhodes family.)

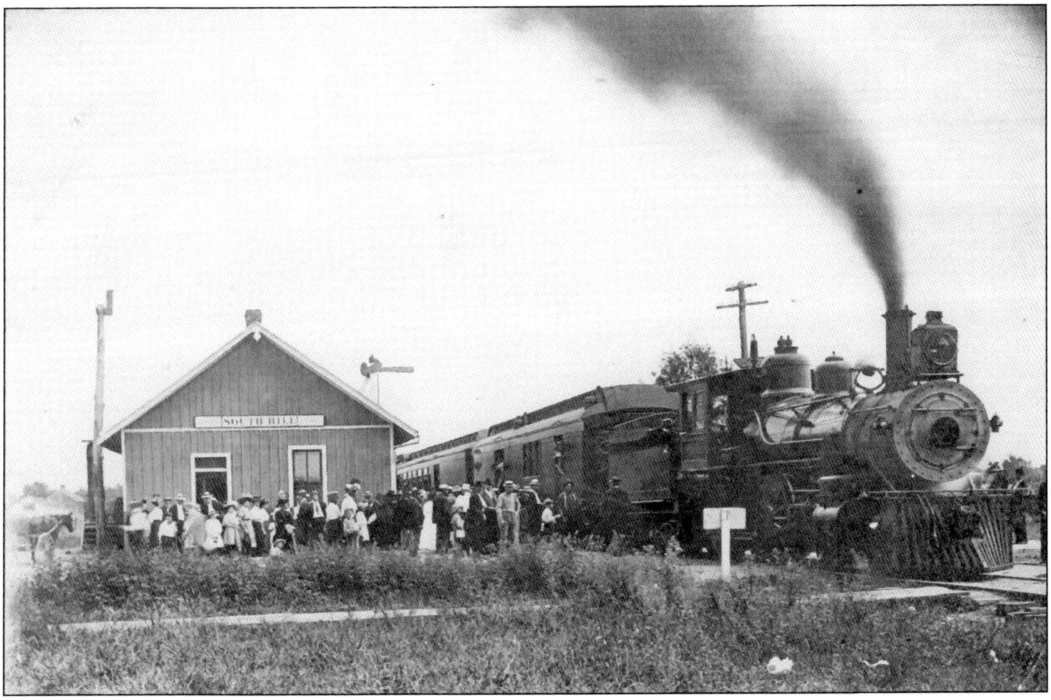

Eastern Mecklenburg County changed dramatically in 1889 with the arrival of the Atlantic and Danville Railroad. The 55-acre platted parcel of Harris was becoming a community, but very slowly. In 1902, there were three warehouses and six or seven businesses, most of which were in small wooden structures. As seen in this photograph above of the Atlantic and Danville station passenger terminal, it appears to be located in a field. Barely visible in the foreground is the old Boydton Plank Road. The first public school in South Hill, shown below, was located on Goode's Ferry Road. A small house was used until the new school could be built and it was completed in 1908. The first teachers were Mrs. L. H. Butterworth and Miss Ella Bustard. (SHM.)

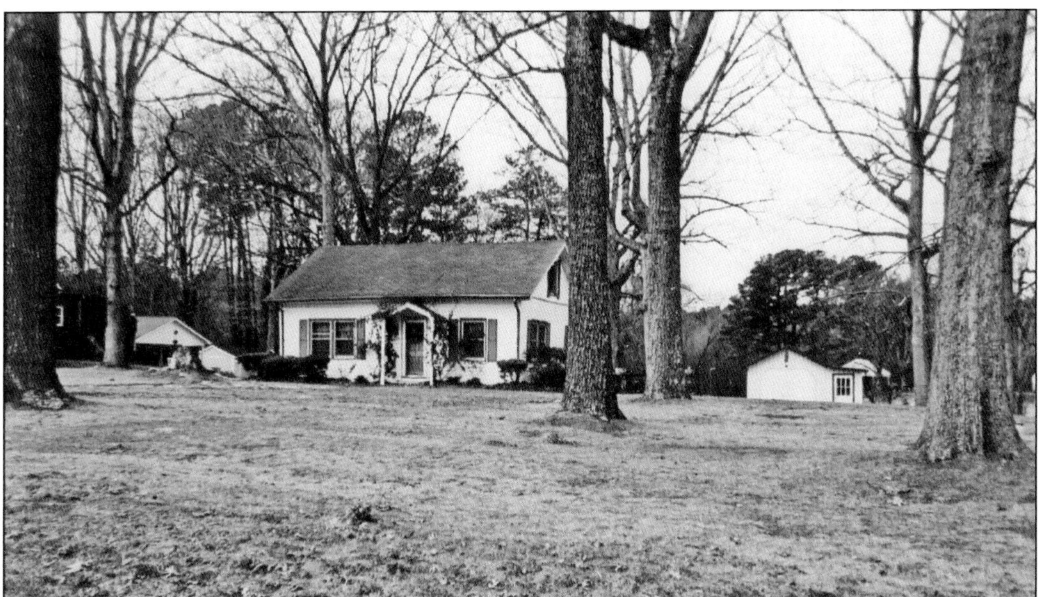

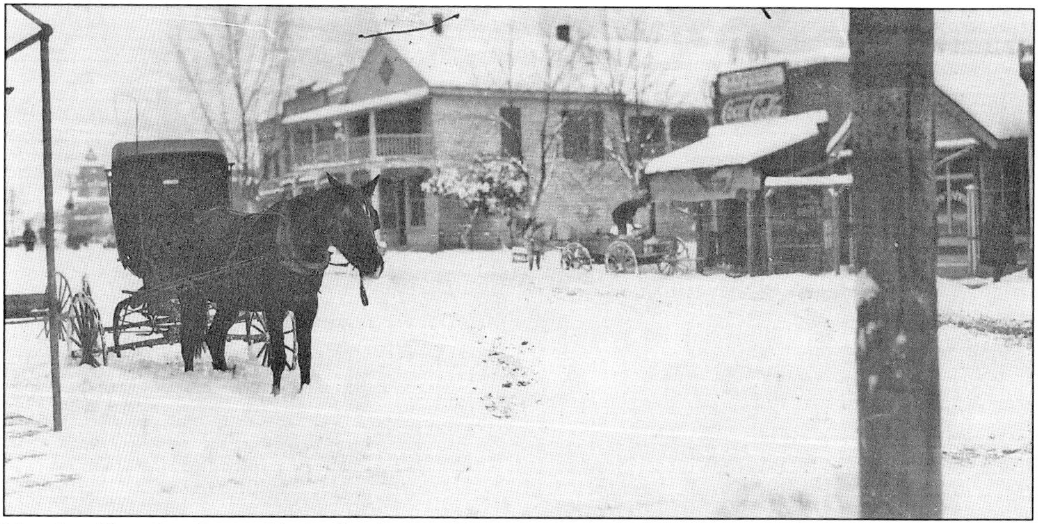

Nearby, Flat Creek established a livery, blacksmith shop, mercantile, dry goods store, water bottling company, gristmill, and more. In South Hill on Mecklenburg Avenue, a local doctor worked from his modest home by buggy. Willie Mangram opened a one-chair barbershop and a two-story boardinghouse (most likely Central Hotel), which was ready to accommodate railroad passengers. (SHM.)

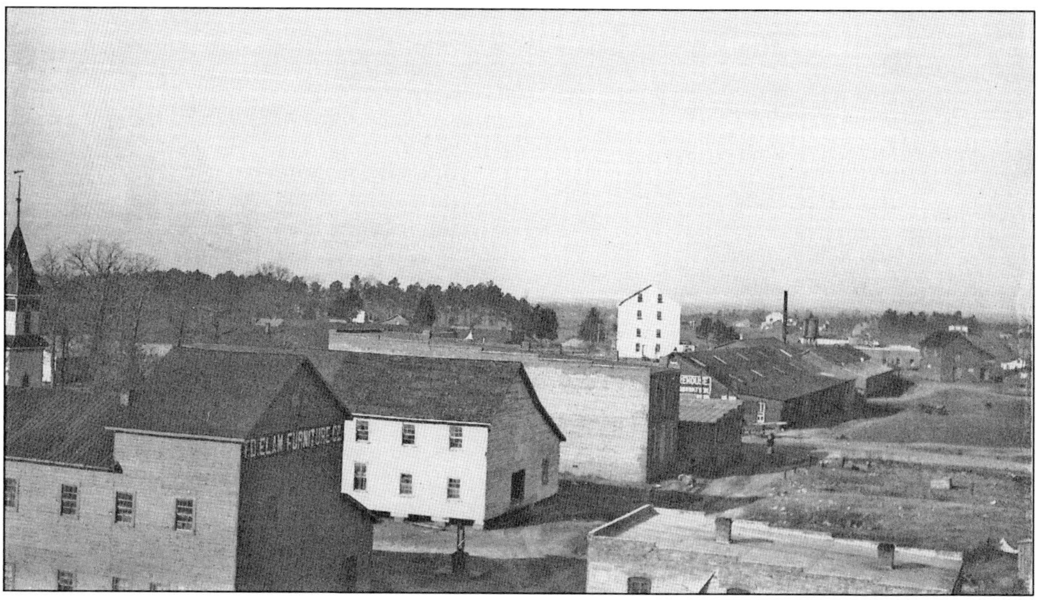

In 1901, South Hill received its state charter. A tobacco warehouse was built by local citizens and a second by an investor. None of the other communities wanted a tobacco warehouse, positioning South Hill to become the tobacco market of eastern Mecklenburg. Over the next eight years, there was a lumber mill, tobacco prizery, and other businesses located along South and North Main Streets, paralleling the railroad. (SHM.)

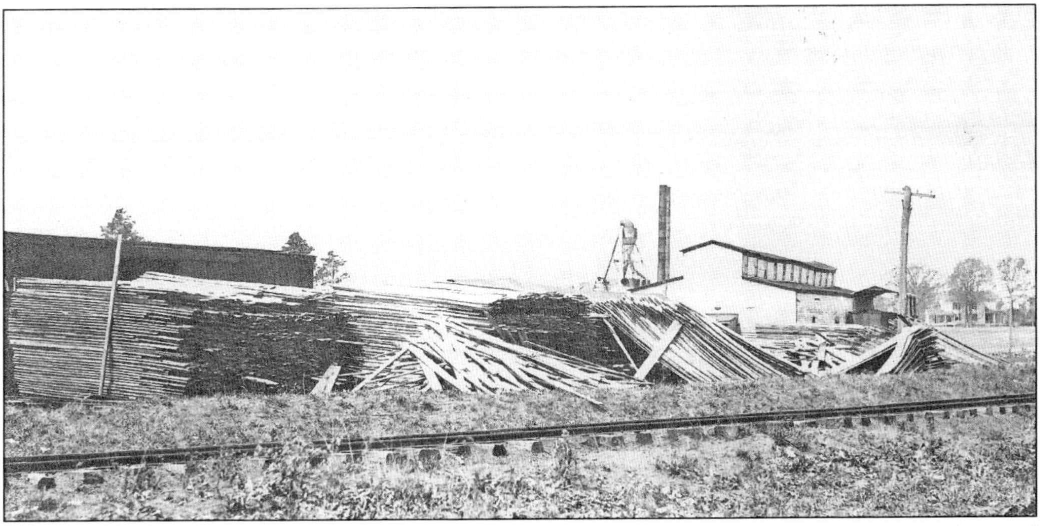

The South Hill Manufacturing Company (1905) by R. E. Yancey and others made lumber and box shooks. Expanding to over 35,000 square feet and employing several hundred persons, it established a power plant in 1922 and sold electricity to the town. Near the plant they built homes for employees to purchase or rent. The plant expanded to Suffolk and Norfolk, Virginia, and to Baltimore, Maryland. (SHM.)

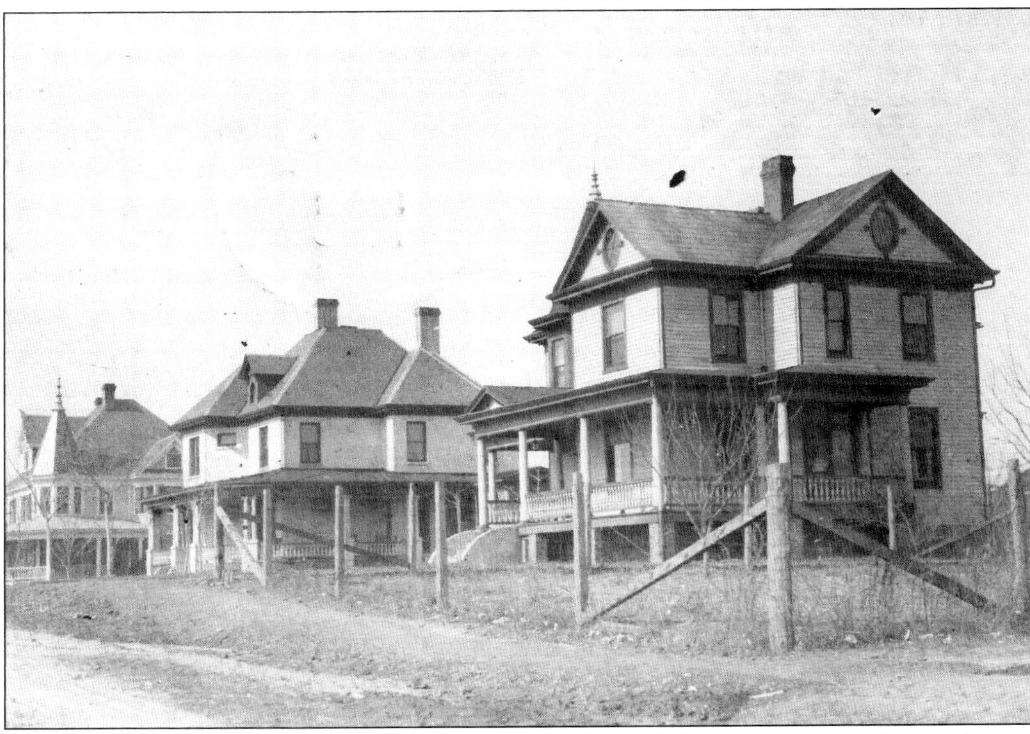

New homes and businesses began to dot the town. In this *c.* 1910 photograph are the new homes, from left to right, of R. E. Yancey, Jim Gordan, and William K. Simmons. These were located on Franklin Street. With the lumber mill in operation and so many people dependent upon it, most stores and homes were built with frame structures. (SHM.)

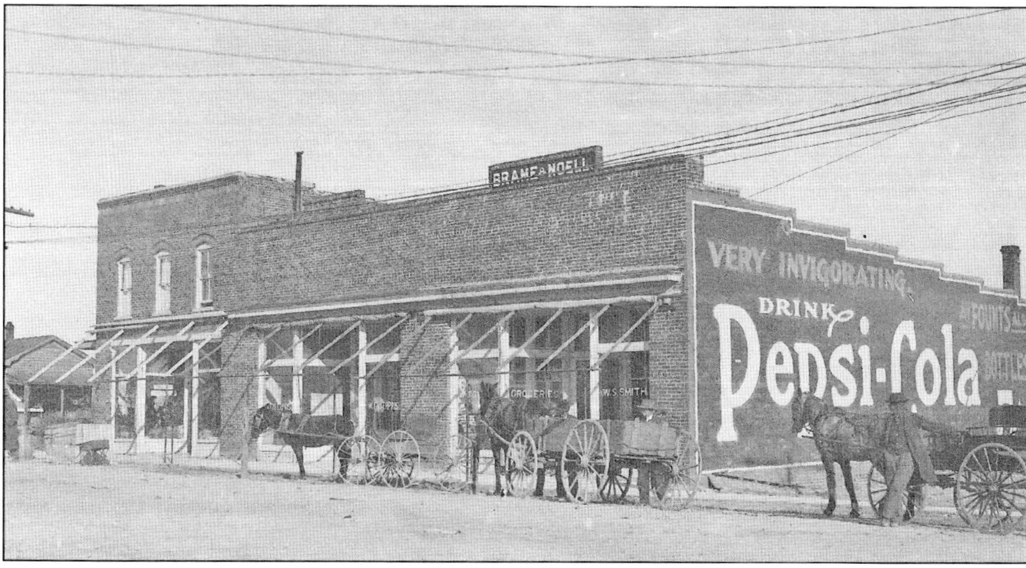

New stores were arriving on Mecklenburg Avenue (Old Plank Road). Some were larger than before, and construction was slowly changing over to brick, as many of the frame stores had burned. In the distance to the left is the two-story brick Bank of South Hill (*c.* 1906) and the new Brame-Noel Building (*c.* 1913), which housed the *South Hill Enterprise* and W. C. Smith Grocery Store. (SHM.)

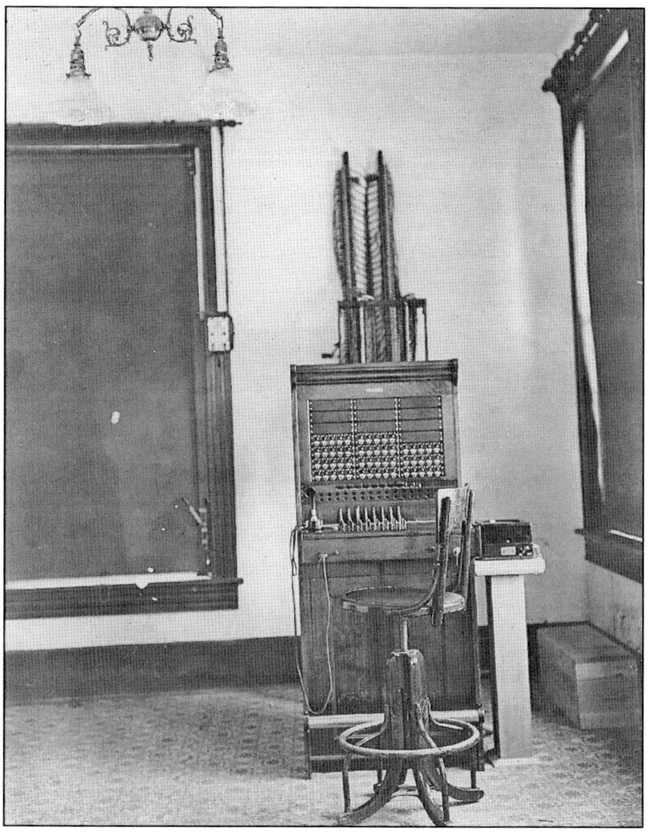

The South Hill Telephone Company began operation in 1909 and was owned by I. T. Nanny, who also owned a local insurance agency. In 1926, they published that they had sold and installed 180 telephones in town. The company, located upstairs in the brick Northington Drug Store building, was sold to a group of investors in 1928. (SHC.)

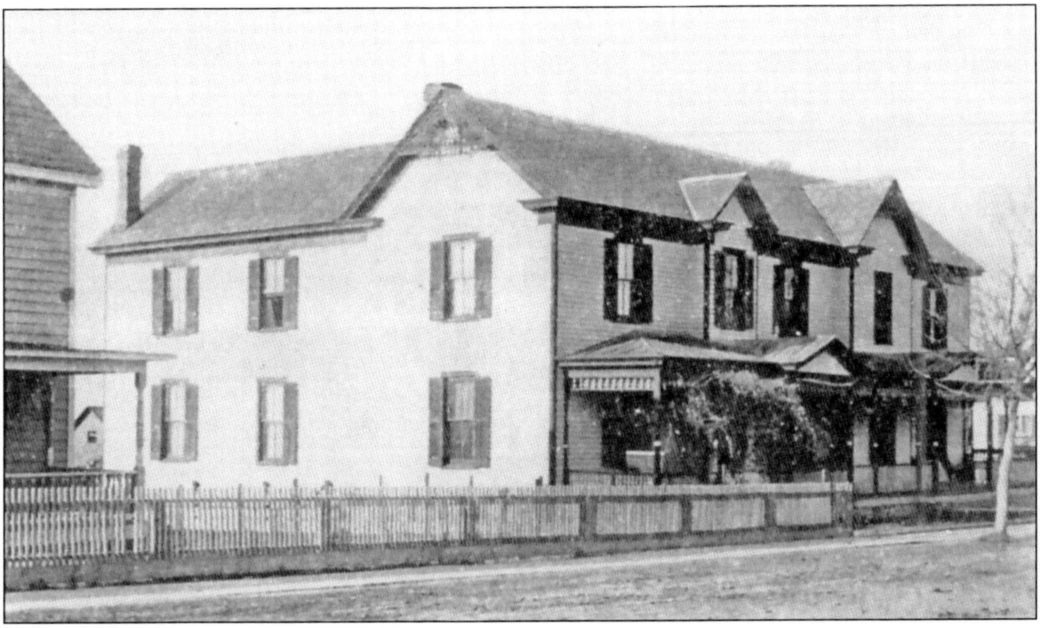

As more and more tobacco was being sold and the warehouses were drawing crowds for a variety of activities, more tourist homes were developed. One of the earliest was the *c.* 1890 Eppes House Hotel, which burned in 1915, but was rebuilt. In 1922, it was sold to a group of investors. (TJS.)

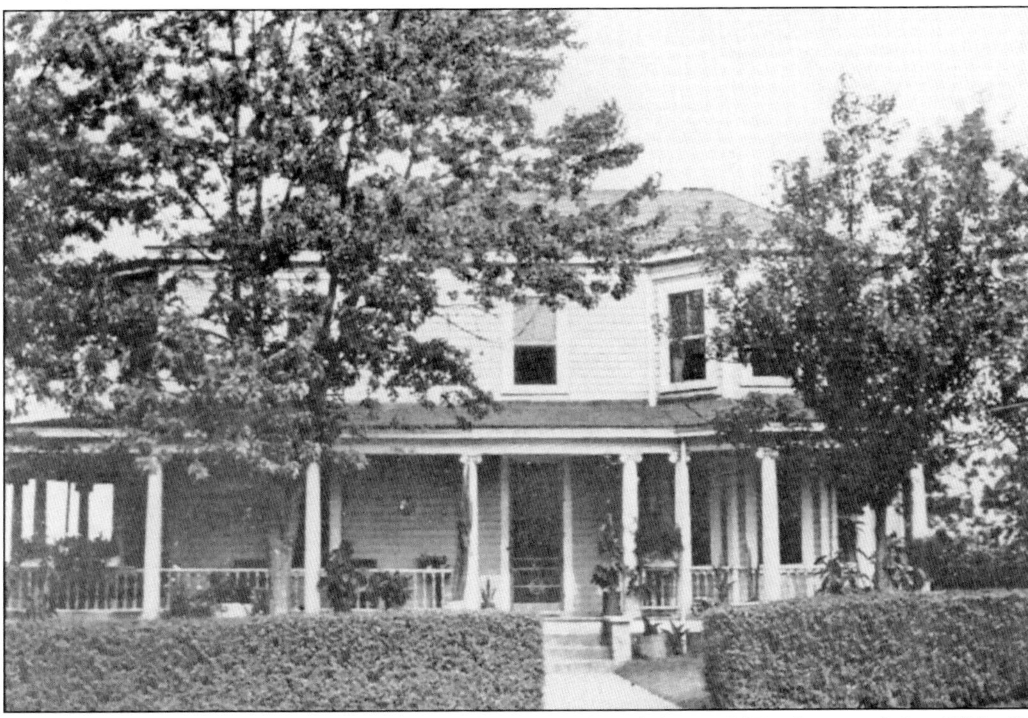

Other establishments included Hotel McAden in 1903 and Central Hotel around the 1890s. By 1913, six passenger trains per day were passing through town. A movie house and bowling alley were built on North Mecklenburg Avenue, but quickly burned. The South Hill Inn, pictured here, was built in 1914. (WCG.)

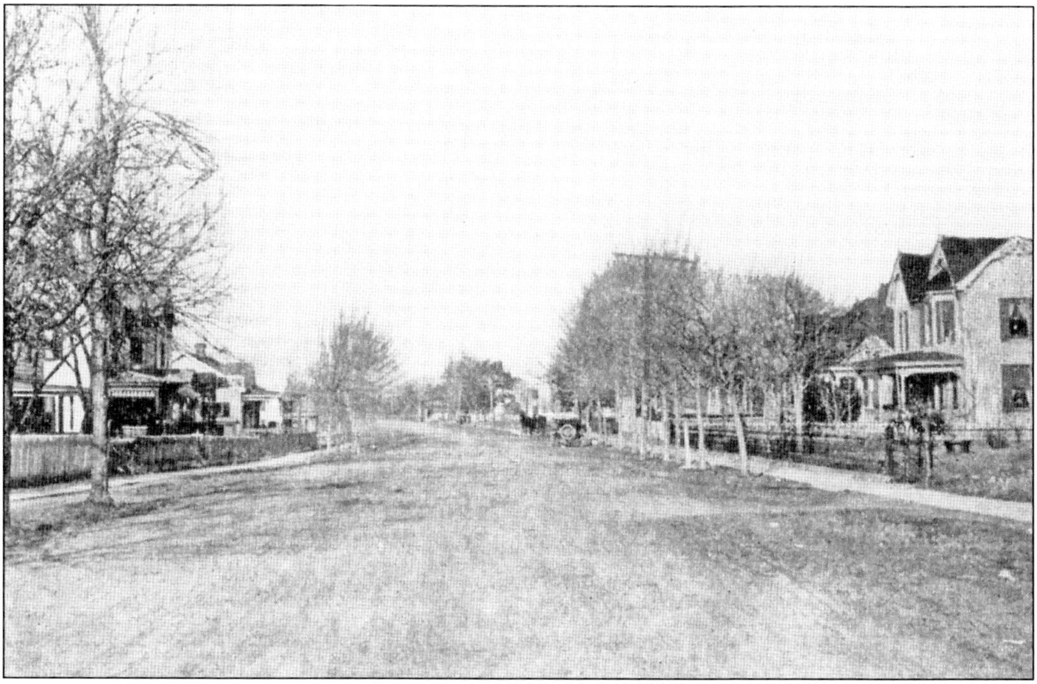

This postcard from 1920 shows that South Hill had become the town of roads, with the railroad, Piney Pond Road to LaCrosse, the Henderson Road, and the Plank Road to Petersburg. The back of the card reads, "Lighthouse—try our famous chicken in a basket." (WCG.)

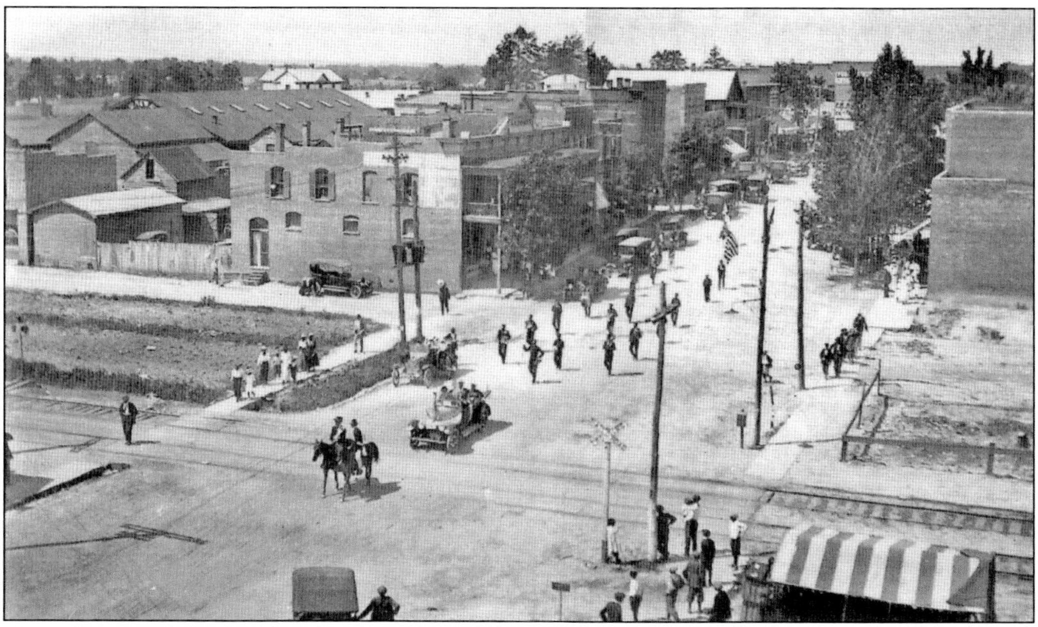

This 1917 parade in South Hill is in celebration of the grand opening of the Bankhead Highway (Route 31, known locally as Route 1), later called the Washington, D.C., to Atlanta Highway. The stately building on the left is the Crowder "First Cash Store" Mercantile. Originally the front was on Main Street facing the railroad, but in 1910 it was remodeled to face Mecklenburg Avenue. (SHC.)

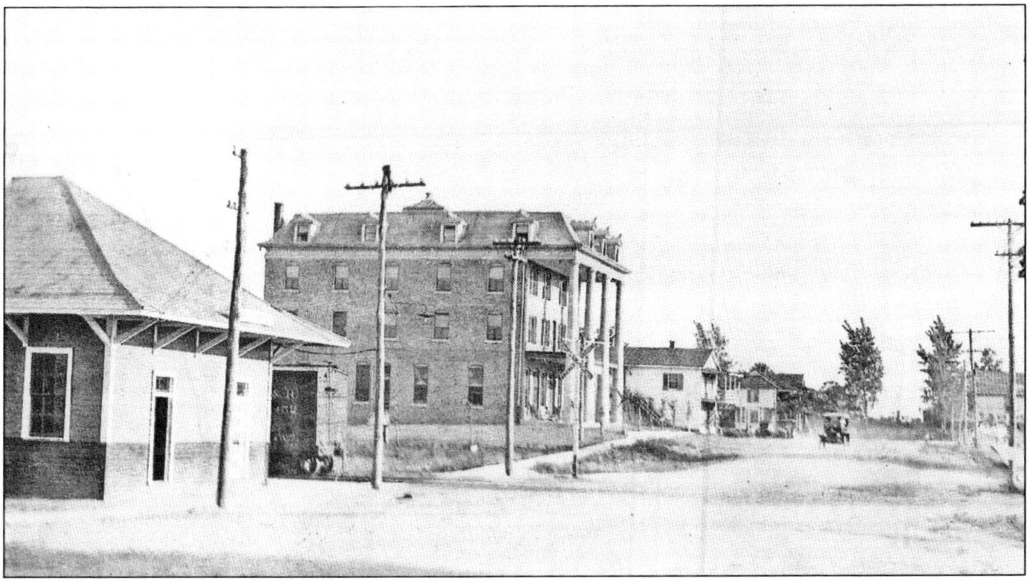

The railroad built a new passenger station closer to Mecklenburg Avenue in 1912. Nearby, a new hotel called The Nordan (first three letters of Norfolk and Danville) was completed that year. Next door was a home/bakery, and at the end of the street was the home of S. J. Bugg, a local businessman and prominent carpenter of the Flat Creek community. In this photograph, the home was occupied by his widow. (Richard Burnett.)

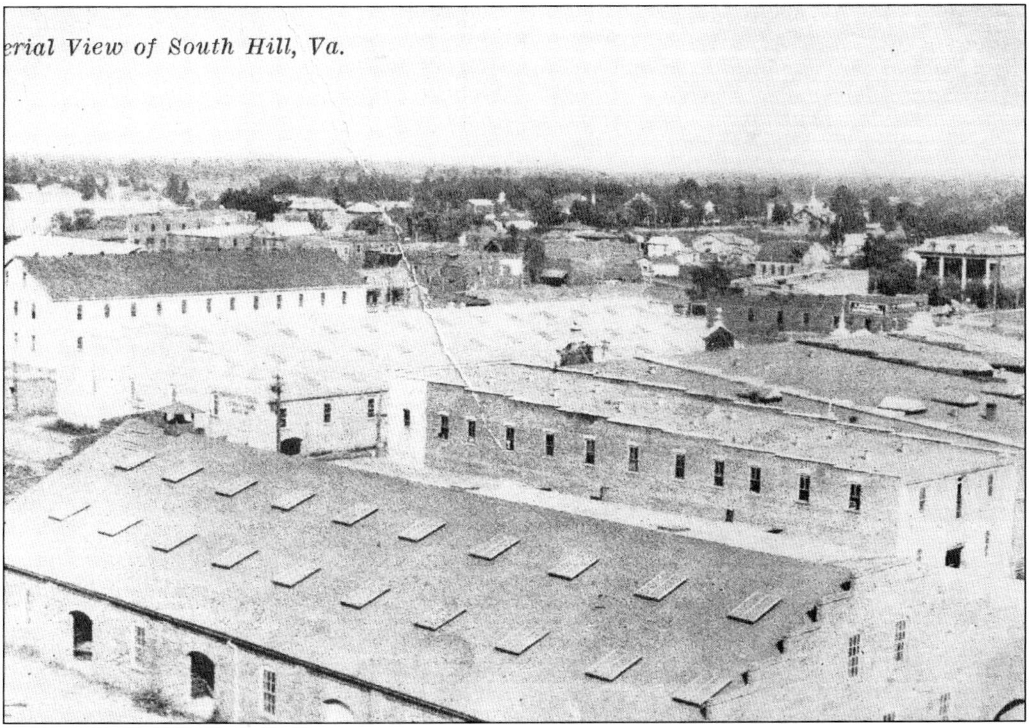

The tobacco market had grown to processing and selling over 200,000 pounds in the four warehouses of town. This photograph gives a bird's-eye view of three of the warehouses and support buildings. In the center to the left is the warehouse owned by S. Matthews. (SHC.)

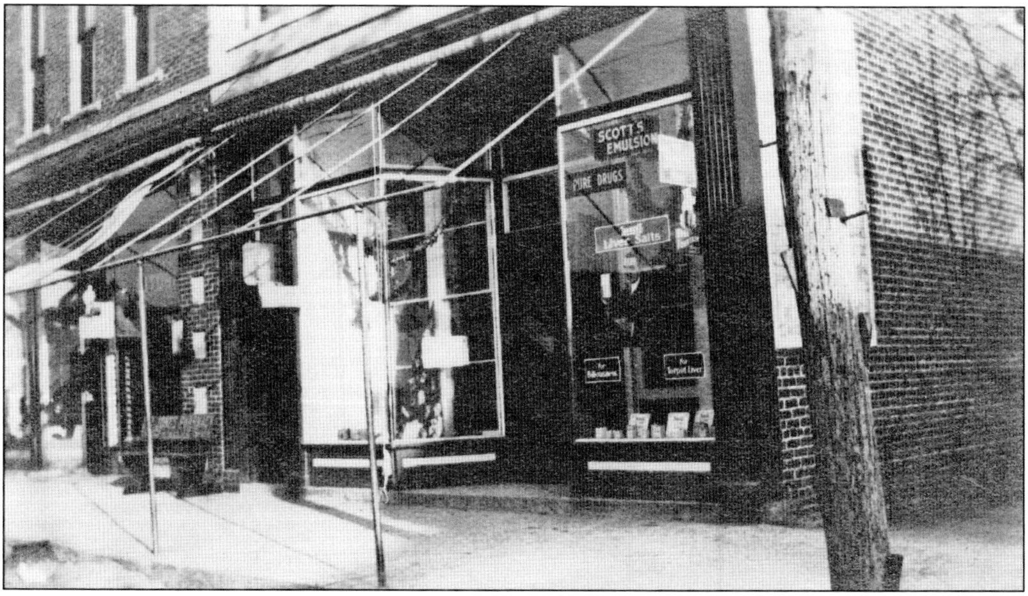

This photograph shows the newly completed Turner Jewelry Store (1914) situated alongside, from left to right, R. E. Yancey's general merchandise, a ready-made clothing and millinery shop (1903), and the Northington Drug Company (1901), with the telephone company upstairs. These are on North Mecklenburg Avenue. (James Lewter.)

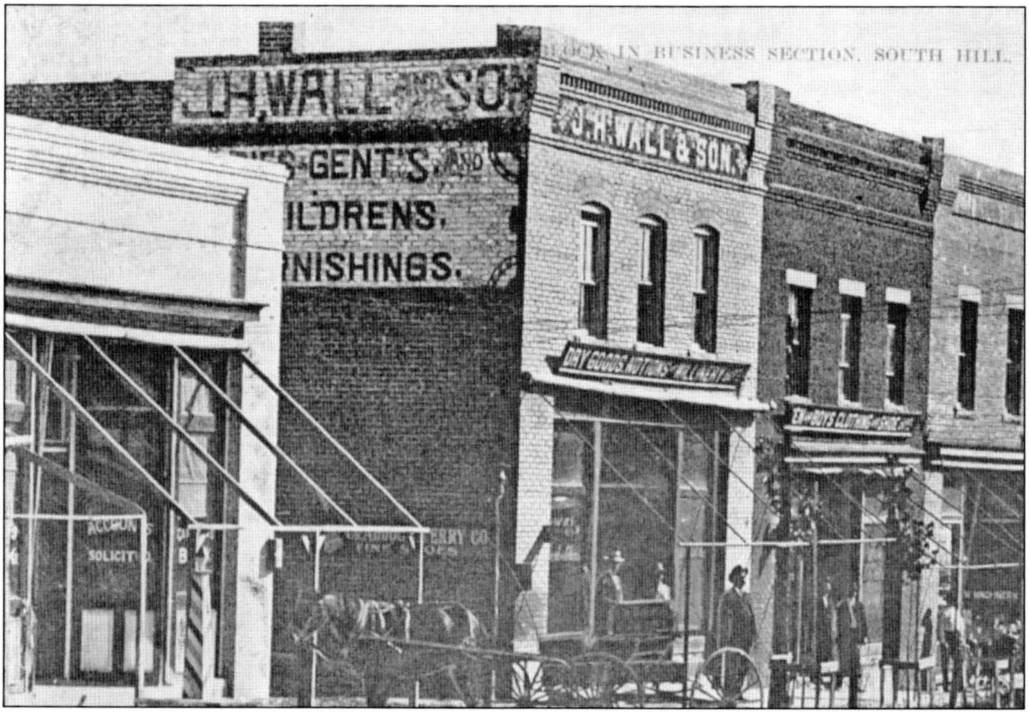

Across the street on the northwest corner of North Mecklenburg Avenue are, from right to left, the stores of Wartman Hardware (1902), A. Fine Department Store (1904), J. H. Wall and Son Dry Goods, Notions, and Millinery (1903), and the new Citizens Bank (November 28, 1908) with a new barbershop next door. (TJS.)

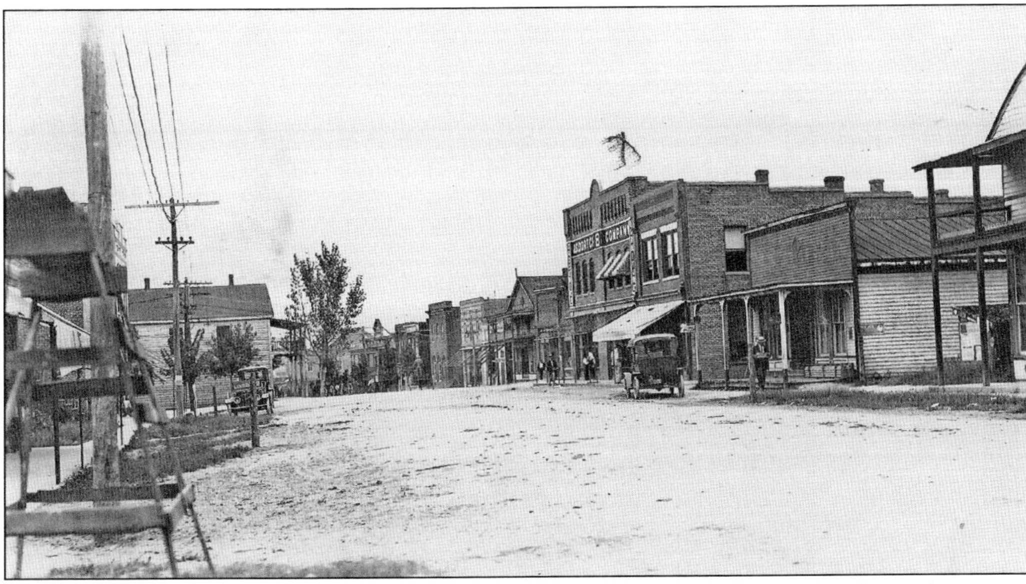

West Danville Street (to Henderson Country Road and to Goode's Ferry Road) was beginning to develop in response to the growing tobacco district. By 1916, this street contained the new brick H. P. Bugg's dry goods store, L. Davis Department Store, the Harness Shop (at the corner of Brunswick Street), and George Smith, dealer in Maxwell cars. (SHM.)

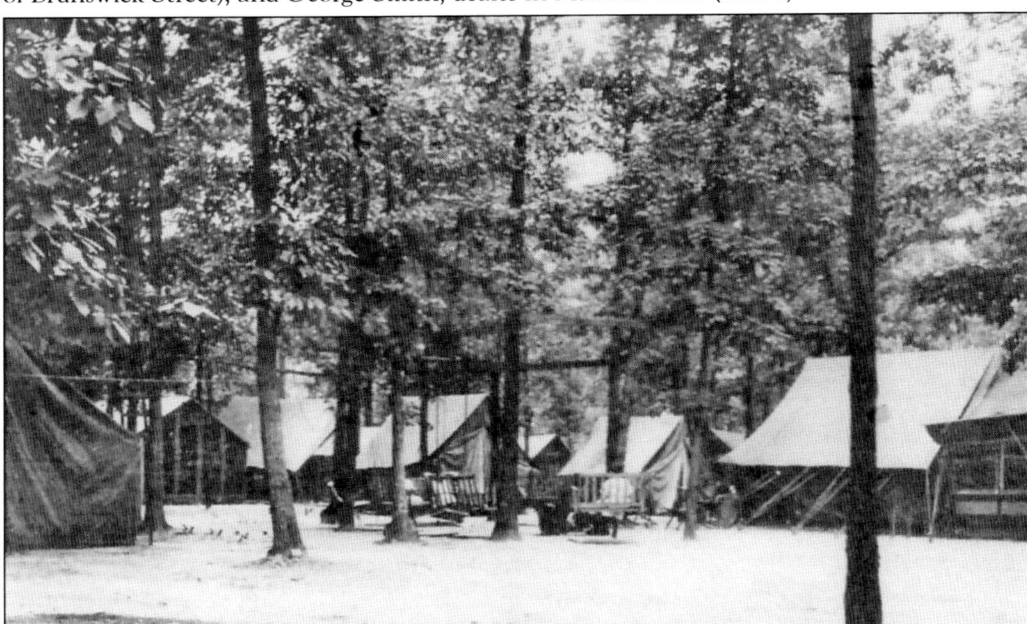

By 1914, the highways were beginning to be frequently traveled. Bear in mind they were not paved or graveled, and the average rate of speed on the open road was about 8 to 12 miles per hour. From Petersburg to South Hill (65 miles with streams, hills, and no bridges), the trip would take at least seven to eight hours in clear weather with dry roads. Break areas with campgrounds, such as the one pictured here, began to line the highways at strategic points for weary travelers. They were simple and modest, but provided water, a bathhouse, and a camping area. Many offered a home-cooked meal and boxed lunches. (TJS.)

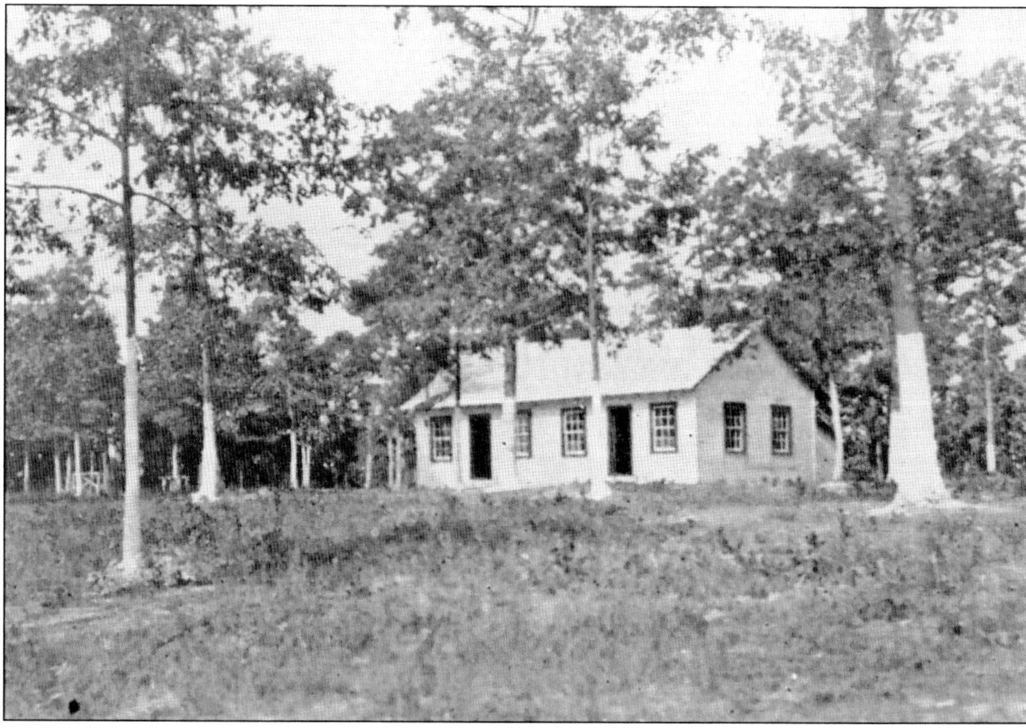

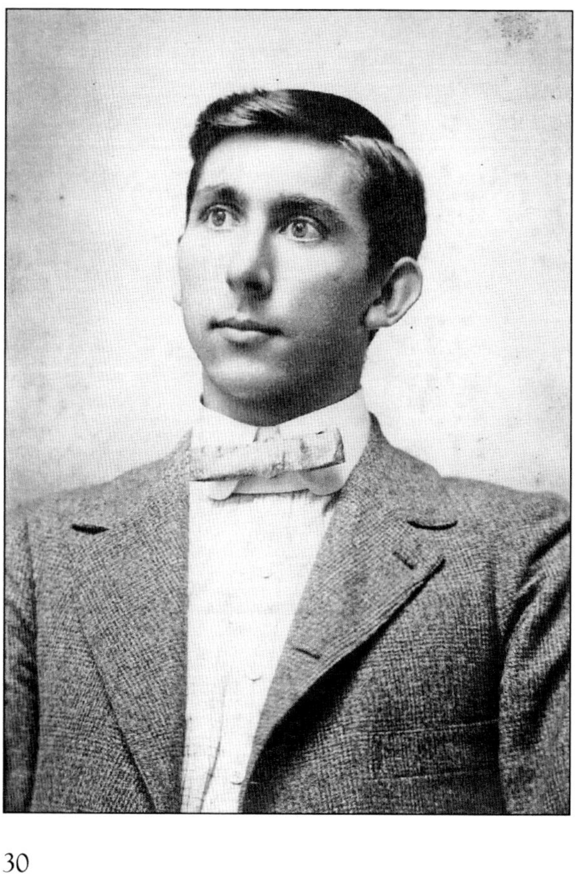

On Goodes Ferry Road (as a layover for the ferry across the Roanoke River), adjacent to the annexed Flat Creek, was the W. H. Butterworth dairy and farm. In 1915, Oakdale Campground opened on this farm and advertised "two big restrooms with water, lights, heat, toilets, shower baths and telephone all for fifty cents per night per car." The dairy and campground closed in 1929. That same year he opened a cheese factory, but it closed in 1932. (TJS.)

In 1908, Howard N. Beales was elected Mecklenburg County treasurer—the longest serving county treasurer (40 years). He, along with the county board of supervisors and planners, pursued continued growth spurred by the railroad and the highways. Western Mecklenburg County was established, and the eastern part of the county was rapidly catching up, but with a whole new theme—tourists and travelers. (Walter Beales III.)

Two

RAILROAD COMMUNITIES

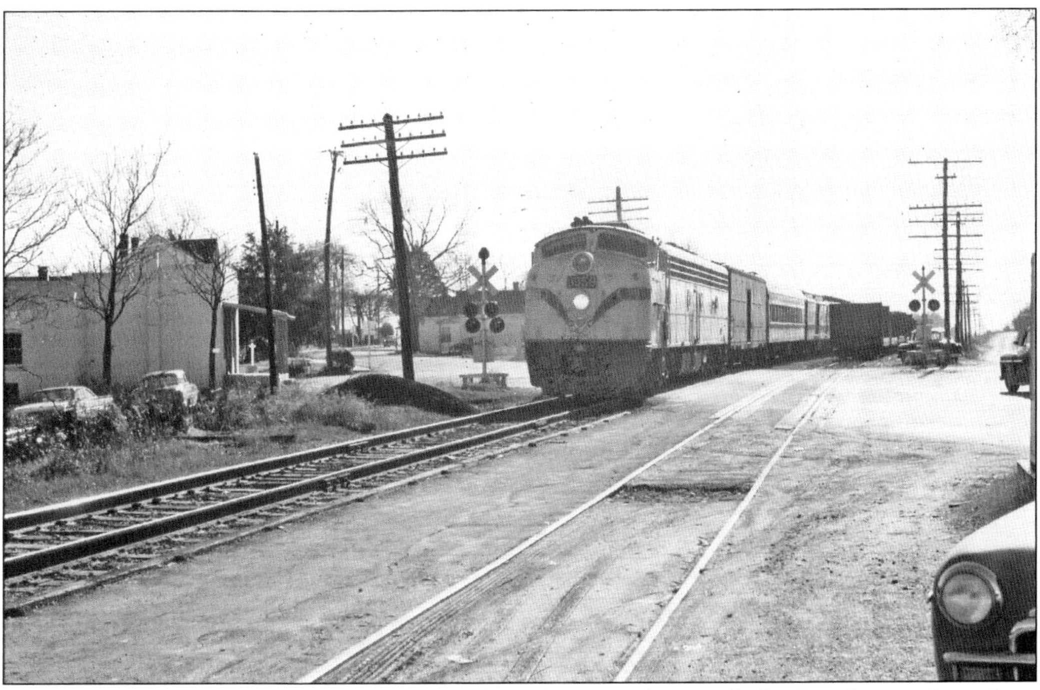

Along Piney Pond Road east of South Hill, the Atlantic and Danville Railroad came through in 1888 and changed the name to LaCrosse. A post office was established at the railroad station, with D'Arville Northington serving as the first postmaster in May 1890. When platted in May 1894, the name again changed to Lacrosse. (PMA.)

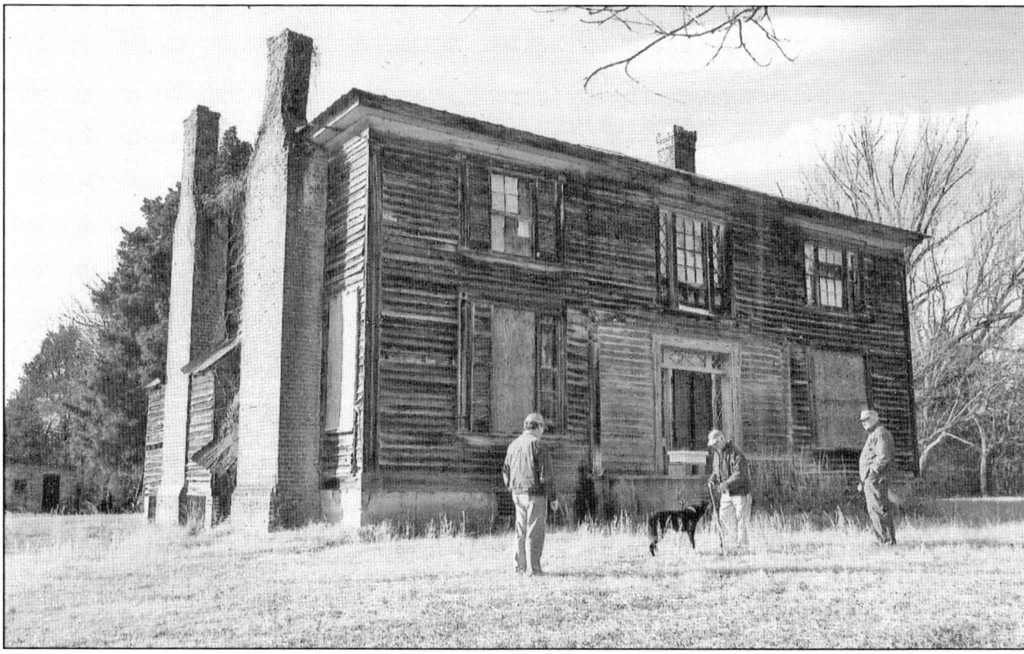

Buena Vista was situated on a 2,000-acre patent to Col. J. P. Goode (Virginia's 18th Regiment Militia). The home was built in 1840, and during the Civil War, Goode's two sons, David and Charles, served gallantly in the Confederate Army. (John E. Goode Taylor.)

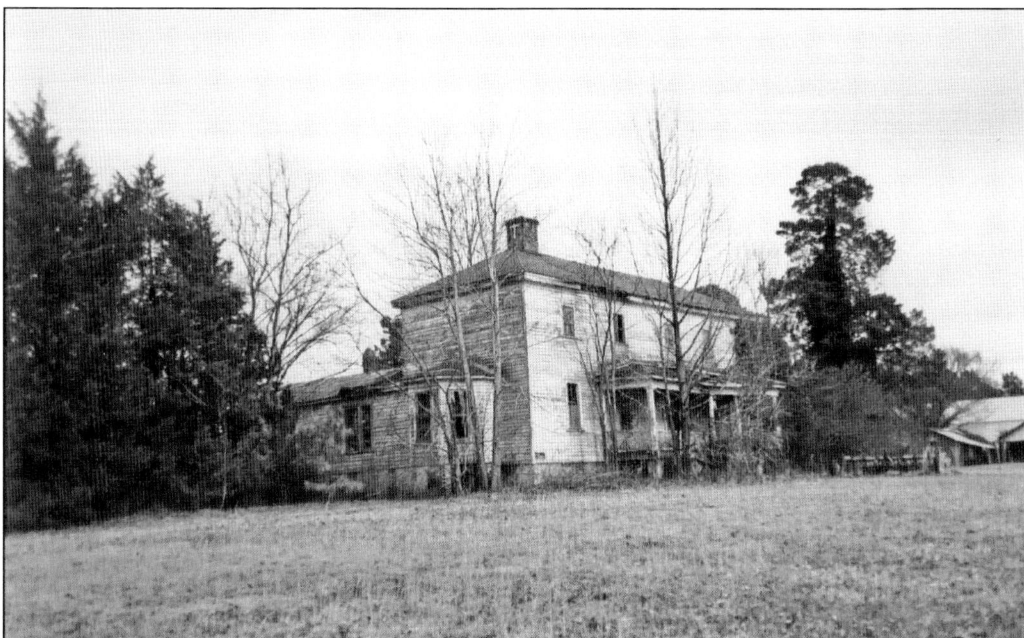

Near the southern end of Goode's Ferry Road was Invermay, the *c.* 1777 home of Col. Samuel Goode. He established the ferry and served in the House of Delegates from 1778 to 1785. In 1789, Goode became the high sheriff for Mecklenburg County and served in that capacity until 1791. The home served for many years as an ordinary for travelers crossing the Roanoke River. In April 1894, it also became a post office operated by Mary Baskervill. (JC.)

One of the first arrivals to Lacrosse was Dr. William W. Wilkerson, who lived in this very stately home in town in the early 1890s. He immediately began working to build the community and have it organized and chartered. It was incorporated in 1901, along with South Hill. One of the few sidewalks in town, it was a perfect place for James B. Cook Jr. to take his little sister Page Cook Axson McGaughy for a ride on his tricycle. (PMA.)

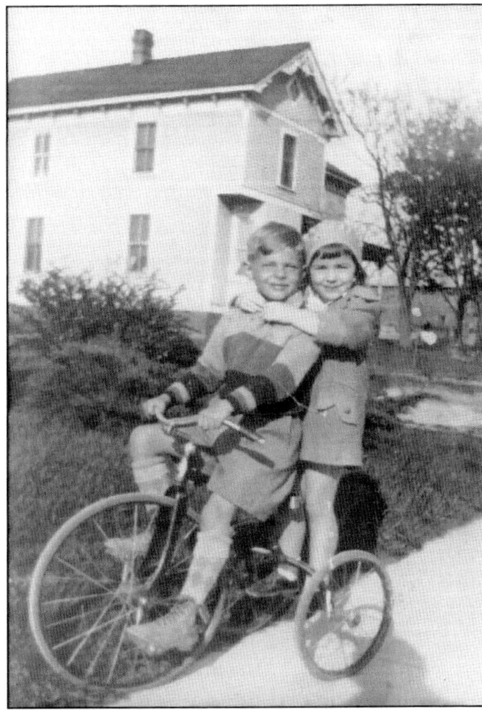

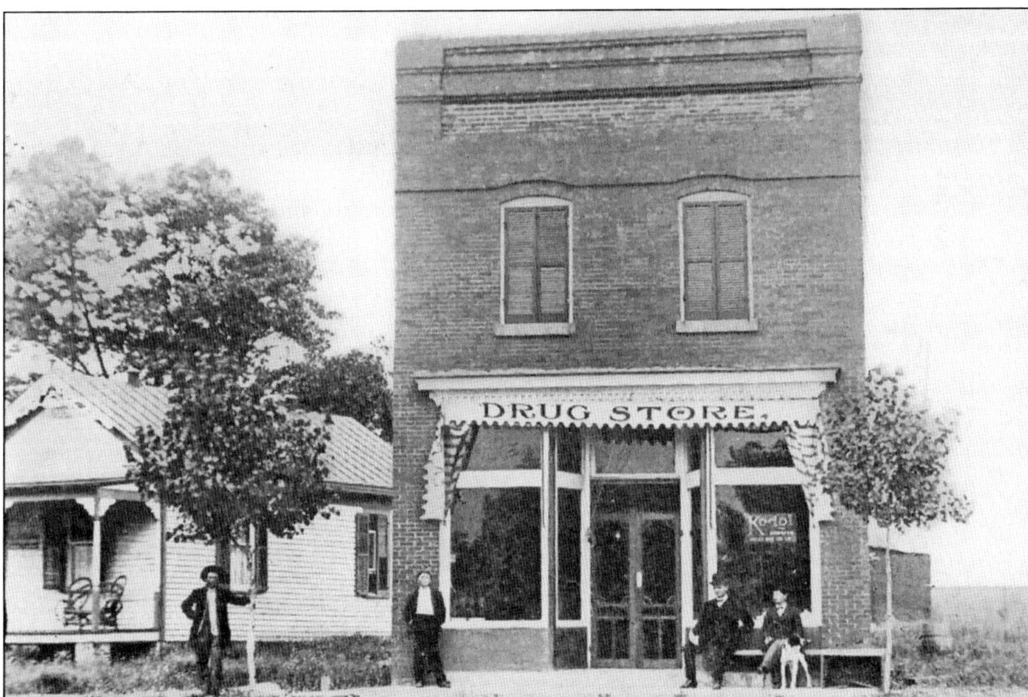

To facilitate growth, Dr. Wilkerson built the first drugstore in town, where he also had his medical practice, in 1901. He continued his practice from this building until the 1940s. Piney Pond Road became Coastal Highway 12 in 1917, leading into South Hill. In the 1940s, it became U.S. Highway 58. (WCG.)

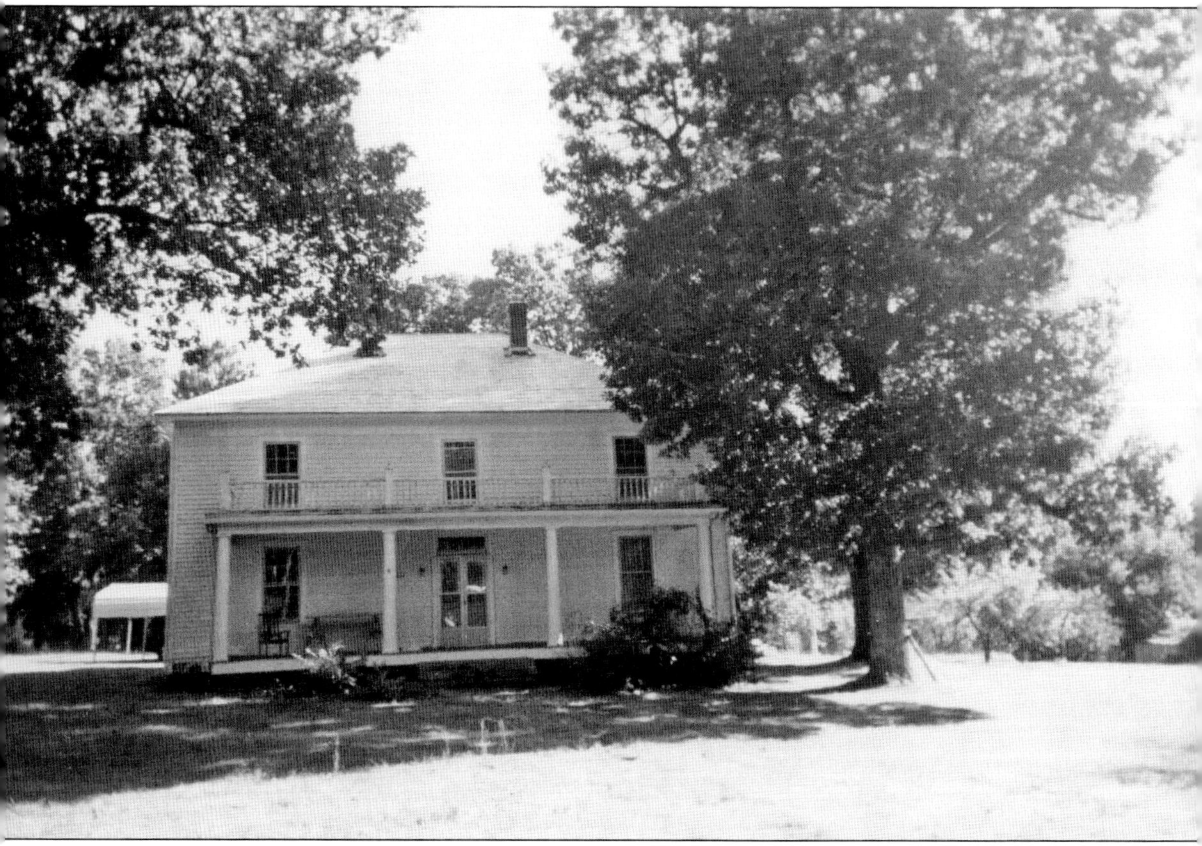

Also in 1901, the LaCrosse Academy was chartered and opened its doors to boys and girls. The boys lived upstairs and the girls in a dormitory across the street. It was chartered as a school for grades 1 through 11 and a college through doctor of philosophy and law. It had three classrooms and three instructors, along with a music teacher. The principal was Prof. J. K. Walker, and the president was M. W. Tanner. Unfortunately the school failed in 1903. (JC.)

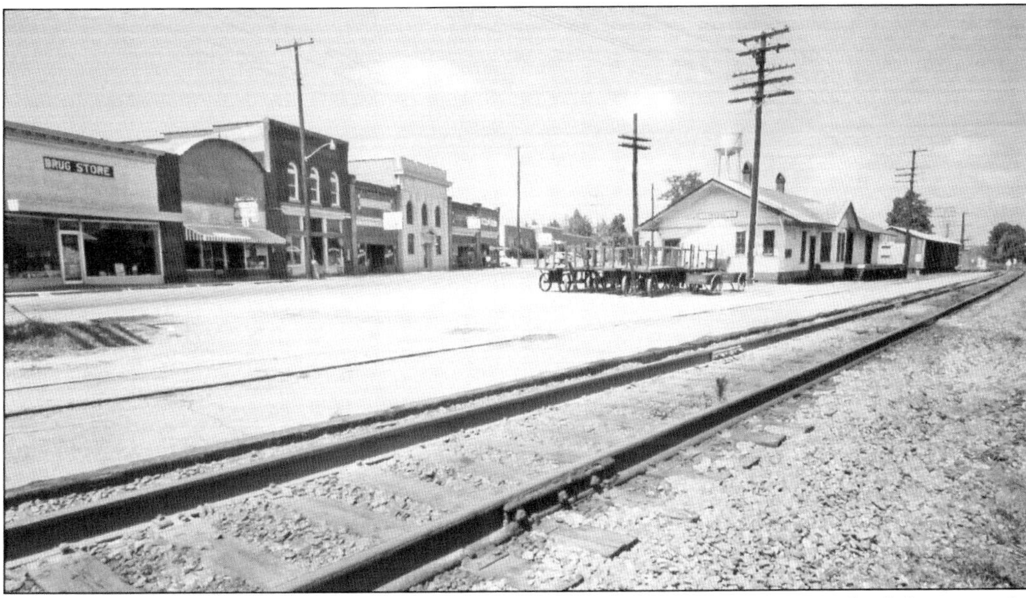

The impetus for Lacrosse in 1901 was a second railroad coming to town, which became the Seaboard Air Line Railroad. The Atlantic and Danville Railroad traveled east and west, but the Seaboard went north and south. A new passenger terminal was constructed near the intersection of the rail lines. Nearby, three saloons, a blacksmith shop, and a log jail were built the same year. The Bank of Lacrosse opened in February 1913 by G. A. Saunders and Robert Montgomery and was only one of two banks in the county to survive the Depression. (PMA.)

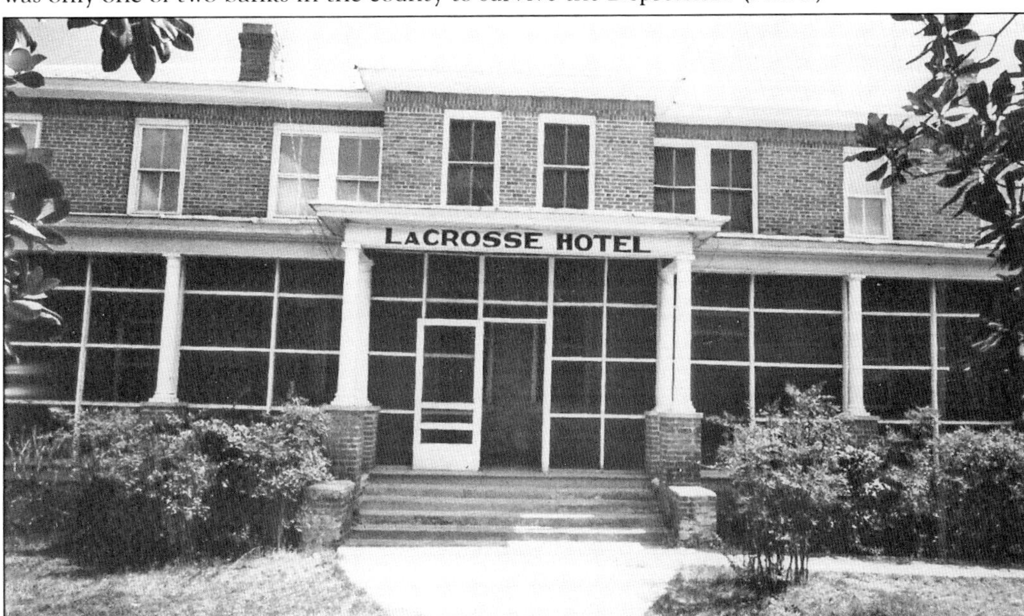

The LaCrosse Hotel, a frame structure, was built in the 1890s. By 1914, the town council was concerned about the small hotel and the large number of passenger trains coming through town with connecting travelers. John Coulter purchased the hotel in 1917, razed it and built the new brick hotel. Ophelia Colley, directress of shows in town, was a frequent visitor in the 1930s. She is most often referred to as Grand Ole Opry's "Minnie Pearl." (SHM.)

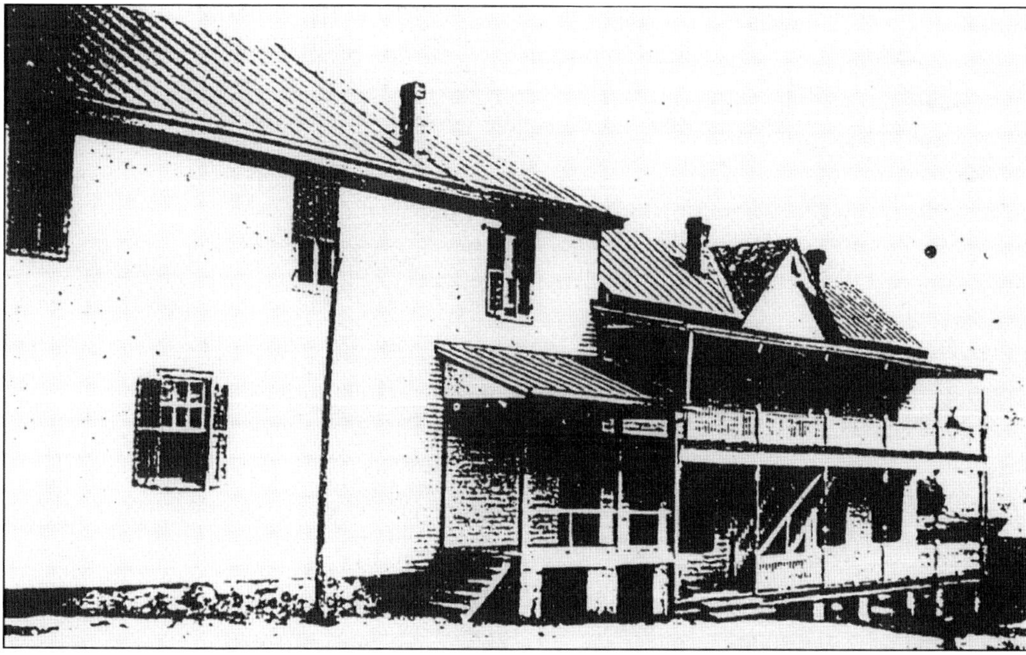

In 1916, Dr. Wilkerson's nephew built a hotel and called it Willis Hotel. A frame structure near the LaCrosse Hotel, it included a wing of stores and shops. Downstairs were Tanner's Retail Store and LaCrosse Candy Company, and upstairs were apartments. This is a sketch of the hotel, which burned on December 16, 1926. (L. Ryland Rash Jr.)

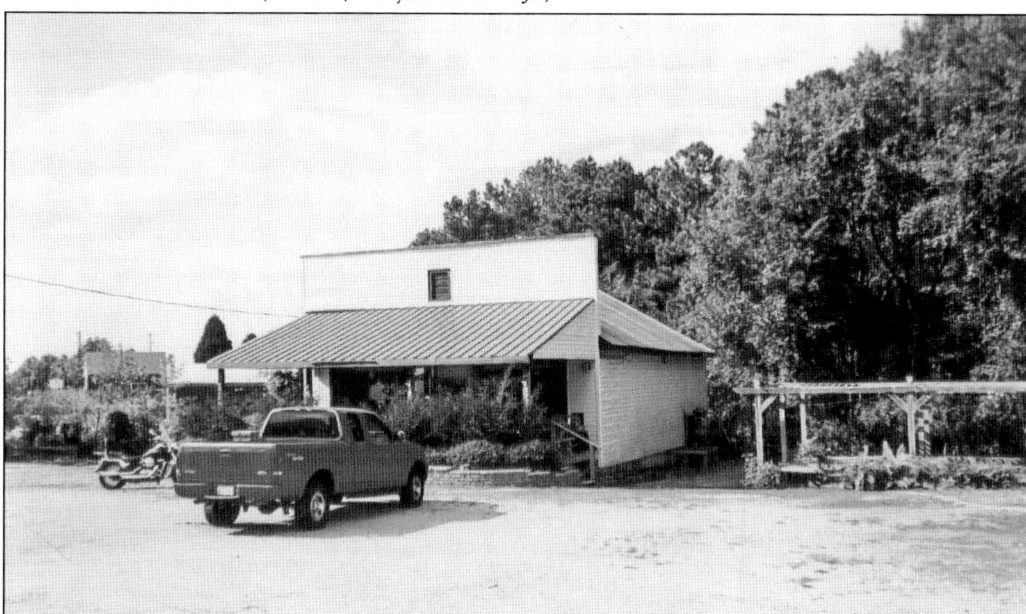

Along the south Seaboard Air Line Railroad was the Blackridge and Rehobeth M. E. Church. Next to the church, D. D. Jones rebuilt his store in 1935 after a band of gypsies came through, robbing and burning the store, which was initially built in 1915 on the foundations of a former store from the 1860s. It is said he chased them down and retrieved his merchandise. The Rehobeth School of 1867 was being rented as a public school in 1910. (JC.)

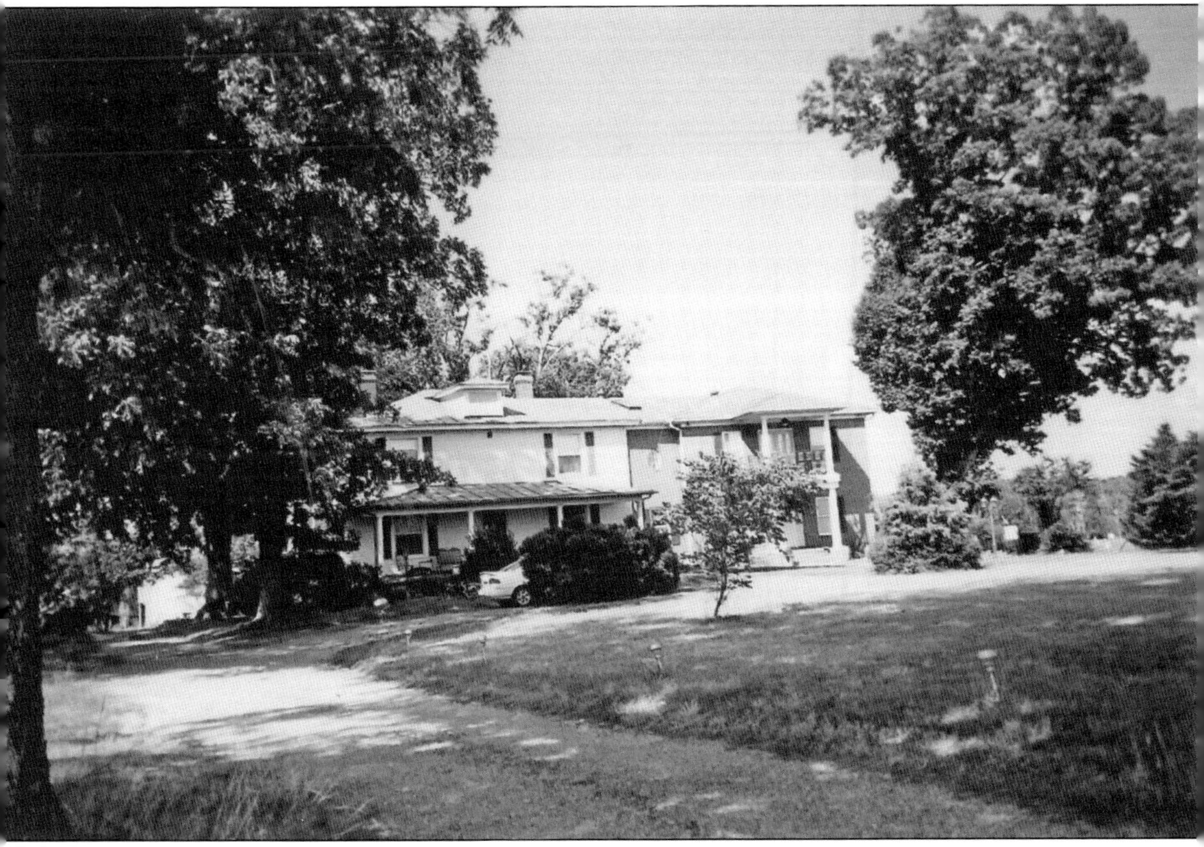

A short distance away was the new home (built in 1916) of Finley Gray Rose Jr. Carrying on the family tradition of truck farming, he found a good market in Washington, D.C., when the National Byway came through in 1917. He purchased a truck and hauled his produce to market in D.C. for many years. Even though he lost his arm in a farming accident around 1920, he continued to make the trip weekly during the season (imagine the times). The section to the left is original. (Finley Gray Rose.)

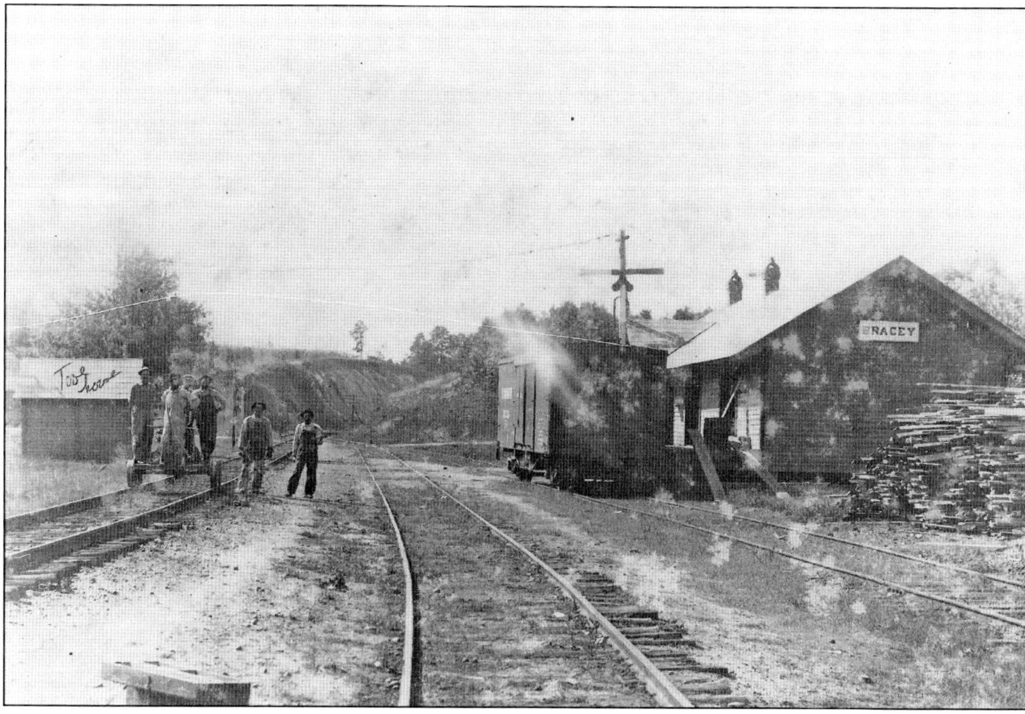

As the Seaboard Air Line Railroad proceeded south in 1900, they stopped about a mile from St. Tammany and established a new terminal. The new community was named Bracey. In July 1900, the post office in St. Tammany, established by John C. Courtney in October 1795, was closed and moved to the Bracey Railroad Station. In short order, Waller T. Bracey became postmaster. (TJS.)

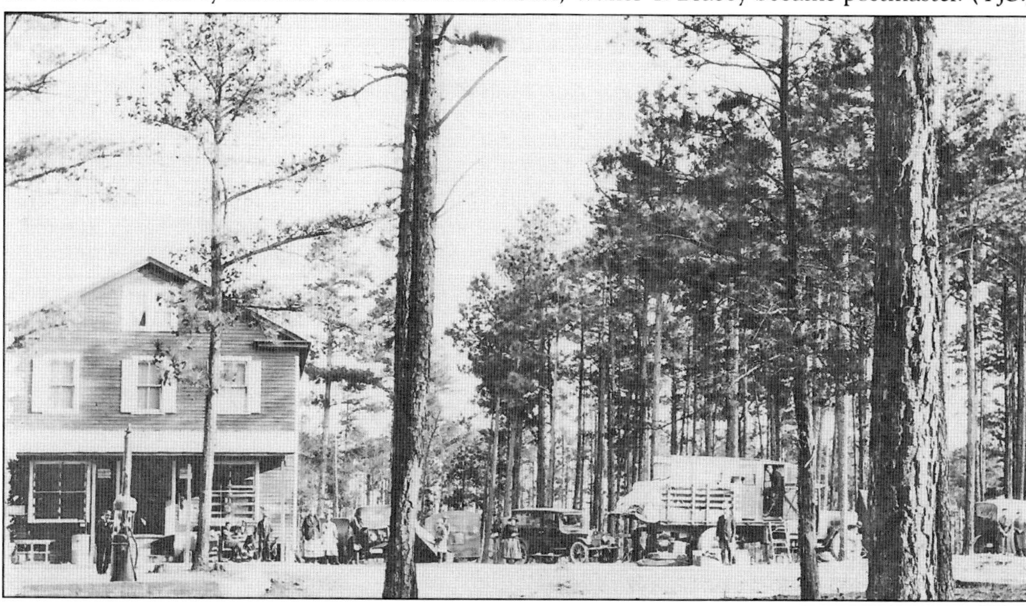

North of LaCrosse on the Seaboard Line was a spur for a water tower near the Meherrin River to replenish the steam engines—this area became Skelton and was on the National Byway. A country store and campgrounds were established in 1917. On October 25, 1932, the "Roosevelt Special" made a stop for water, and Pres. F. D. Roosevelt gave a short address to the onlookers. (TJS.)

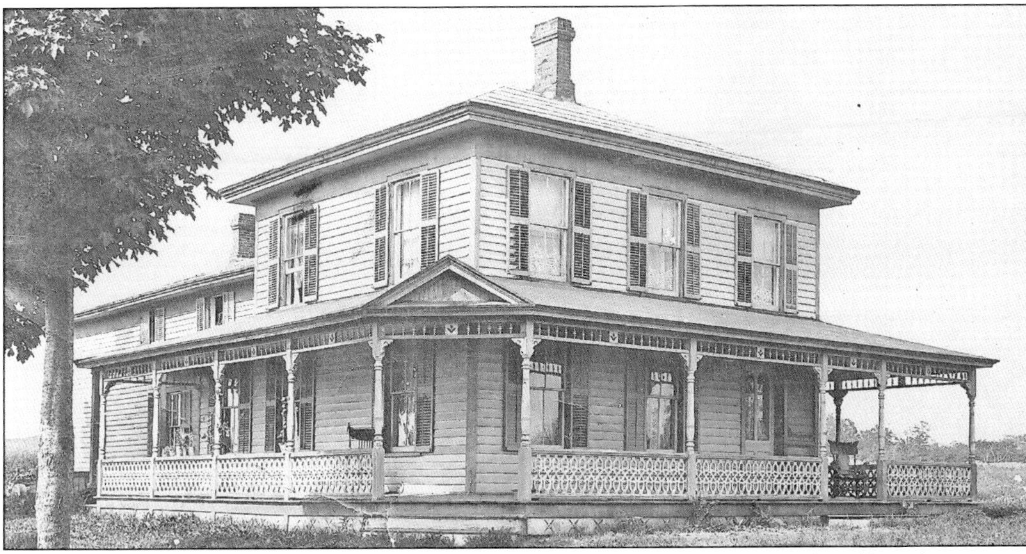

A mile south of Skelton on Old Plank Road (National Byway) was Forksville. This was an old highway intersection community established with a post office in October 1831 by Phillip Pennington. On this postcard from the early 1900s is written, "How do you like my new house?" This home resembles the homes of Gilbert A. Saunders, Esq., and Dr. Tanner, both still in Forksville. (TJS.)

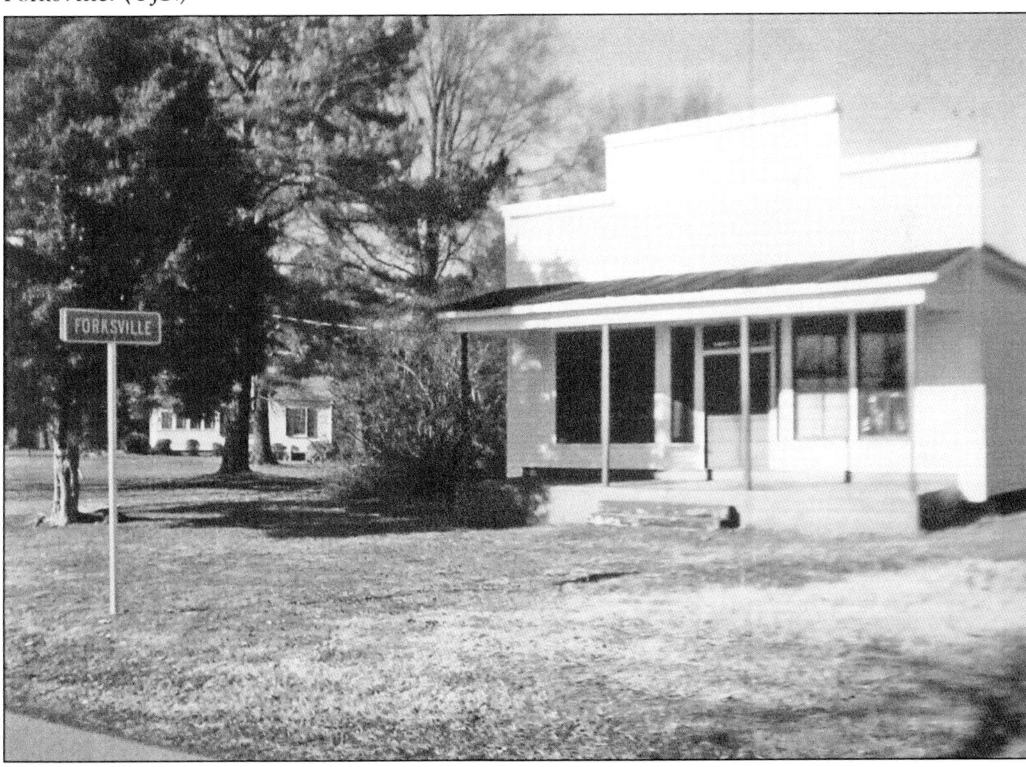

The community developed with the introduction of automobiles. By 1917, a general store, post office, service station/store, and tourist cabin were built, but when the National Byway came through the same year, it bypassed the community. (BMC.)

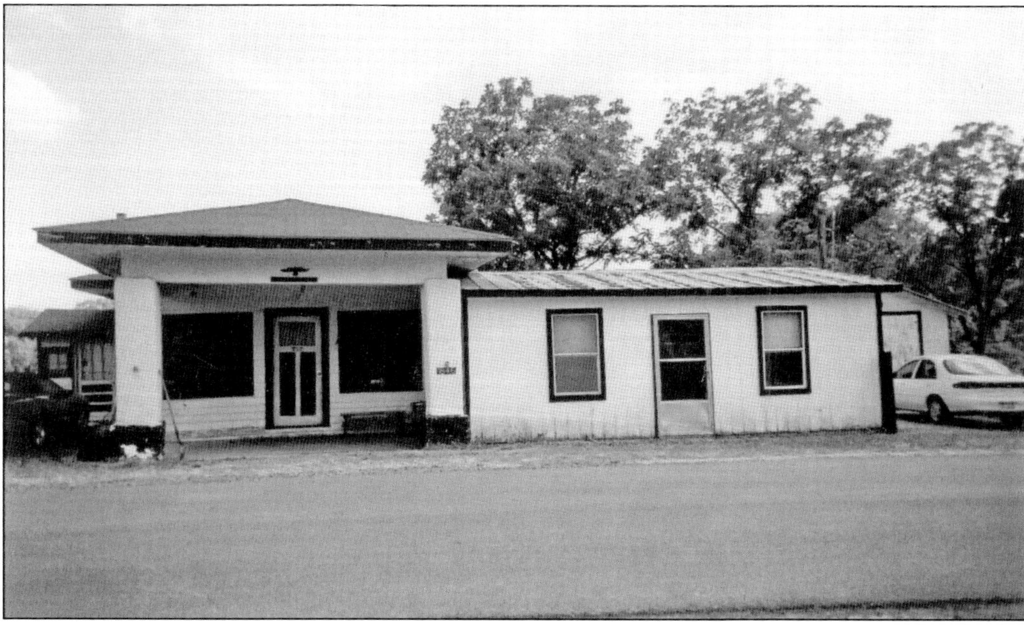

Two general stores and a post office served the community for several years, but following the Depression, the store and cabin closed. It became a tourist attraction on July 16, 1924, (between 5:00 and 6:00 p.m.) when residents and nearby train passengers noted spaceships landing. Actually, after investigation, four large meteorites hit Forksville over a span of a few minutes, drawing national headlines. The old, local "Grange" is in the back. (BMC.)

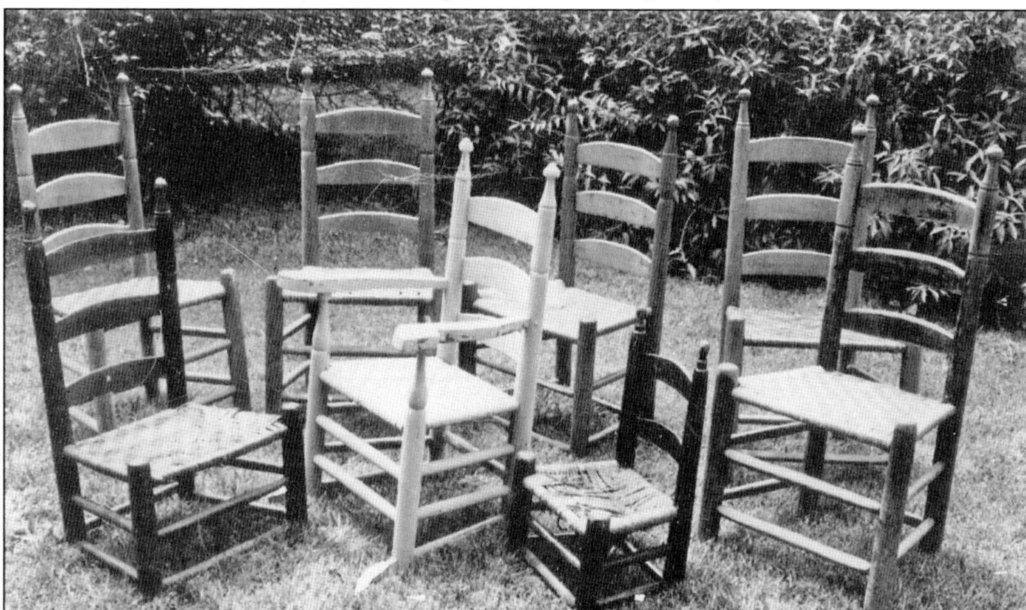

At the opposite end of eastern Mecklenburg is the home of the locally famous Johnson chairs. Thomas Johnson began making chairs in Wightman around 1800 and taught his son Warner K. Johnson, who took their chair-making business to the commercial level in the 1840s. Today the chairs sell at auction for thousands of dollars. This photograph depicts some of the most common Johnson chairs. (Virginia Dare Wright.)

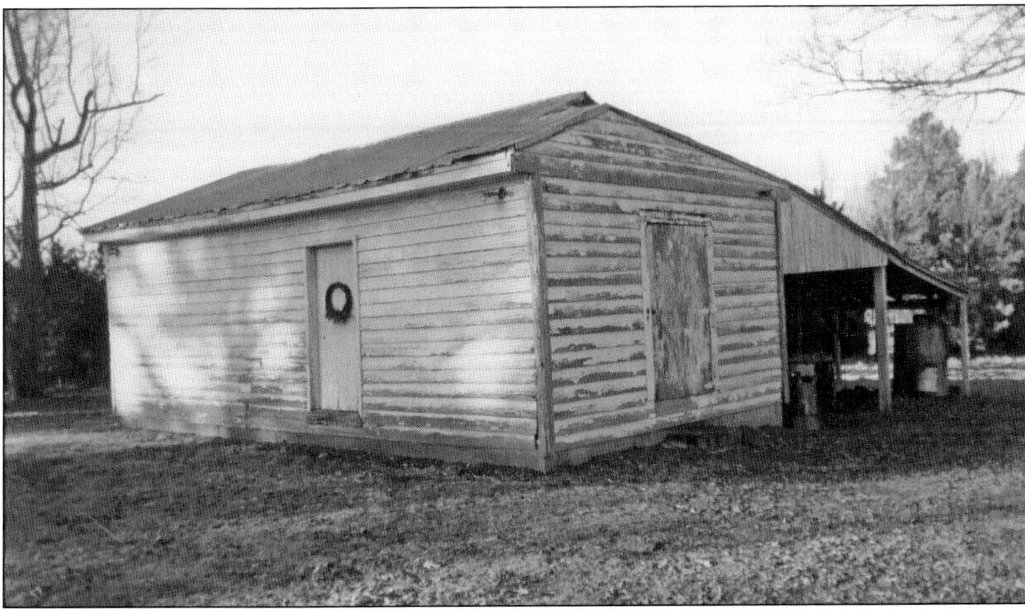

In 1881, R. H. and M. E. Johnson established a store in Wightman. In 1887, they built this post office adjacent to the store. Robert H. Johnson became the postmaster in January 1888. The post office served the community with mail, and this also became a meeting lodge for the Chase City Order of Free and Accepted Masons for several years. (Mary Alice Reamey.)

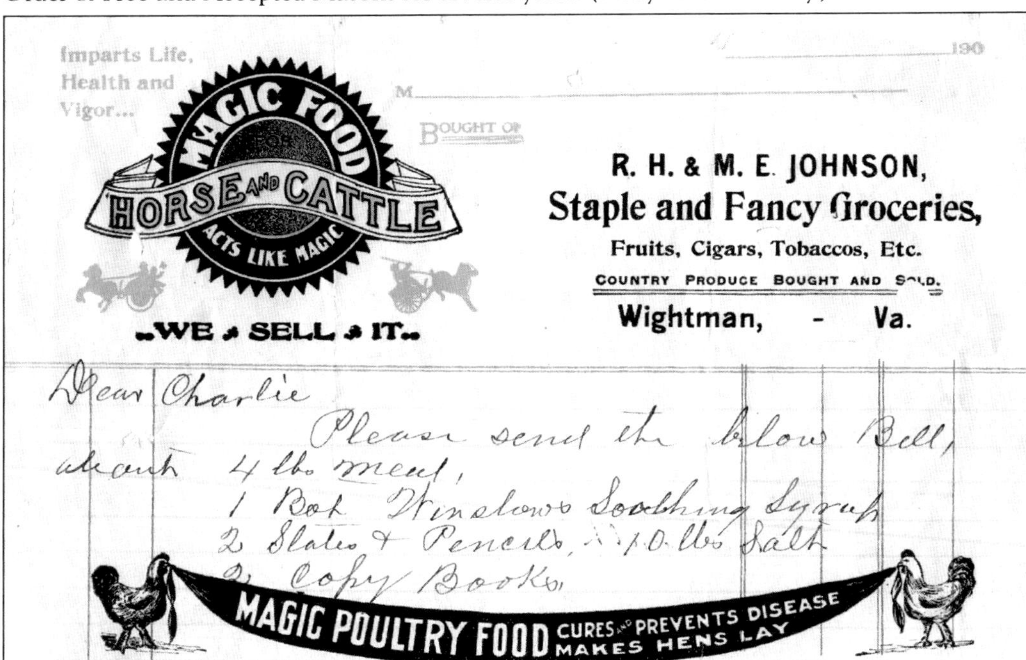

Imparts Life,
Health and
Vigor...

MAGIC FOOD FOR HORSE AND CATTLE
ACTS LIKE MAGIC
..WE SELL IT..

190

M

BOUGHT OF

R. H. & M. E. JOHNSON,
Staple and Fancy Groceries,
Fruits, Cigars, Tobaccos, Etc.
COUNTRY PRODUCE BOUGHT AND SOLD.
Wightman, - Va.

Dear Charlie
Please send the blow Bill,
about 4 lbs meal,
1 Bot Winslows Soothing Syrup
2 Slates & Pencils, 10 lbs Salt
2 Copy Books

MAGIC POULTRY FOOD CURES AND PREVENTS DISEASE MAKES HENS LAY

The store and post office were located on the old Buckhorn Road. As roads changed, a new South Hill Road was established in the late 1930s to connect directly to Chase City and west. Two new stores emerged in Wightman. With the customer base and service, Johnson's store lasted for over 90 years before being torn down to widen the highway. This note from 1905 shows a customer had sent in an order to be delivered. (Mary Alice Reamey.)

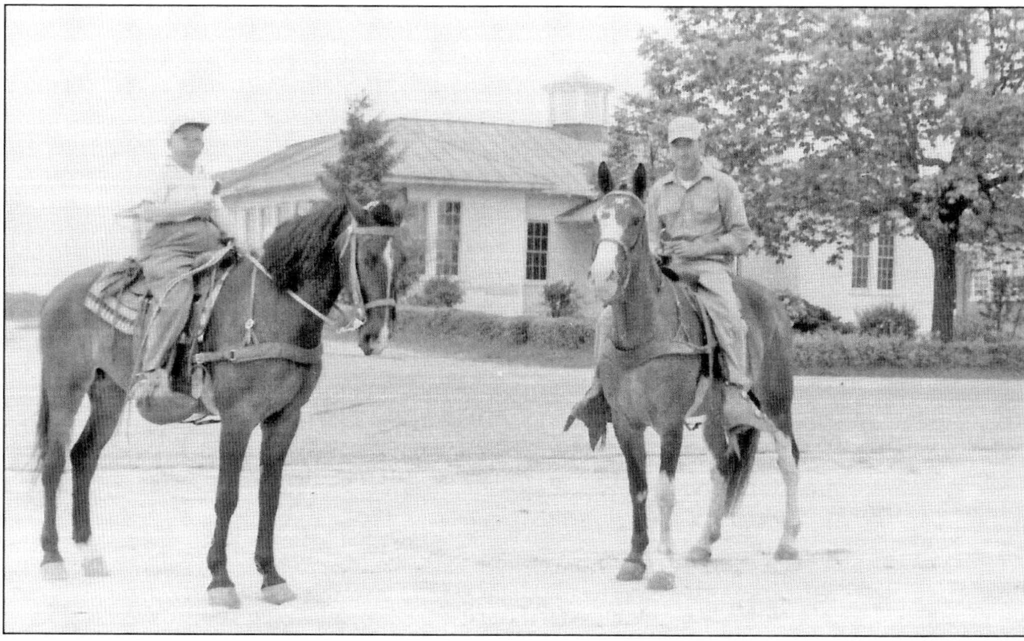

Near Wightman was the Buckhorn community. Pictured here is Louis Thompson on Lady and Bob Watson riding Stardust. They are in the parking lot of Sam Well's store across the road from the 1908 Buckhorn School. The first principal was William N. Willis. The school district was established in 1886 as an academy with Miss Goode as principal and Mary Buchanon as a teacher, but no professors. (CST.)

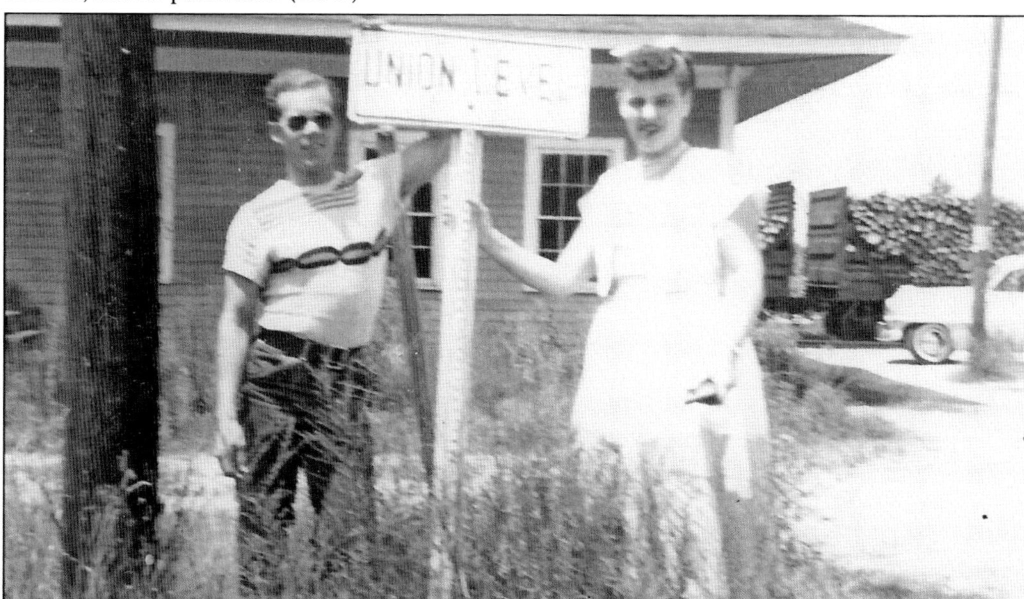

Southwest of Buckhorn was the community of Union Level. Established with a post office in January 1836 by James Bridgeforth, the community was a way station at an intersection for stagecoaches. In 1890, with the arrival of the Atlantic and Danville Railroad, the community moved near the new station. In front are C. W. Johnson and Ethel Thompson. Note pulpwood is being loaded onto flatcars in the rear. (CST.)

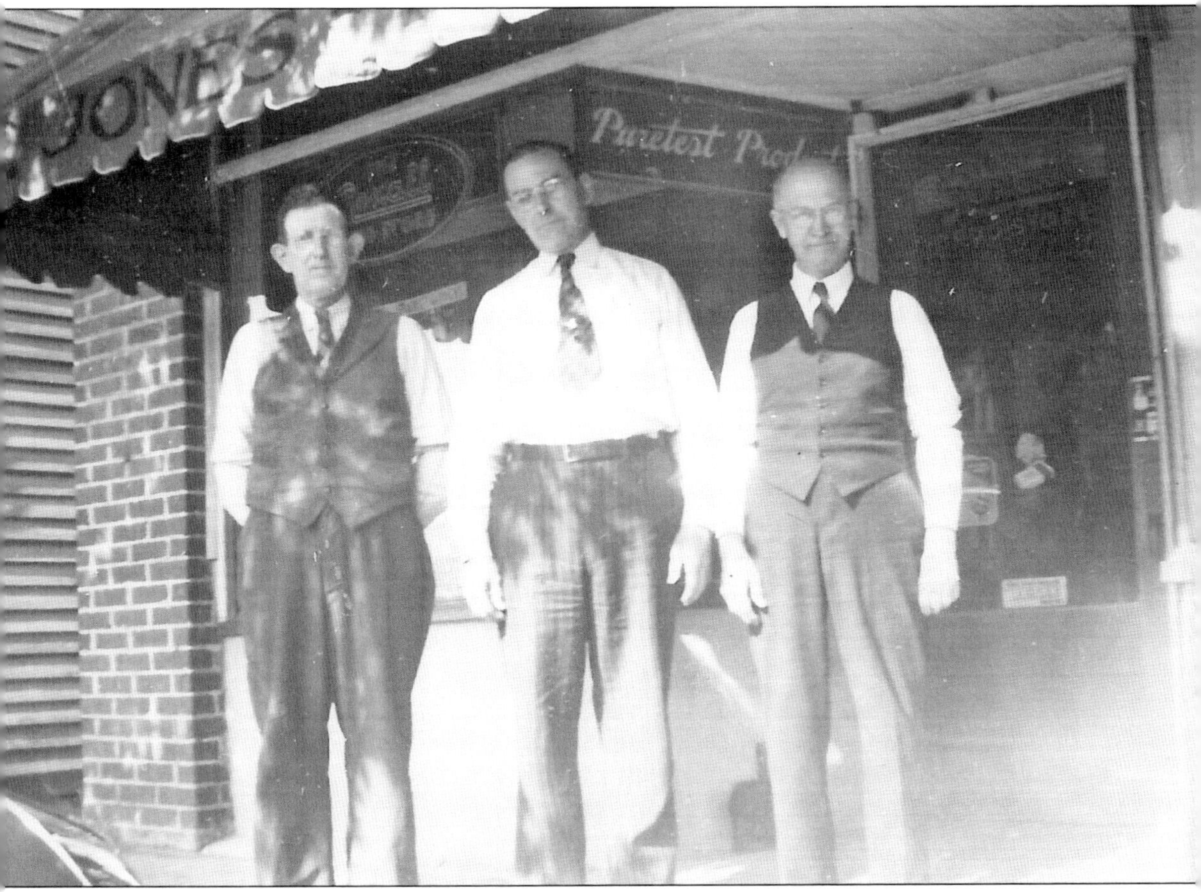

Cornelius P. Jones joined his brother John in their store in 1894. The store burned, and Cornelius rebuilt it in 1900 as a drugstore. He hired help and studied from them, passing his state test as a druggist in 1912. In 1914, C. P., as he was called, purchased a second drugstore in South Hill but returned to Union Level in 1922. In front of the store are, from left to right, John E. Smith, John A. Thompson (Jones's new partner), and C. P. Jones. (CST.)

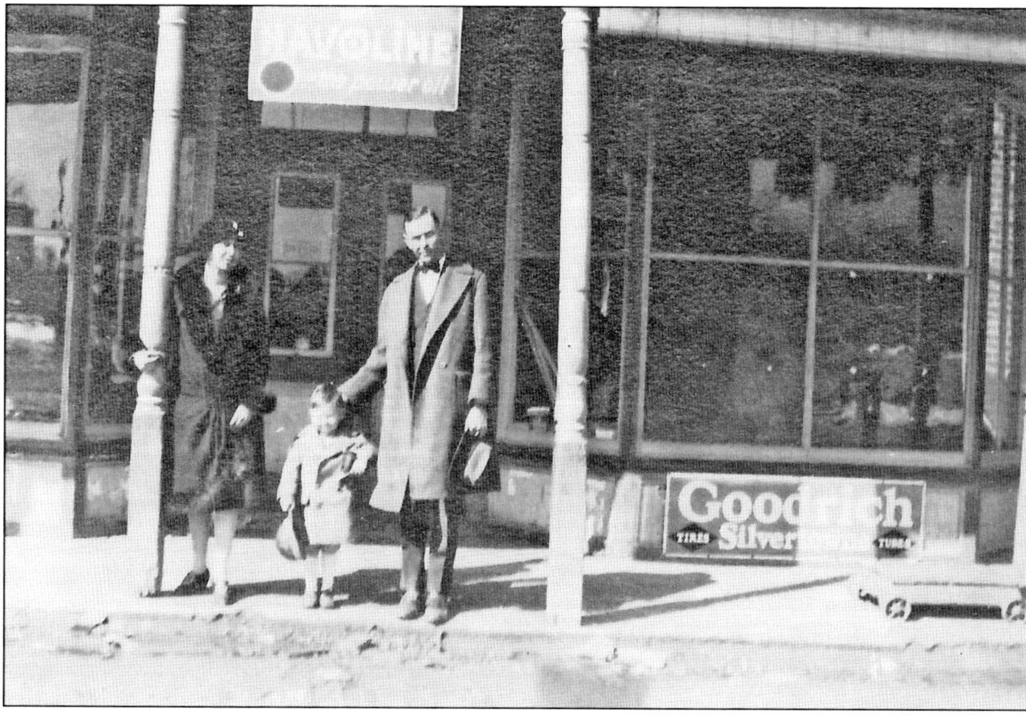

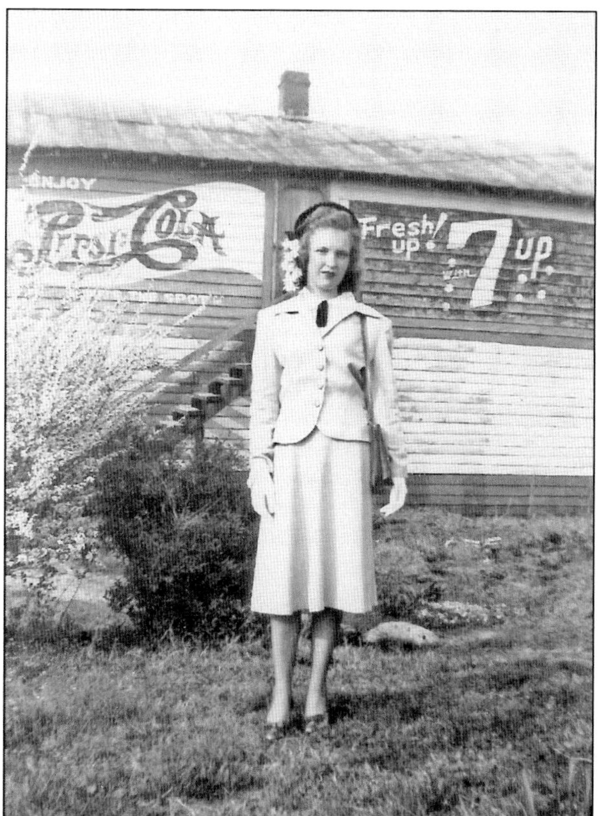

In 1908, Cornelius Jones built a frame general store next door with a doorway connecting the two. The second floor became a millinery shop operated by Margaret Thompson when her husband, Edward, purchased it in 1920. The millinery was converted to an apartment after being purchased by Ashby Thompson and his son John A. Thompson in 1926. (CST.)

L. W. Lett purchased the general merchandise store (established in 1905) from Katherine Davis (widow of James Davis) in 1929. Upstairs became an apartment and the backroom was the voting precinct. The store became a school bus stop, so it was always busy with neighborhood children. Nancy Johnson is seen at left in front of the merchandise store. (CST.)

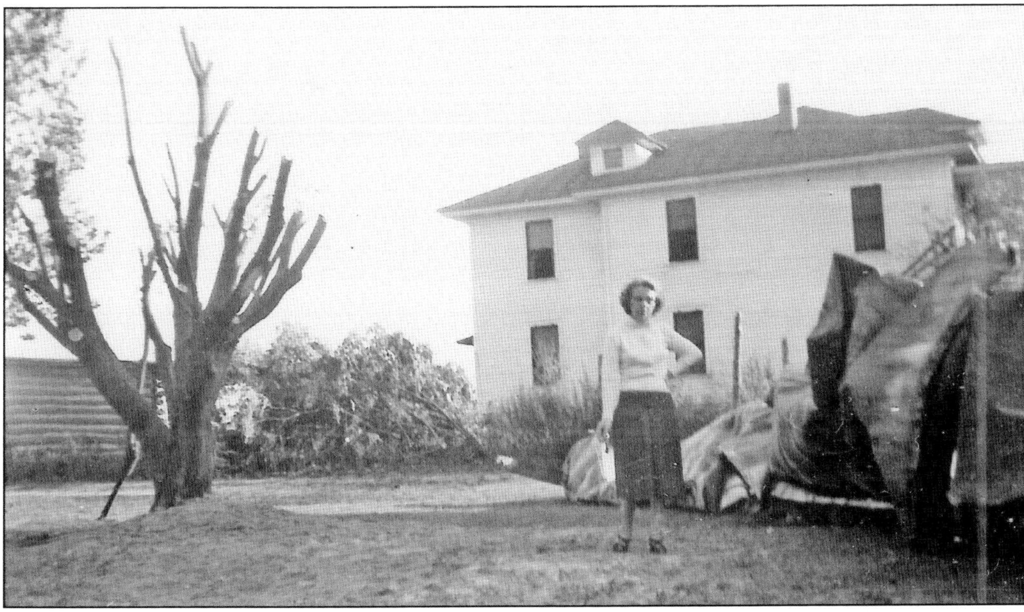

In 1920, N. W. and Georgia Ross purchased the local gristmill with 10 acres. In 1925, they purchased a parcel to build a boardinghouse (originally a hotel) for travelers. Following the Depression, it became apartments. Clara Thompson is shown above standing next to the roof from the building across the street. The roof was ripped off during Hurricane Hazel in August 1954. (CST.)

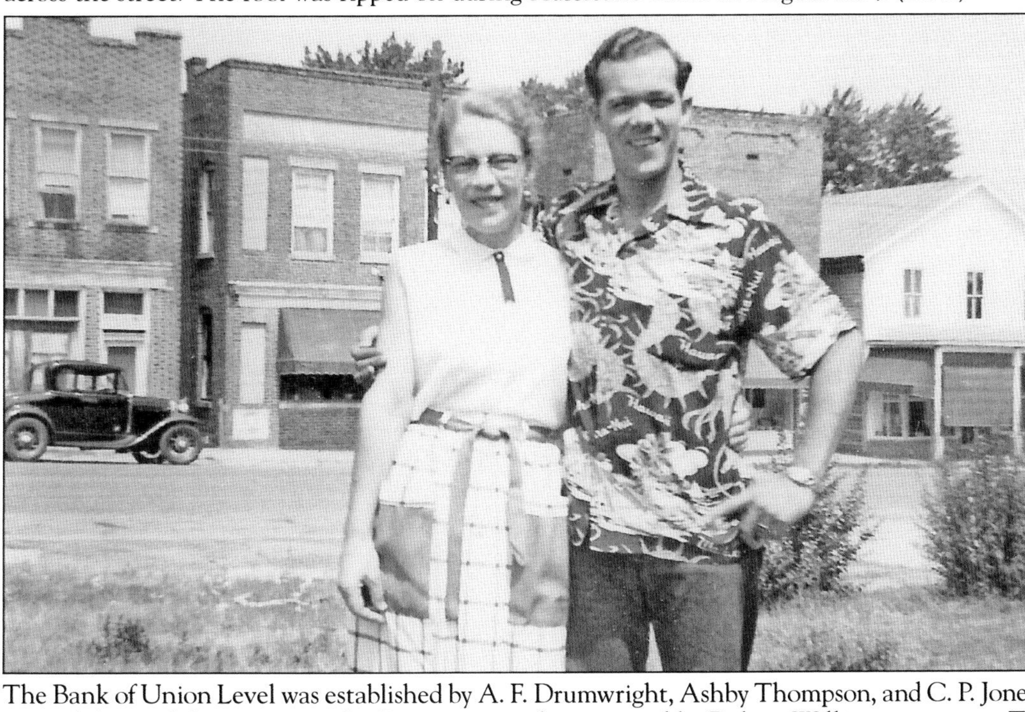

The Bank of Union Level was established by A. F. Drumwright, Ashby Thompson, and C. P. Jones in 1915, but it did not survive the Depression and was rented by Robert Williams as a store. To the left of the bank were the general store and upstairs apartment of Archie Ferguson Jr.; to the right was the mercantile/millinery of Drumright and Williams. Pictured here is Clara Thompson (aunt of the famed F. Lee Bailey) with C. W. Thompson. (CST.)

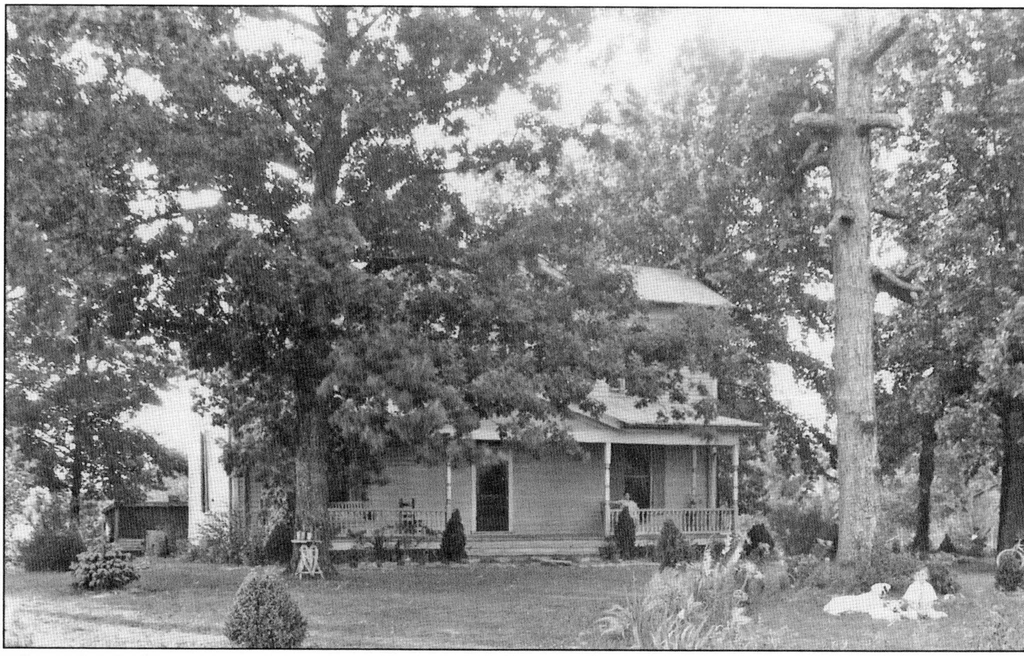

The 1875 Oak Grove of Archie Ferguson (a veteran of the Confederate States of America, CSA, 3rd Virginia Cavalry) was purchased by Martha Saunders around 1890 with her two daughters, Lucy and Alice. They became school teachers for the Buckhorn Academy (about 2 miles away) until it closed in 1908. Margaret Thompson is on the porch with Louis and Petro (his dog) on the lawn. (CST.)

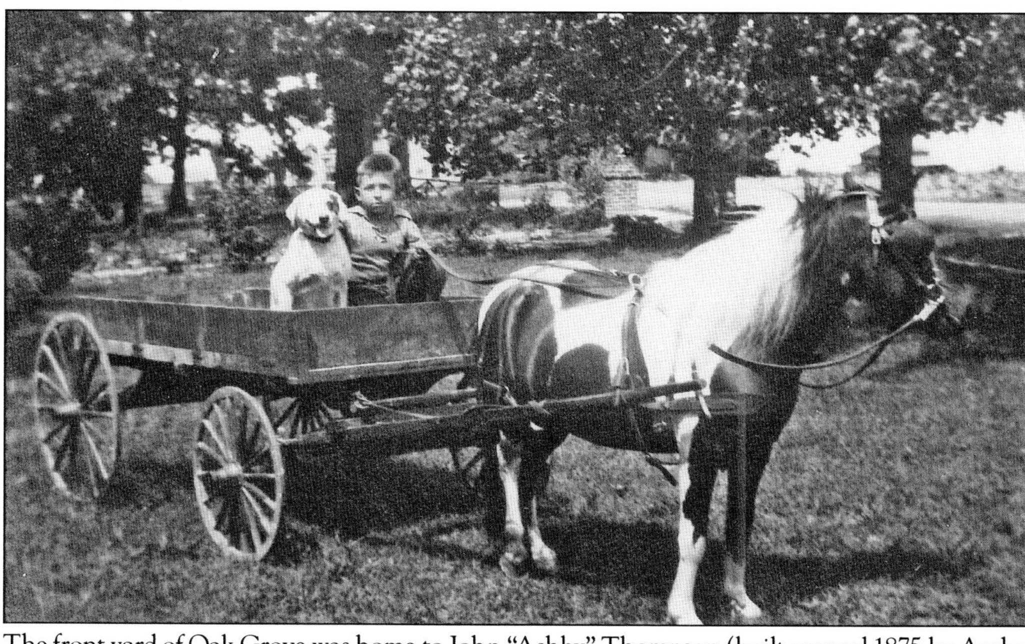

The front yard of Oak Grove was home to John "Ashby" Thompson (built around 1875 by Archer Ferguson) and his family in 1929. Ashby was the owner of the Union Level Mercantile. His son Louis is going for a stroll around the property in 1931 with Petro, and his pony Dot is pulling the wagon. (Spot and Clara Thompson.)

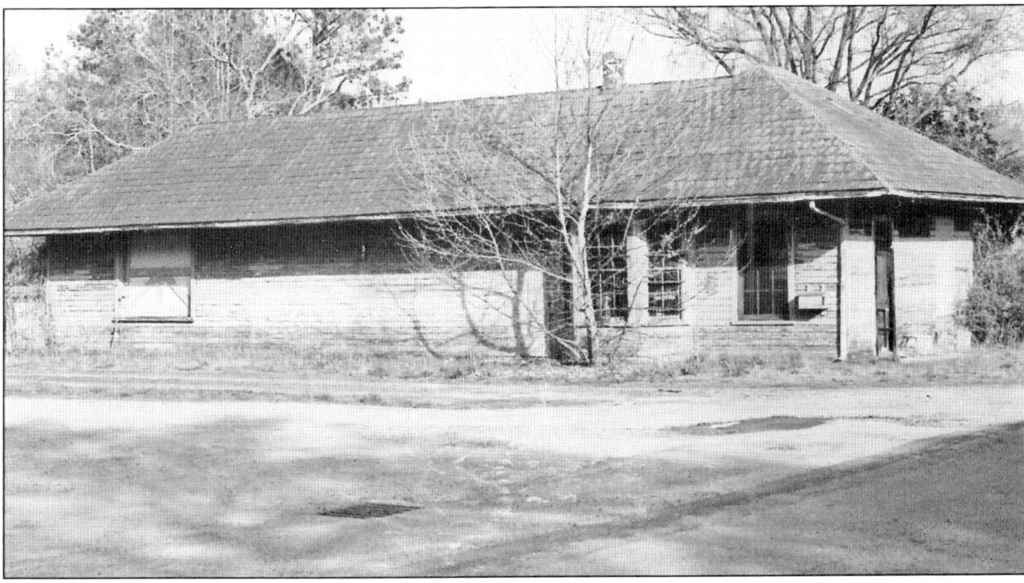

The Atlantic and Danville Railroad arrived in another community in 1890. The railroad physician, Dr. Robert R. Baskervill, named the community "Baskerville." The depot was established with a front entrance for whites, a side entrance for blacks, and a holding pen for livestock below. It was a telegraph station, and a post office was established in June with Sterling N. Hutcheson as the first postmaster. Hutcheson had to move the post office from his store to the station. (CST.)

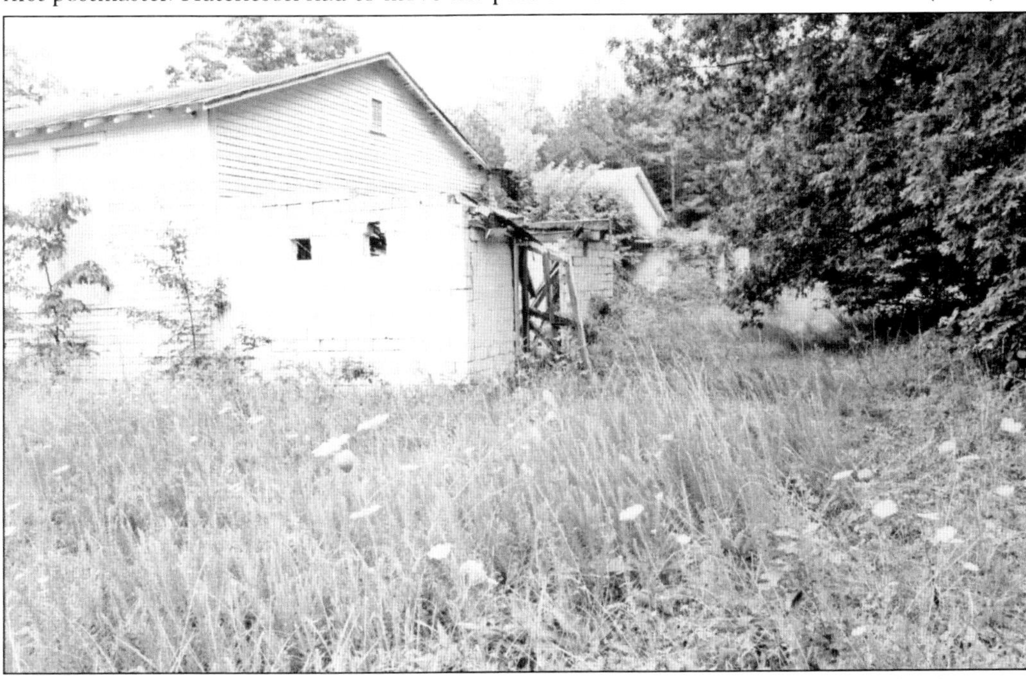

South of the Roanoke River, Palmer Springs began to develop with a new public school in 1904. By 1907, Palmer Springs received the fourth-largest funding from the county's school budget. The teachers were W. B. Poggin, Mattie Epps, and Helen Hayes. Having closed and been consolidated in 1955, this is a photograph of the remains, which became Rick Hendrick's first automobile workshop. (Hendrick Motorsports.)

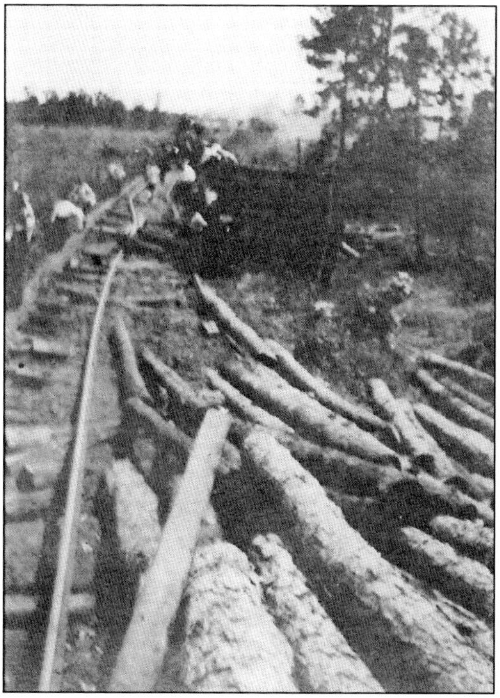

The Atlantic and Danville and the Seaboard Air Line Railroads were both accident prone. Records indicate they experienced at least one crash or derailment every year, some serious. This derailment in 1923, coming into South Hill, provided excitement for the community and was well attended. There were no injuries. (SHM.)

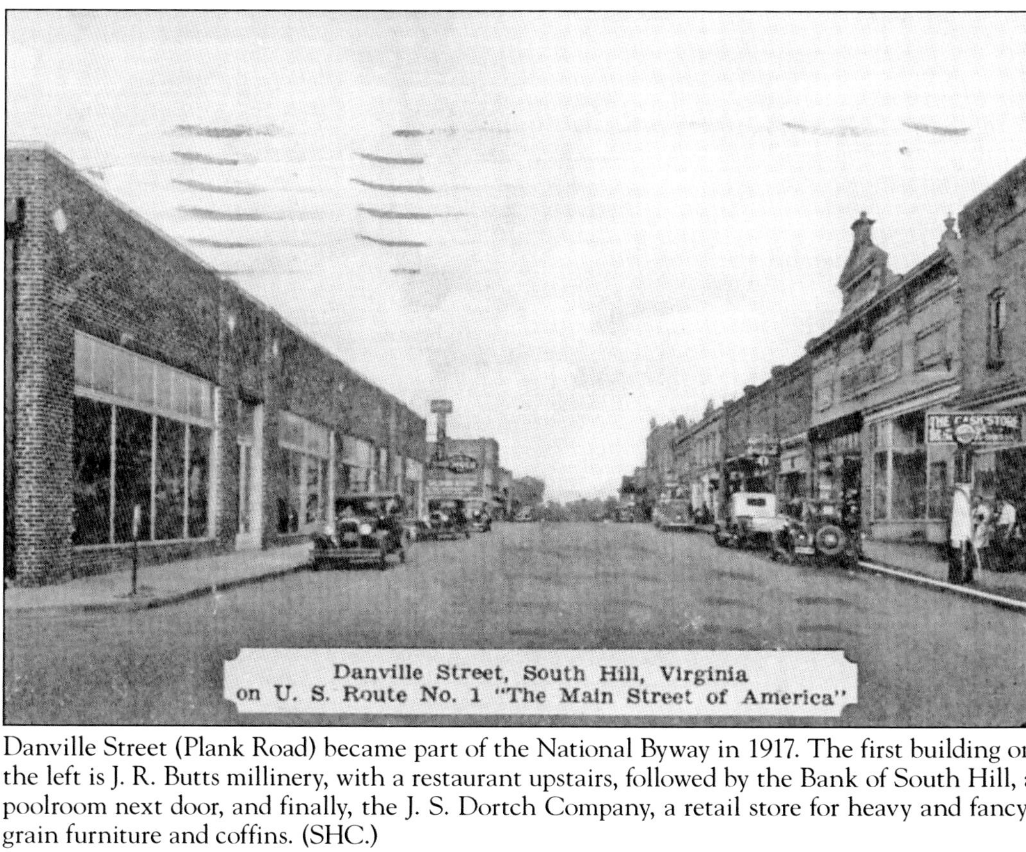

Danville Street (Plank Road) became part of the National Byway in 1917. The first building on the left is J. R. Butts millinery, with a restaurant upstairs, followed by the Bank of South Hill, a poolroom next door, and finally, the J. S. Dortch Company, a retail store for heavy and fancy-grain furniture and coffins. (SHC.)

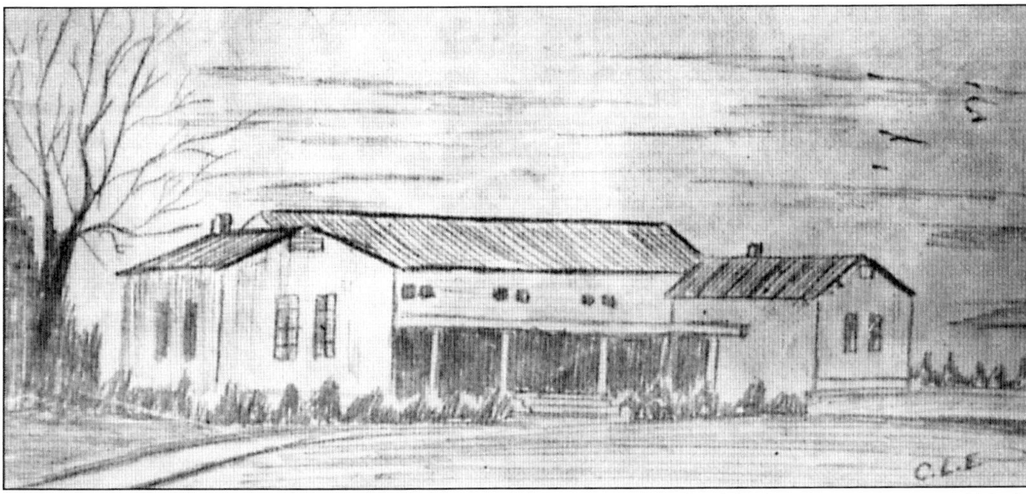

This was a sketch for a Rosenwald two-room school built for the black community in 1918. In 1920, with the support of the county school board and community citizens, the Mecklenburg County Training School was constructed (comprised of three frame buildings). It opened in 1925 with 200 students enrolled in grades one through seven. In 1927, the old South Hill cannery next door was purchased for a home economics program. (SHC.)

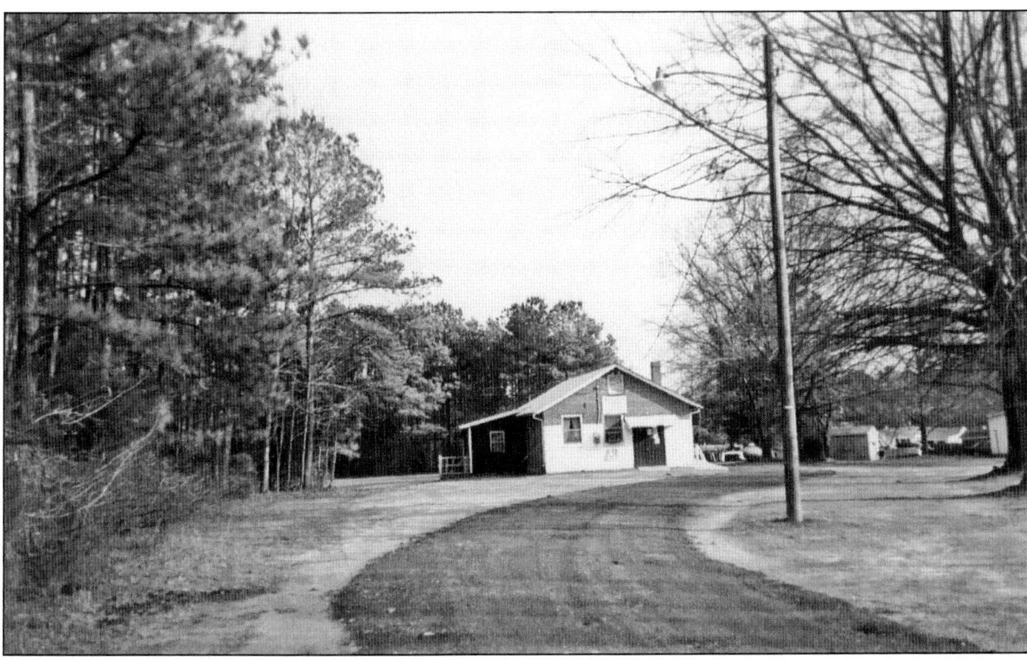

Also in 1927, the agriculture building was added and the cannery became a cafeteria. The three frame buildings had extensive damage from a fire on December 22, 1942, which closed the school. The cannery was eventually removed, and the agriculture building serves as community center for a senior citizens. (JC.)

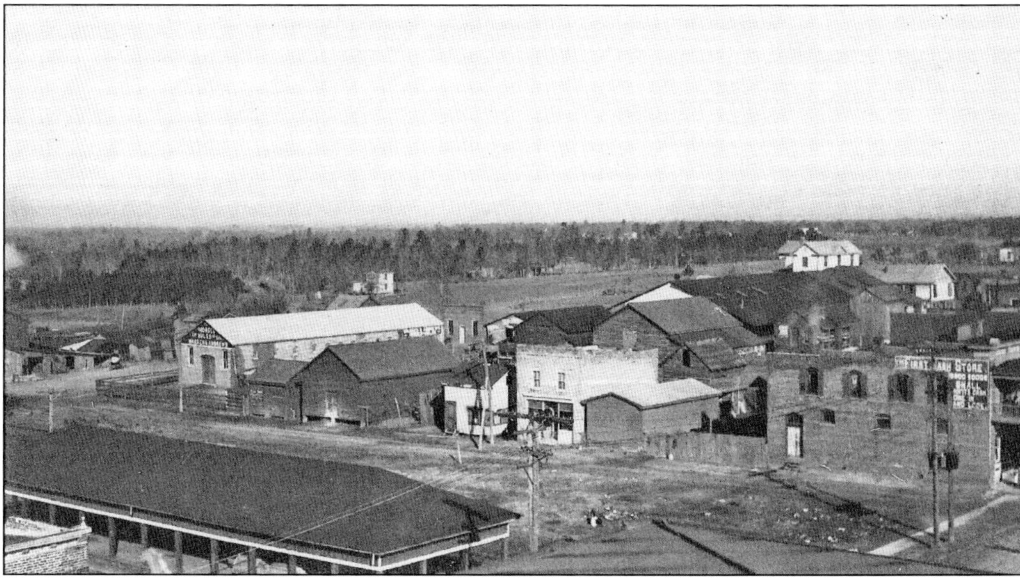

Seen at the far right on North Main Street, along the railroad tracks, is Crowder's First Cash Store, which now faces Mecklenburg Avenue with a livery stable in the rear. The next store is a saloon, then a warehouse, an unidentified structure, and finally, the last building is believed to say "Horses, Mules & Supplies, Warren and Spencer." (SHM.)

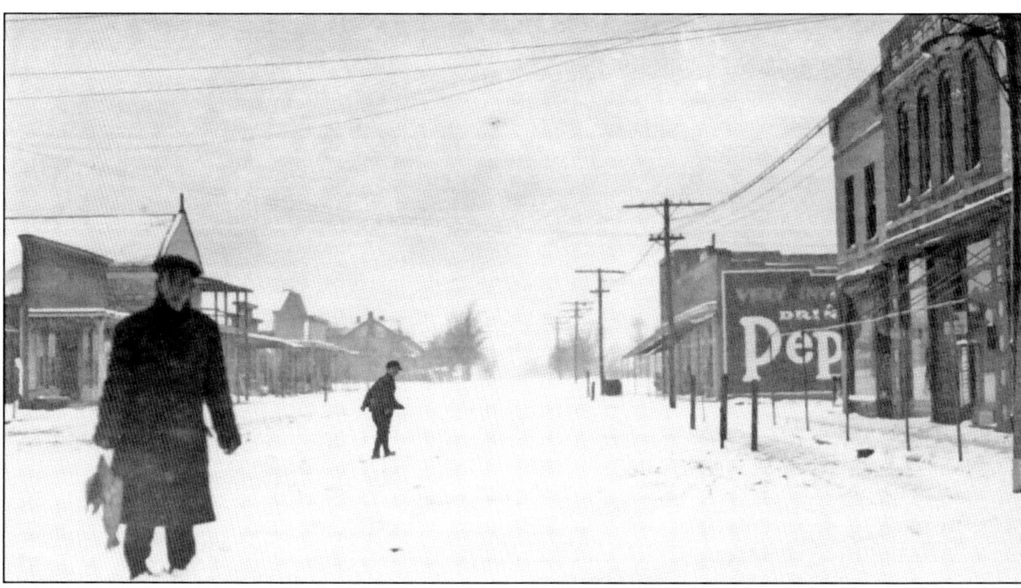

The blizzard of April 2, 1915, did not stop local citizens from fishing the "crappie run." On the left in the foreground is an unidentified man with a stringer of fish on North Mecklenburg Avenue. Note the shops on the streets have hitching posts in front of the plank sidewalks. (SHC.)

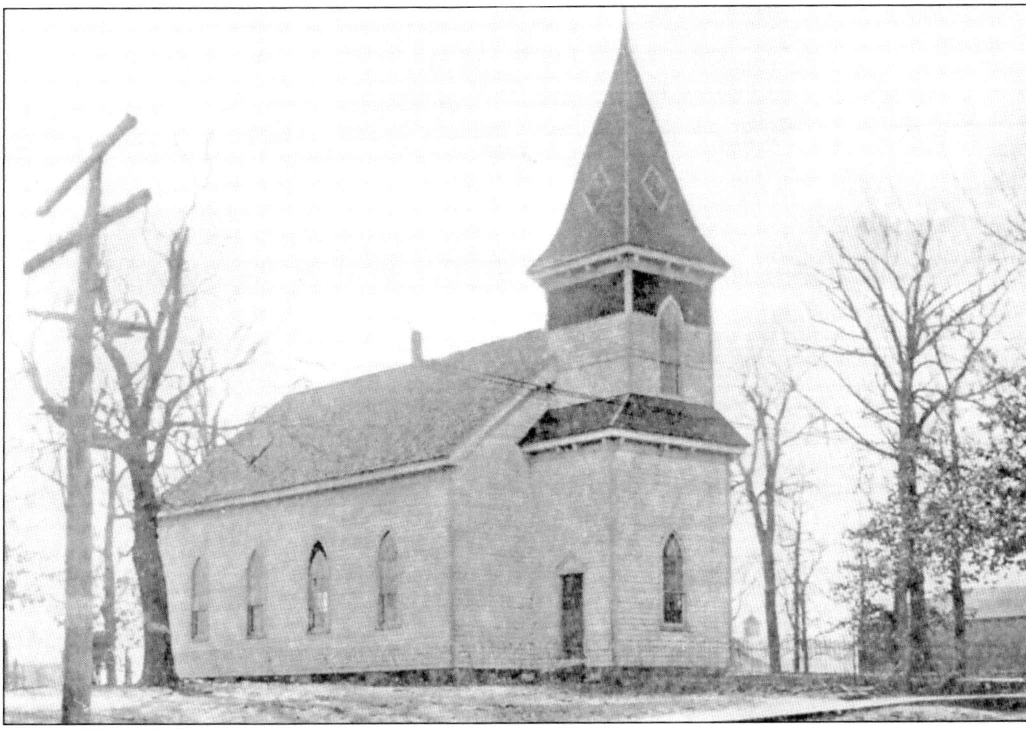

The South Hill Methodist Church was dedicated in 1903 on Danville Street, but by 1917 the congregation decided it needed more room. They built a new sanctuary that was dedicated in December 1919. The old church would become the building site of a new hotel. (SHC.)

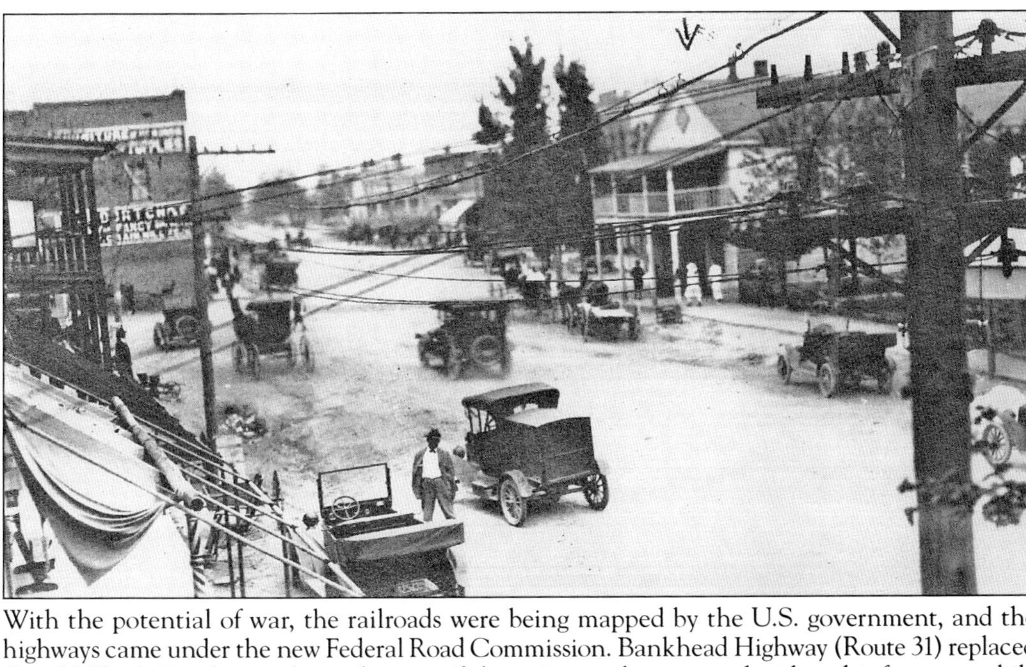

With the potential of war, the railroads were being mapped by the U.S. government, and the highways came under the new Federal Road Commission. Bankhead Highway (Route 31) replaced the old Plank Road, straightened many of the twists and turns, and widened it for automobile travel. Many stores lost their front awnings, porches, and balconies. (SHC.)

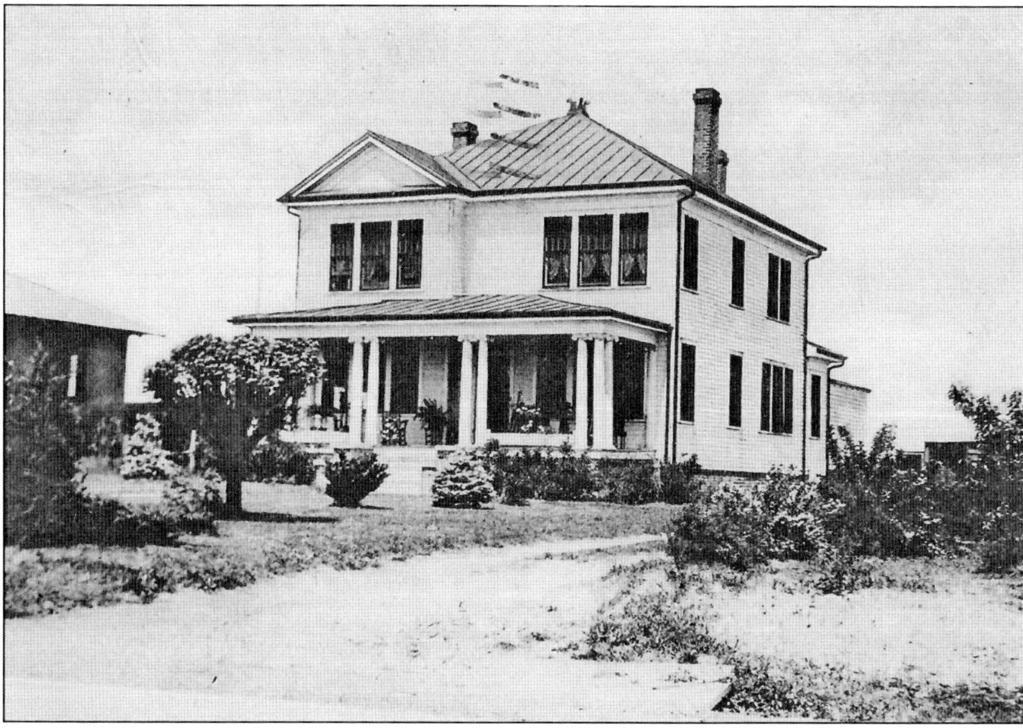

To embrace the new highway, many new homes were being built as tourist homes. This is the Sunnyside Inn built by H. C. Coleman. He advertised "AA rating by National Red Book—rooms and meals." (TJS.)

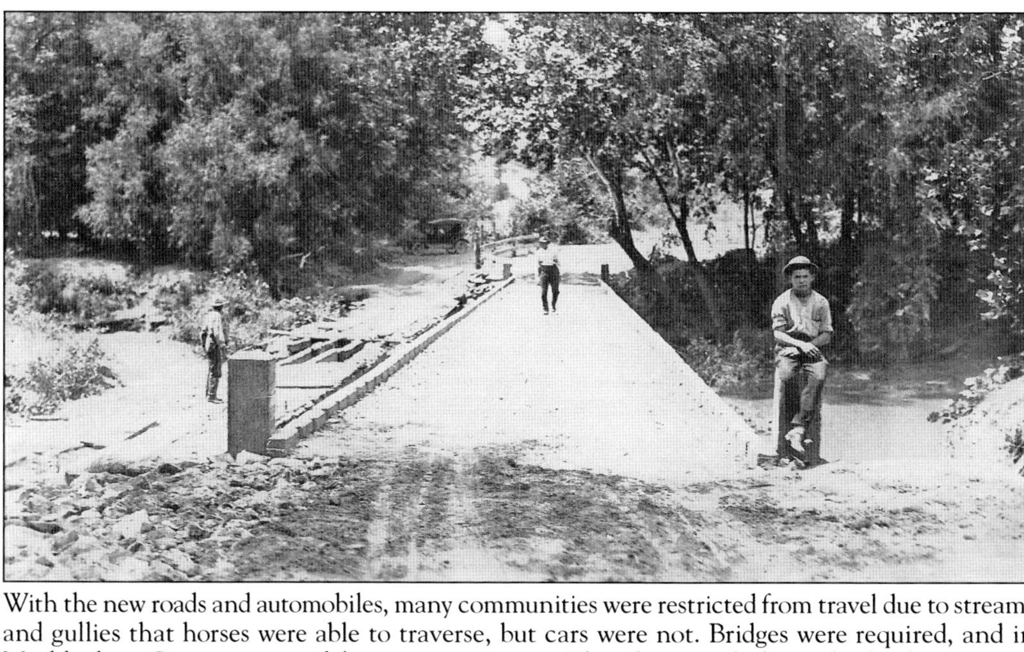

With the new roads and automobiles, many communities were restricted from travel due to streams and gullies that horses were able to traverse, but cars were not. Bridges were required, and in Mecklenburg County, many of them were necessary. This photograph shows the final inspection of the Union Mill Bridge on December 23, 1923. The individuals are unidentified. (SHM.)

Three

Growth during the 1920s

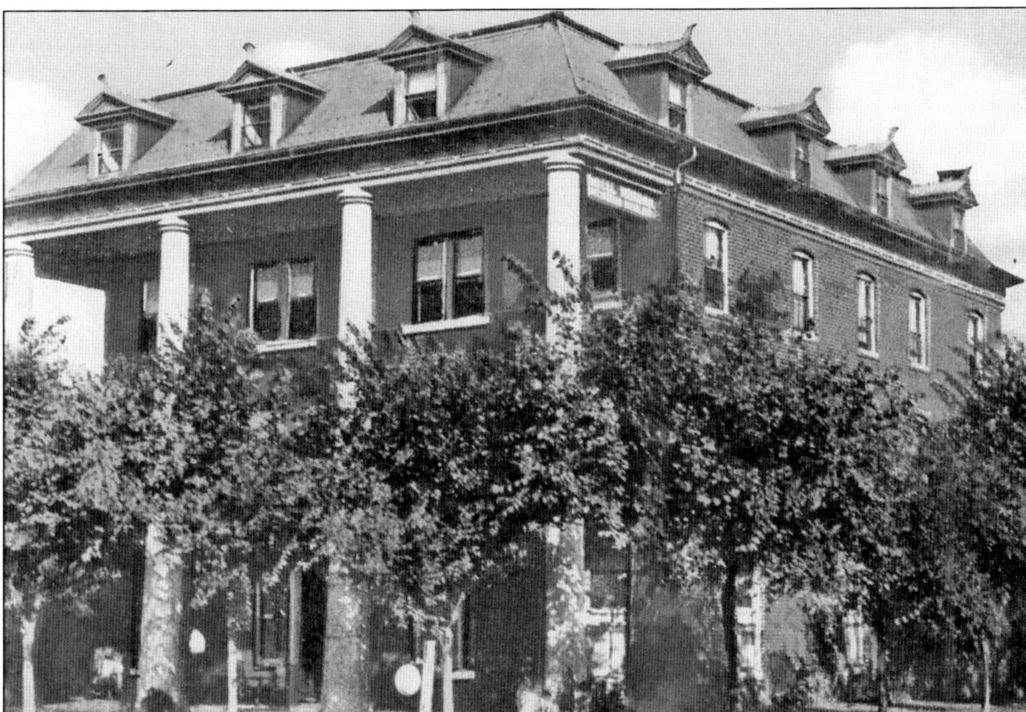

The Nordan Hotel was fully remodeled and landscaped. It became a well-known stopover for couples on their honeymoon. It also became a destination for business travelers. Lumber and tobacco were in great demand, both of which were plentiful in eastern Mecklenburg County. Many business negotiations took place in this hotel, and the entire county benefited from its prosperity. (WCG.)

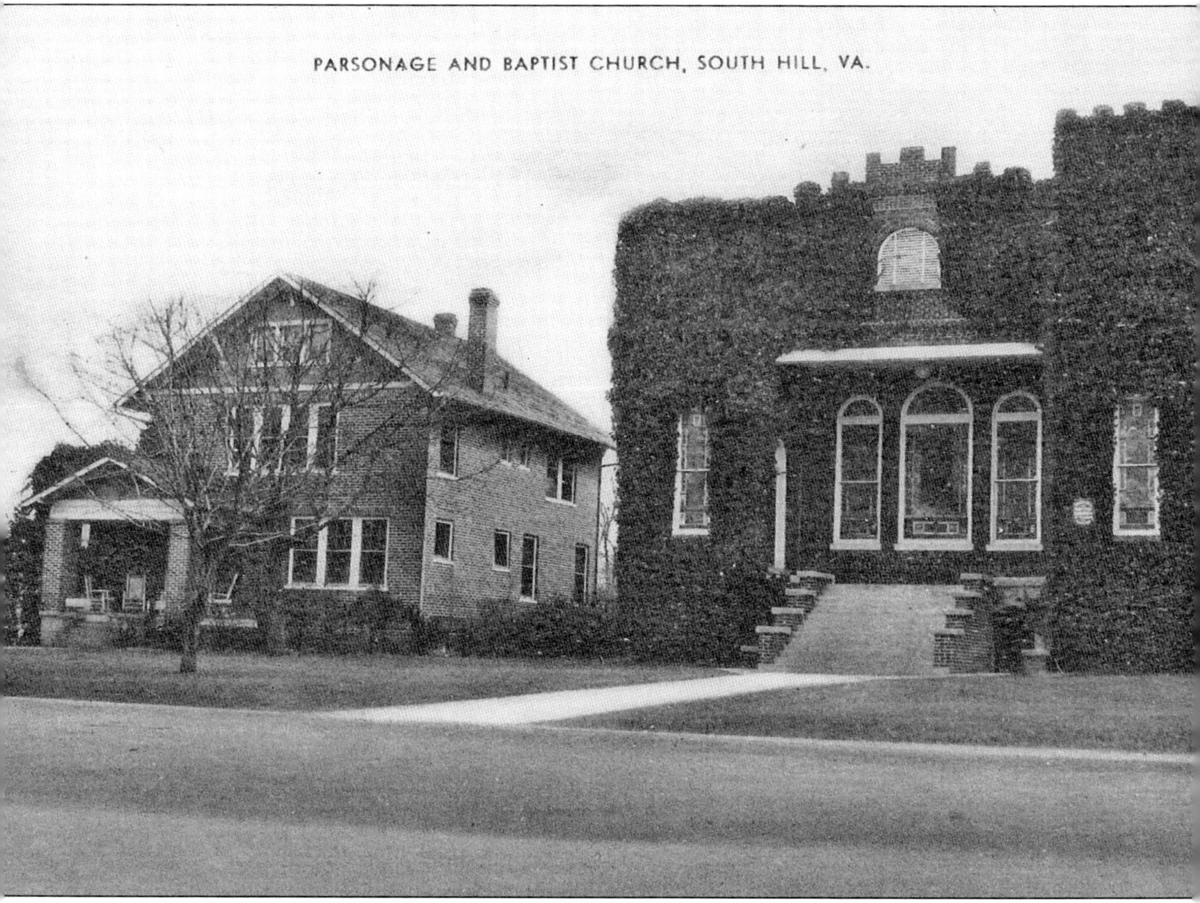

The Baptist Church of South Hill continued to grow and required a new sanctuary to be built in 1920. This postcard is from the 1940s, as the church did not add the parsonage next door until 1942. (TJS.)

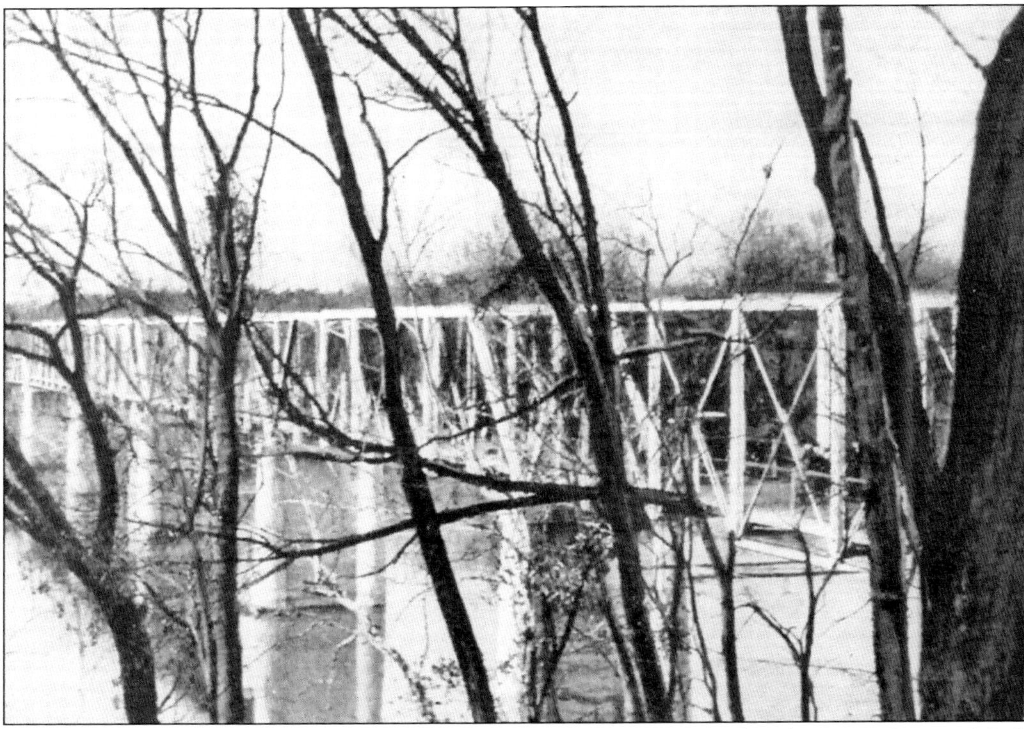

On February 21, 1921, the South Hill–Henderson Toll Bridge opened with Henry Owen of Gold Leaf as the first keeper. It shortened the travel from Richmond to Raleigh by over 20 miles (using the Clarksville Bridge), and a great deal of time was saved from using the ferries. South Hill was now host to three highways, two rivers, and a railroad. (TJS.)

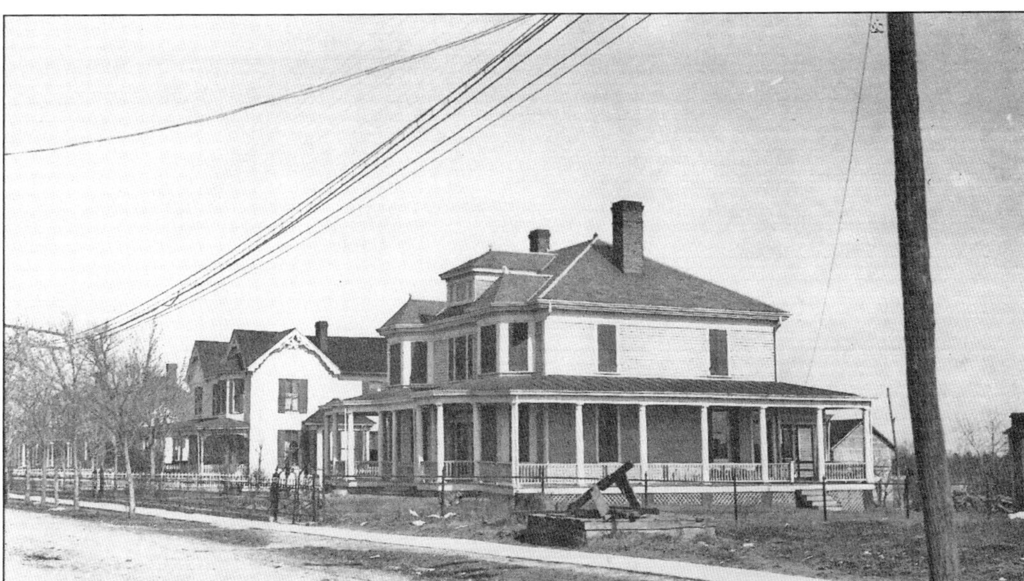

Several more tourist rests were opened by local citizens. This postcard shows the home of Mrs. W. A. Wartman. She advertised private baths, steam heat, and garages, and her telephone number was 92. With a population of 1,047, South Hill was united in its effort to foster tourism. (TJS.)

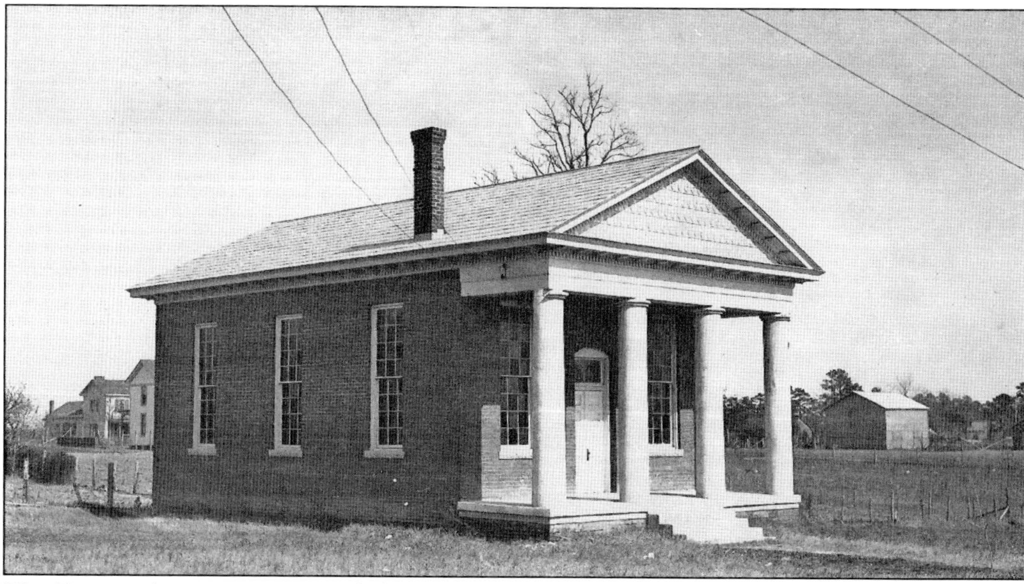

The Episcopal congregation used the sanctuary of the Christian church from its beginning in 1900. As both congregations grew, the Episcopal church congregation believed it was time to have their own sanctuary. In 1922, they built this new All Saints Church on Franklin Street. It partially burned in 1968, but was promptly rebuilt. (SHC.)

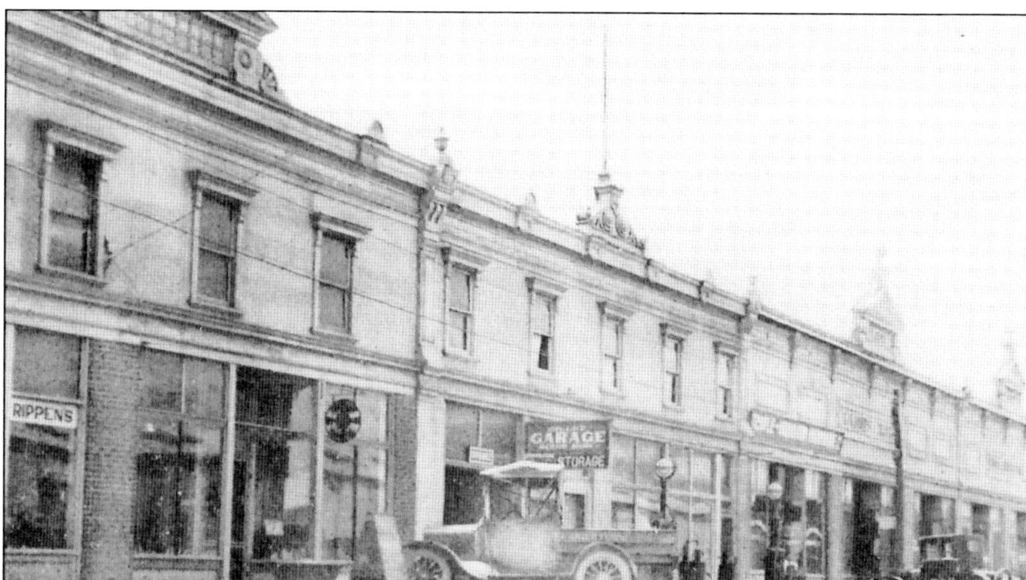

Danville Street lost most of its frame structures in the early 1920s, but the old and new businesses were soon all built from brick. In 1924, the town of South Hill added its first sewer system, which helped the rebuilding of the area. In this photograph are, from left to right, the Rippens Department Store (1924), Collins Garage (1922, later a Plymouth-Dodge dealership in 1935), J. S. Dortch Company (1911), and an unidentified restaurant. (SHM.)

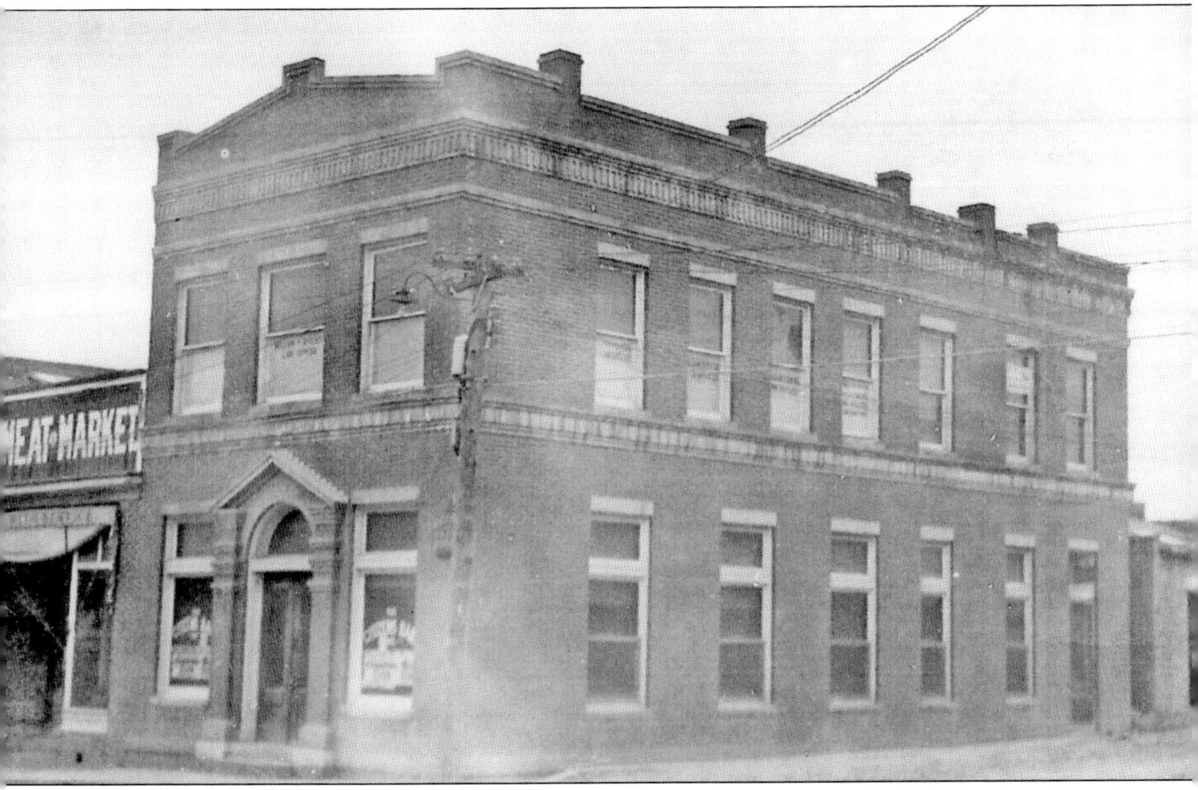

Most of the buildings had offices, meeting rooms, or restaurants upstairs. In this photograph, the new Sanitary Meat Market (a butcher shop) opened in 1928 with offices upstairs, and next was the new Citizens Bank building, which also opened in 1928 and had second-floor office space. (SHM.)

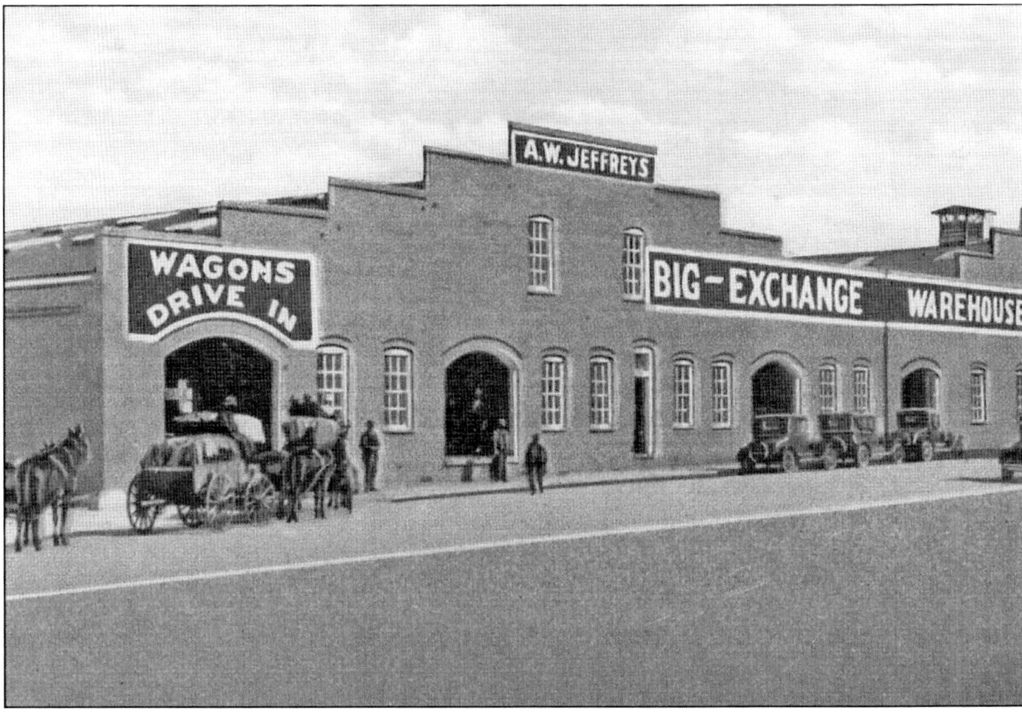

The Big Exchange Warehouse, owned by A. W. Jeffreys and C. H. Harris, opened on Danville Street for the 1922 season. This was the first brick warehouse in town. By the end of the 1920s, tobacco season sales in South Hill had reached the 300,000-pound mark. Half of this warehouse collapsed in 1960 and was removed. (WCG.)

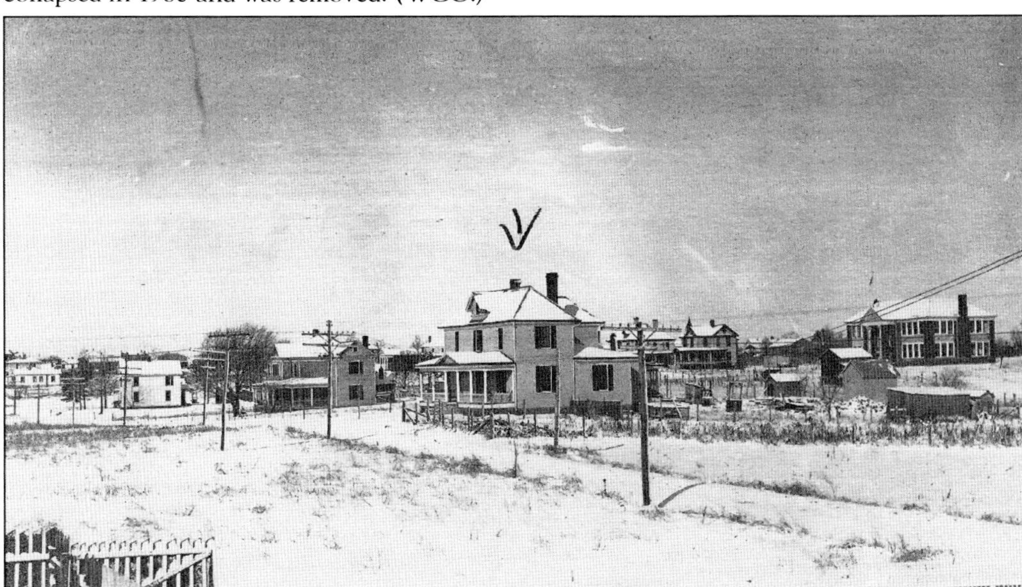

In this photograph, electricity (1922) and a sewer system (1924) have been installed, but dirt streets, plank sidewalks, and wells still remain. In the foreground is one of the wells (privately owned) in South Hill that provided water to residential areas. At the top right is the South Hill High School (1910) sitting in a field (the school burned). (SHC.)

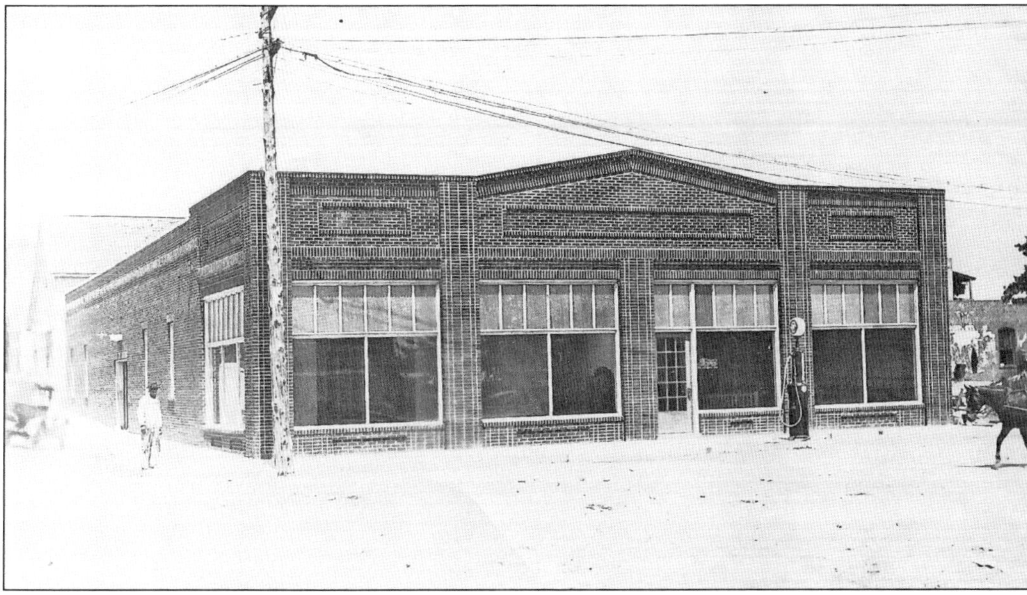

Radcliffe Motor Company (Ford) constructed this new building in 1926 and opened in the same year. The structure served as a showroom on Mecklenburg Avenue. Around the back of the building was a garage and service center. (SHC.)

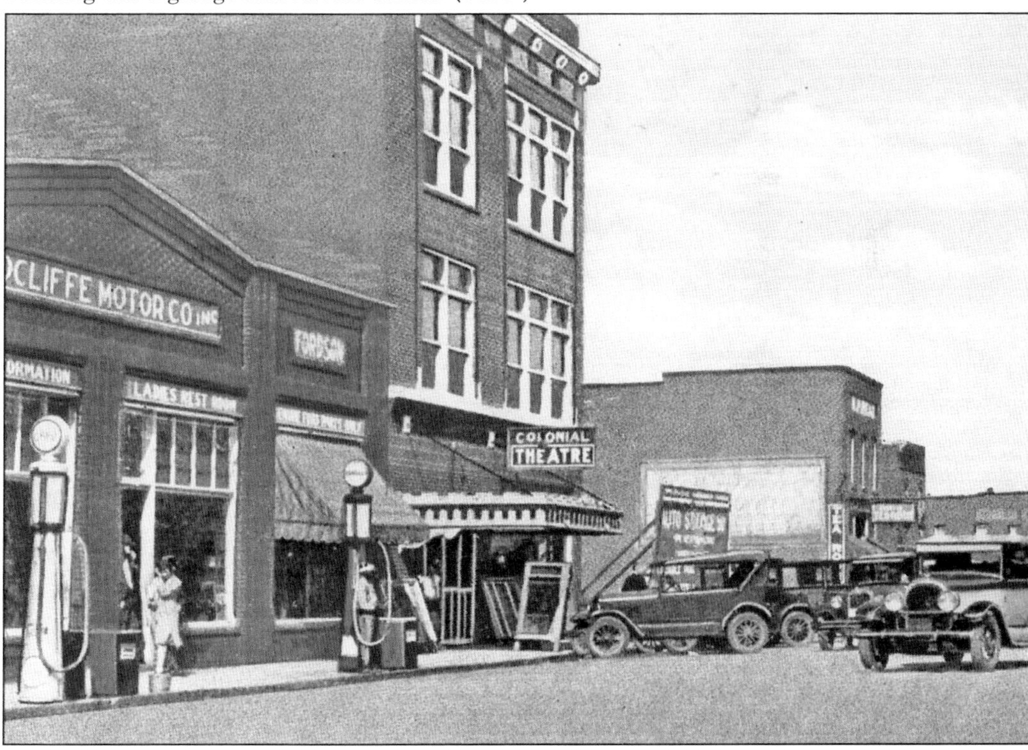

Nearby, G. A. Saunders had built the Colonial Theatre. It opened for business on October 1, 1925. The downstairs housed offices, which were moved to the new location from the old Saunders Building up the street. The upstairs and rear sections were the theaters for both movies and visiting shows and entertainers. (WCG.)

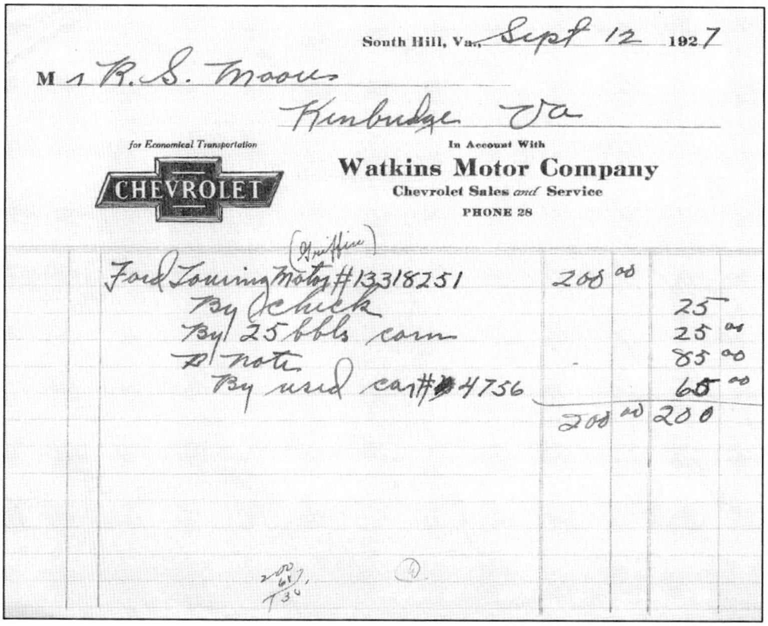

South Hill, Va., Sept 12 1927

M R. S. Moores

Kenbridge Va

for Economical Transportation

CHEVROLET

In Account With

Watkins Motor Company

Chevrolet Sales and Service

PHONE 28

Ford Touring Motor #13318251 (Griffin)	200 00	
By check		25
By 25 bbls corn		25 00
note		85 00
By used car #4756		65 00
	200 00	200

Fred E. Watkins Motor Company (Chevrolet) opened on Danville Street next to the Big Exchange Warehouse in December 1926. This September 12, 1927, invoice shows a completed deal of barter, finance, and trade-in (typical for the day) for a car purchased by R. S. Moores. Note part of the barter was 25 bushels of corn. Watkins opened a second dealership in 1935 in Chase City. (TJS.)

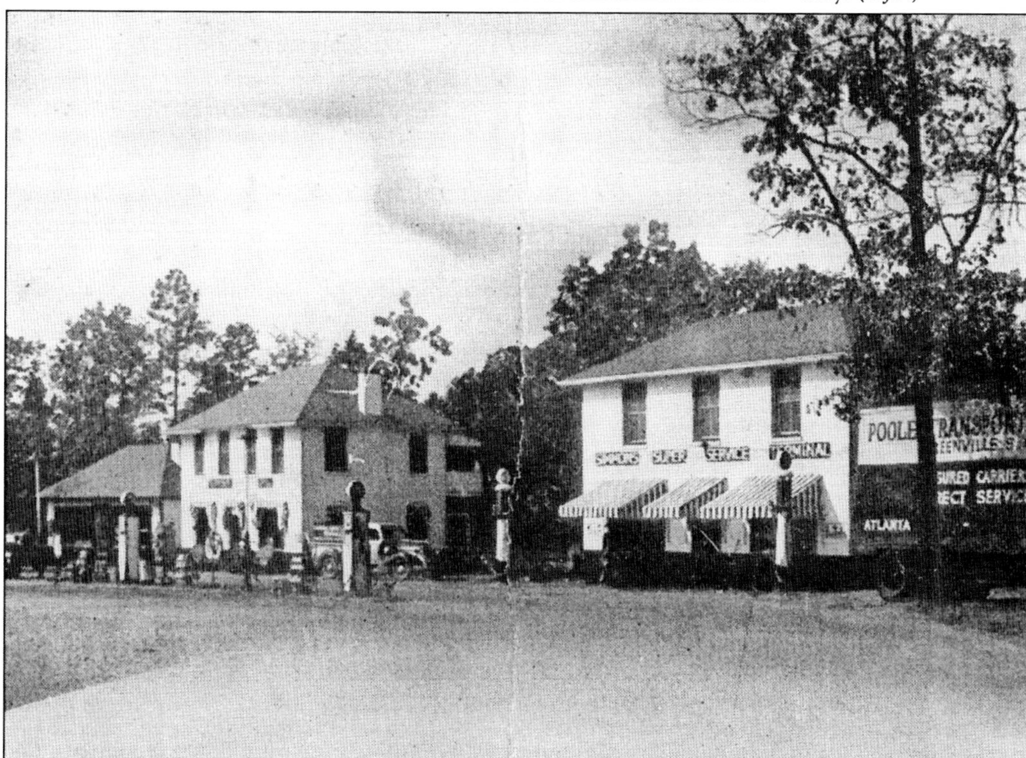

In January 1927, W. L. Simmons of Union Level began a Cities Service petroleum business, and in March, he partnered with Louis Parker Jr. By the end of that year, Parker purchased the entire business from Simmons. In 1936, Parker built a new Pure Oil truck terminal along U.S. Route 1, south of South Hill, which included offices upstairs and a grill downstairs. Several more terminals were added through the following years. (WCG.)

The arrival of U.S. Route 1 was a yearlong celebration in South Hill, but would change the county drastically. Many small communities were bypassed, but tourists came to South Hill by the thousands. On April 18, 1927, the town hosted a state fiddler's convention, which was held in Farmer's Warehouse. This is the cover page of the program. (Glen and Lisa Gillispie.)

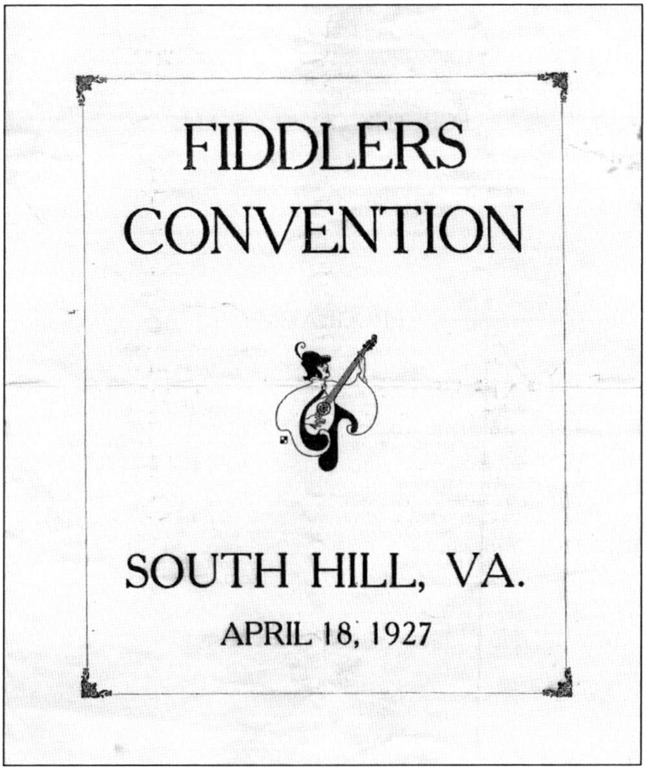

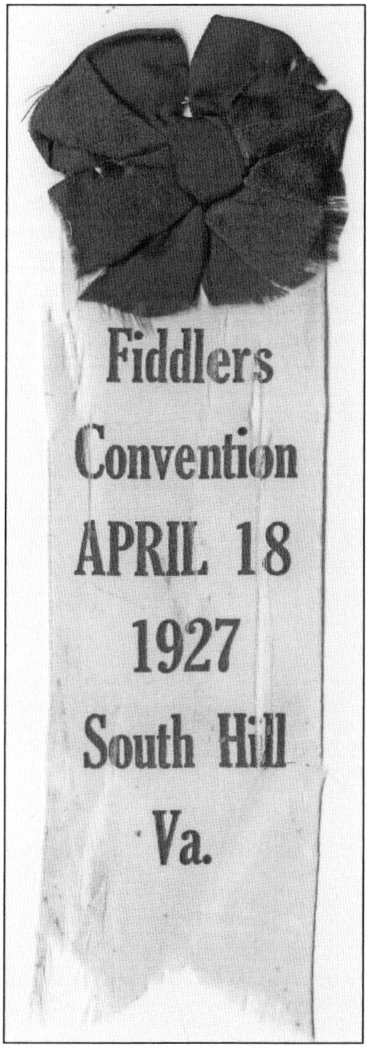

At the convention, this ribbon was presented to all the competitors. U.S. Route 1 became known as the most heavily traveled route in the state, as it spanned from Maine to Florida. Following Old Plank Road to Big Fork, it turns south following the old Henderson Country Road just outside of Palmer Springs, bypassing all of the western part of the county. (Glen and Lisa Gillispie.)

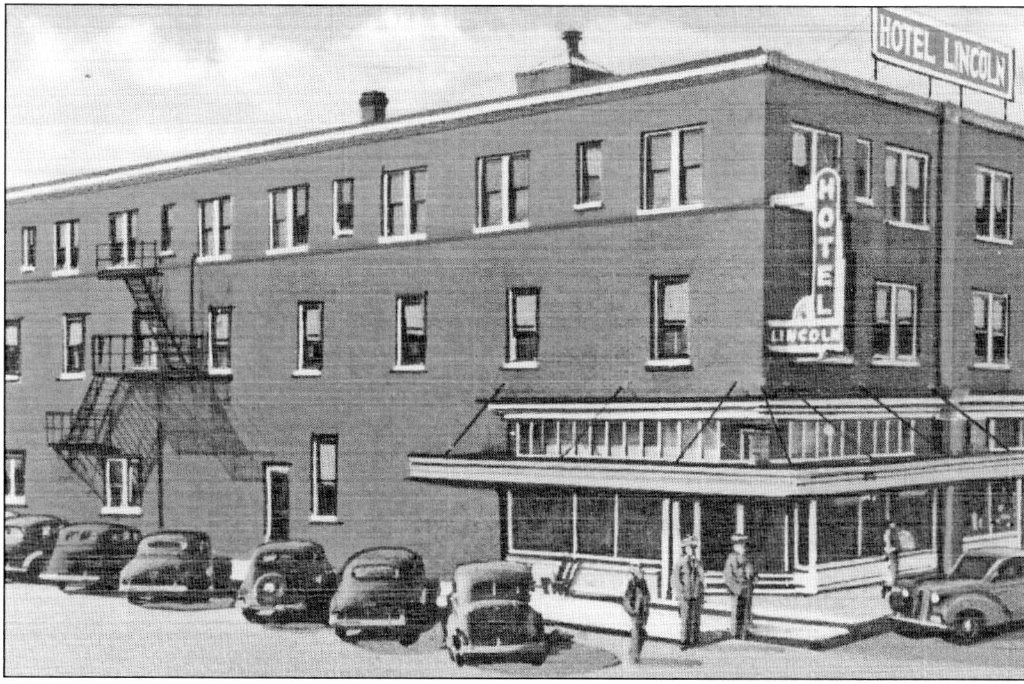

The Lincoln Hotel on the site of the old Methodist church was completed in time for the fiddler's convention, opening on February 2, 1927. Built by G. A. Saunders, the first floor was primarily businesses, with the second and third floors for guest rooms. A parking lot was located in the rear. The restaurant manager was Virgie W. Eppes, and she advertised "oyster or turkey dinners—$1.00 per plate." (WCG.)

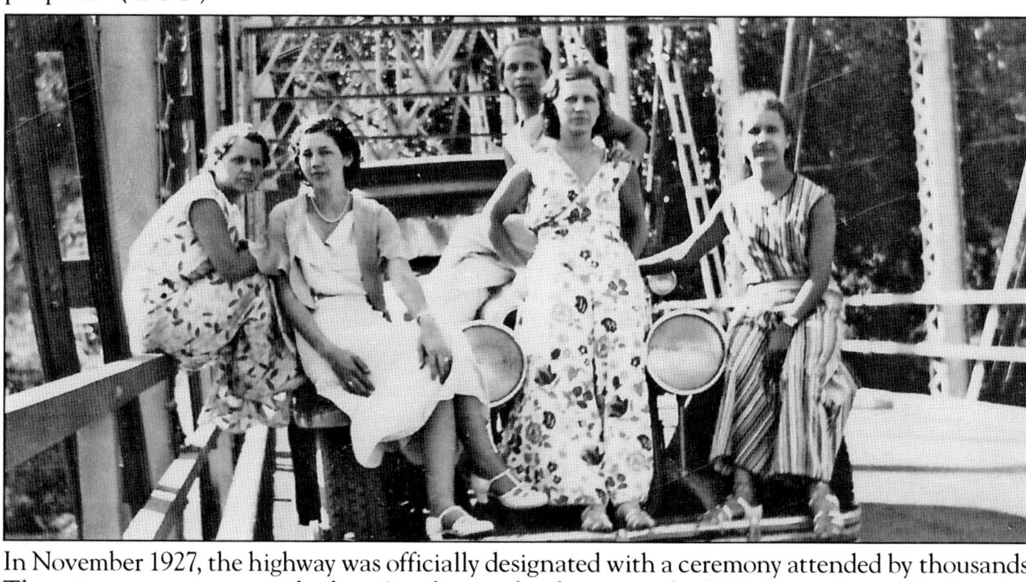

In November 1927, the highway was officially designated with a ceremony attended by thousands. The primary ceremony took place 9 miles south of town at the U.S. Route 1 steel bridge that crossed the Roanoke River. Built by the Henderson Bridge Company and owned by the state, there was no toll. Quickly appearing on either end of the bridge was a country store with tourist accommodations (each with local fame and lore). In the center is Mary Elam Dunn (the rest are unidentified). (Martha Dunn Overton.)

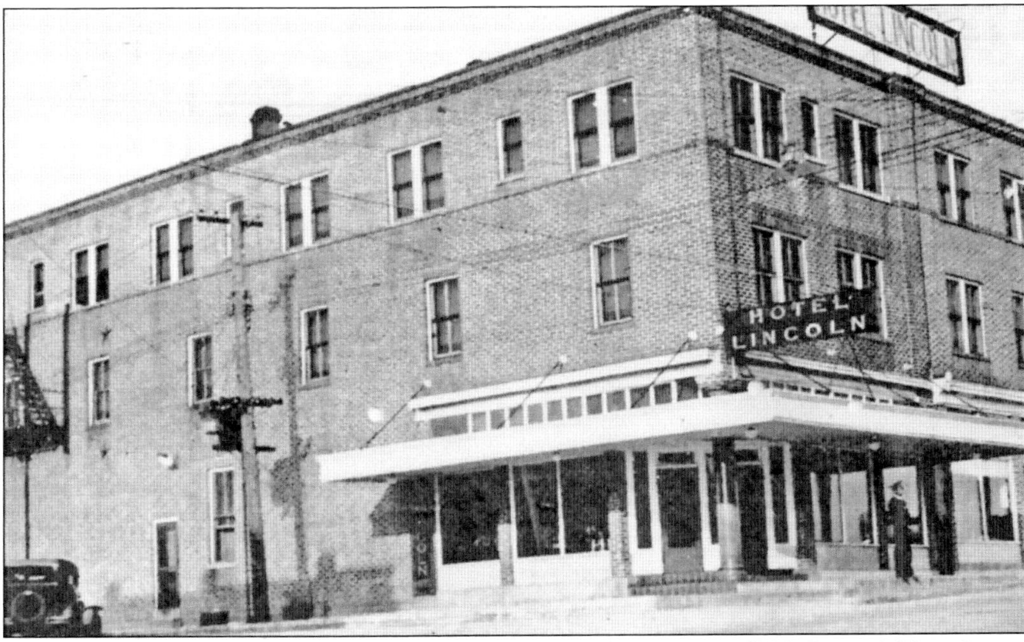

This is a 1928 postcard of Mecklenburg Avenue following the opening of U.S. Route 1. Note the new concrete streets were in place, but the sidewalks were slow to follow. On North Mecklenburg Avenue, many of the stores were still built with frame structures, which have all been replaced. (SHC.)

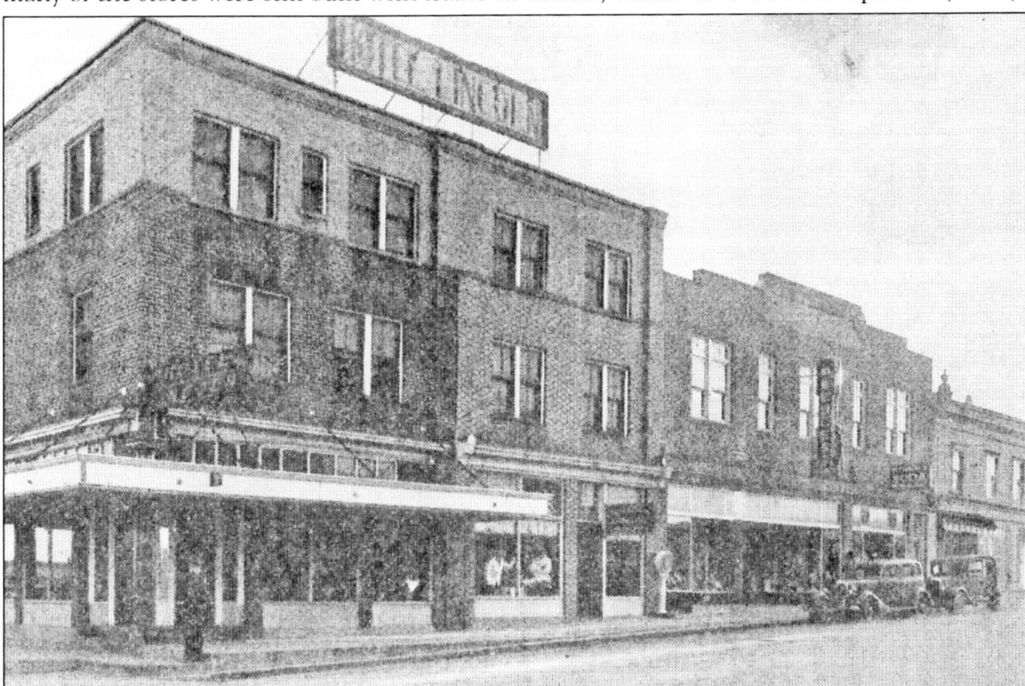

In March 1928, the Peebles Department Store, next to the Lincoln Hotel, purchased the former H. Foreman Department Store, which was in bankruptcy. A Lawrenceville-based company, they opened their second store on September 15, 1928. Today they have stores in over 15 states and have moved their corporate offices and distribution center to South Hill. (WCG.)

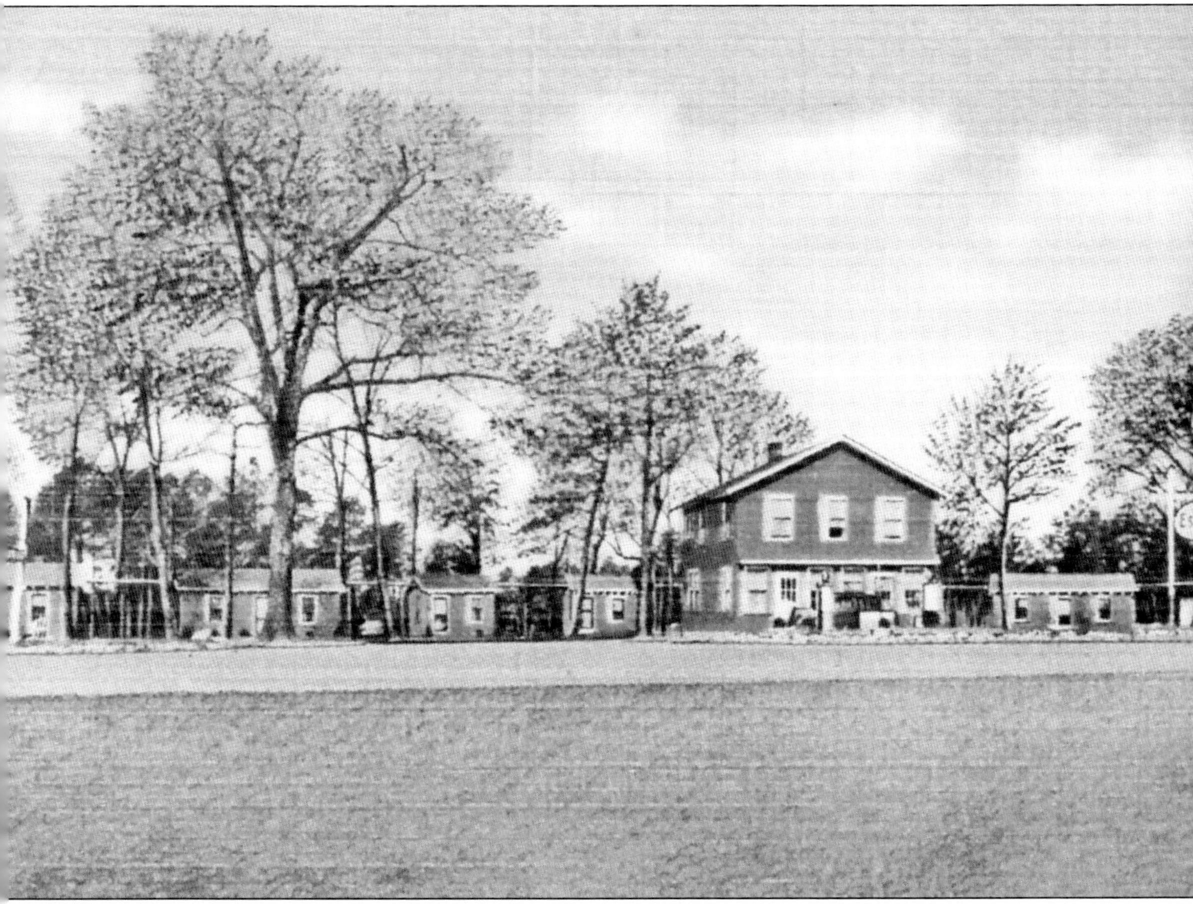

One mile north of South Hill, the Greenwood Tourist Court opened with full amenities, complete with a service station. In addition to the advertising on the front of the postcard, "inner spring mattresses" was included on the back as well as "Southern fried chicken and Virginia ham dinners, our specialty." (Richard Burnett.)

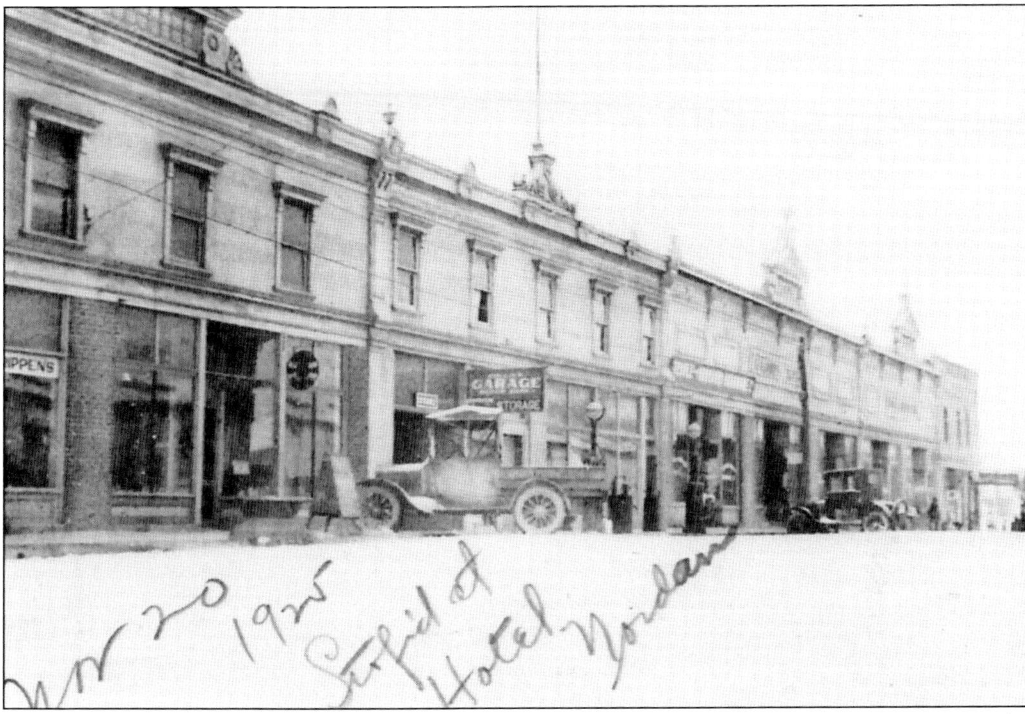

On Danville Street the new cash store opened across from Watkins Motor Company. From this point south on U.S. Route 1 (which also included Coastal to Atlanta Highway Route 12), a number of tourist courts, cabins, service stations, and restaurants opened for business, spanning over a 5-mile distance to Big Fork. (WCG)

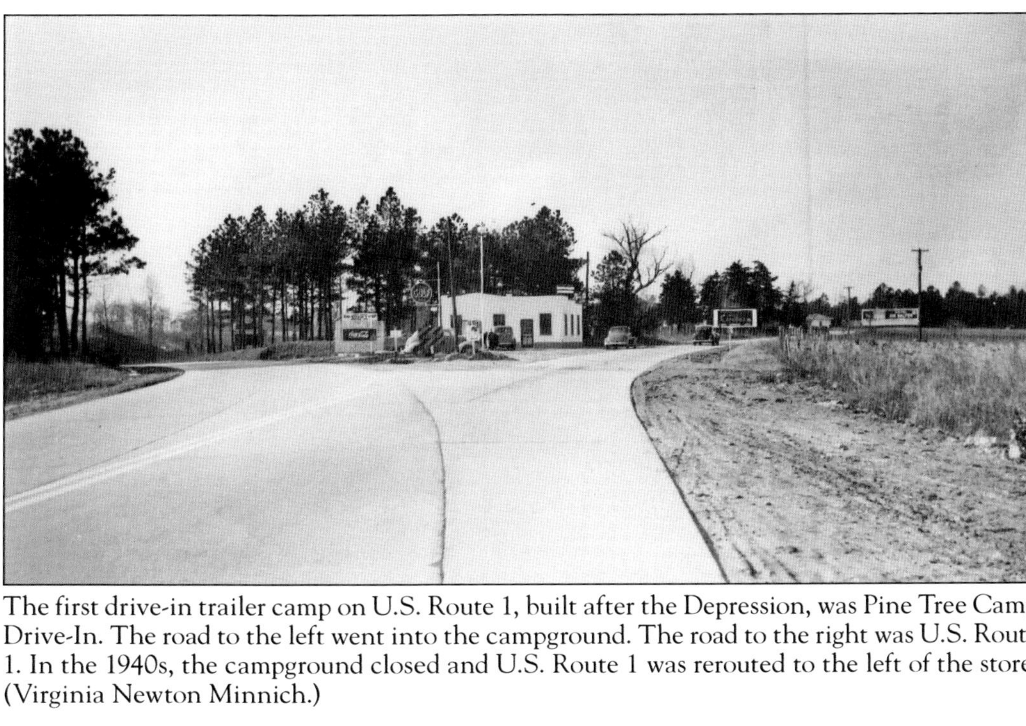

The first drive-in trailer camp on U.S. Route 1, built after the Depression, was Pine Tree Camp Drive-In. The road to the left went into the campground. The road to the right was U.S. Route 1. In the 1940s, the campground closed and U.S. Route 1 was rerouted to the left of the store. (Virginia Newton Minnich.)

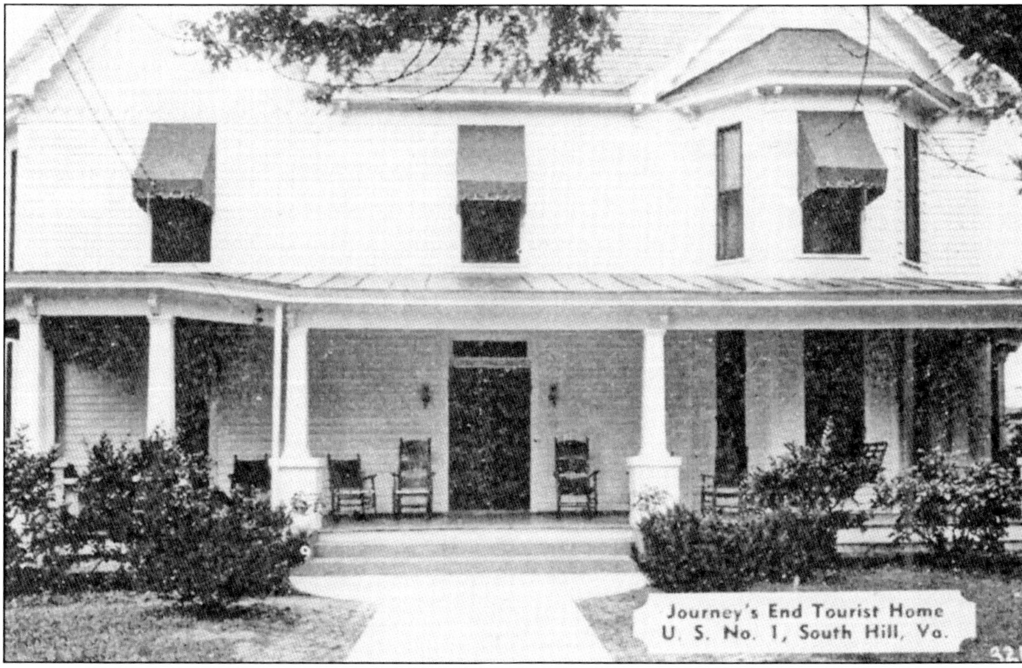

North of South Hill, along U.S. Route 1, tourist homes, cabins, or campgrounds with restaurants and service stations were built for one convenient stop. The focus was on travelers' accommodations. The Journey's End tourist home was a good example. Opened by James Armistead Sr., it advertised steam heat, innerspring beds, free garages, and meals. (TJS.)

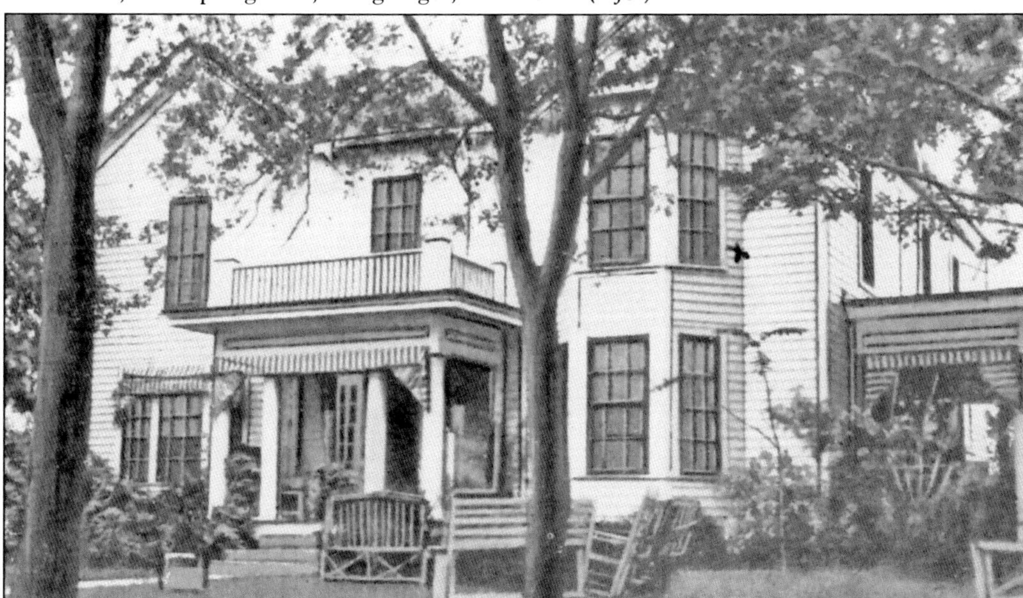

Nearby, the Restful Inn advertised, "A home away from home. Halfway between Raleigh and Richmond. Private garages or free parking. Meals, large rooms and hot water." The examples on this page are just two of the many options available to travelers. Not as congested as south of town where the two highways ran together, there was a 3-mile stretch north of town with many accommodations. (TJS.)

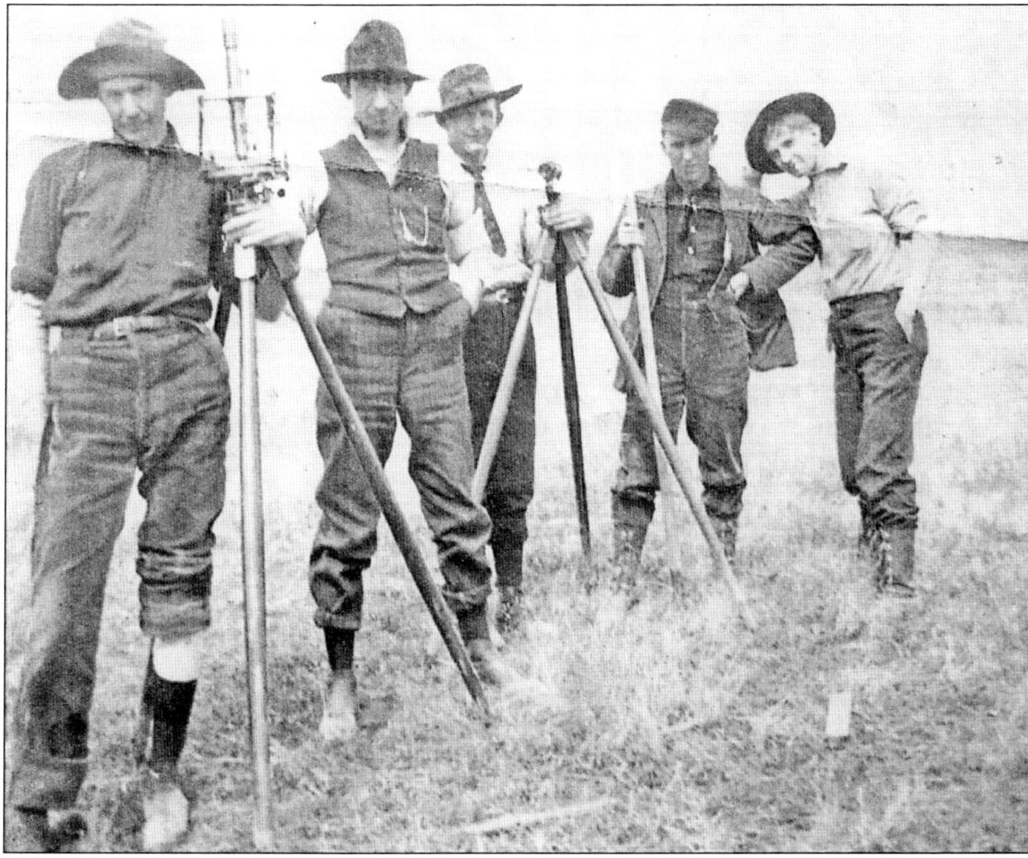

Survey crews were a common sight in Mecklenburg County starting in the 1880s, surveying miles and miles of land for railroad corporations for track placement and especially numerous bridges. Surveying continued into the 20th century for roadways, later with the U.S. Road Commission, and into the 1930s with the Federal Highway Administration. This crew was photographed in the late 1890s working in the soon-to-be Bracey community. (WRH.)

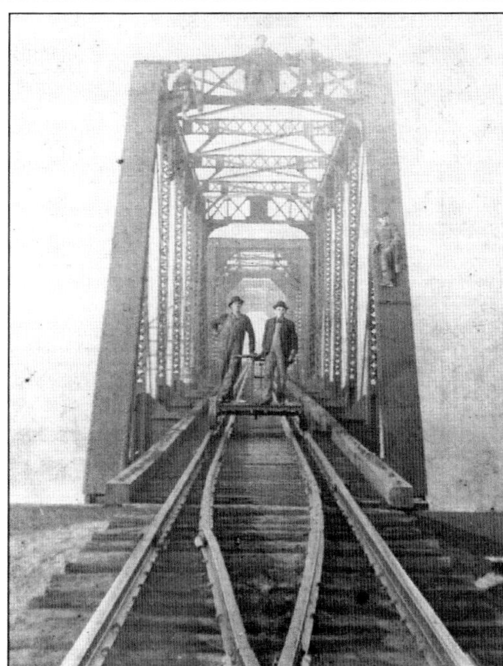

Survey crews and builders photographed much of their work to include in their reports. One of the most complex jobs in the county was the bridge across two rivers in Clarksville. The second was the bridge across the Roanoke River at St. Tammany. This photograph depicts the inspection of the completed bridge at St. Tammany in the late 1890s. The crew is unidentified, but appears pleased with their work. (WRH.)

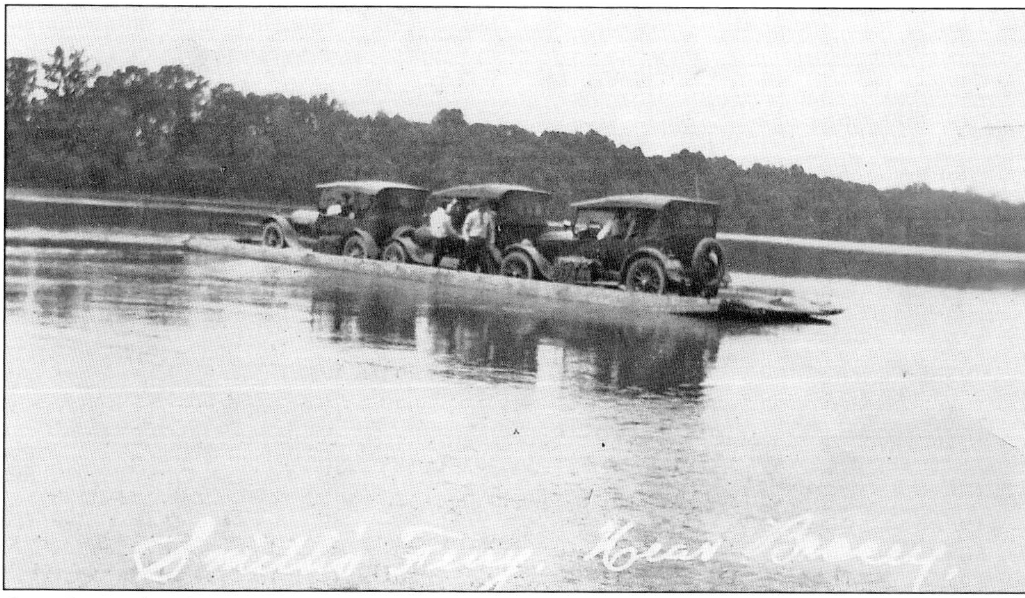

One chain of 14 ferries along the Roanoke River was Smith's Ferry. In 1904, the Clarksville toll bridge opened in the western part of the county (which closed four ferries), but it was not until 1921 that the Henderson toll bridge opened in the eastern part of the county (which closed two ferries). In 1928, the steel bridge on U.S. Route 1 eliminated the tolls and closed the remainder of the ferries. After 1915, most ferry passengers were automobiles with riders. (WRH.)

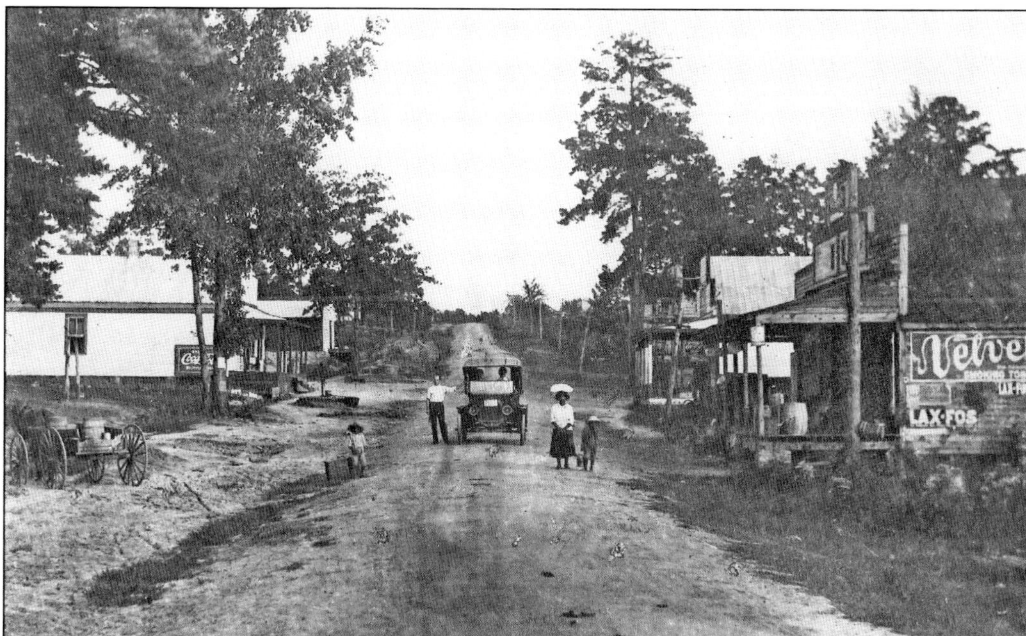

This photograph taken around 1915 shows William "Willie" Harper driving his new car up Main Street in Bracey. The passenger is Waller T. Bracey, and standing outside is John Rideout. All three owned businesses in Bracey. Bracey was a railroad community carved from a parcel of land owned by George Lambert. Lambert also built a store in town. Most of the stores were built between 1901 and 1909. (WRH.)

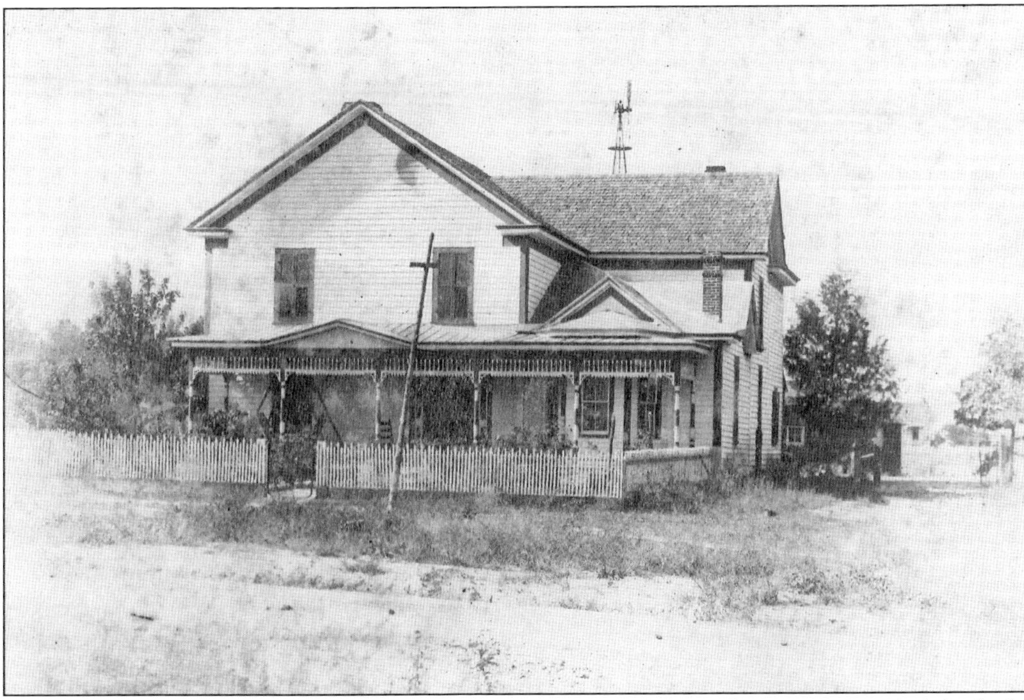

Waller T. Bracey, son of Altamont "Mont" (CSA veteran of the 3rd Virginia Cavalry), built the family home in 1900 and his store the following year. He became the postmaster of Bracey, helped to establish a local public school, and served on the county school board. A boarder in his home was Minnie Pearison, who was a sales clerk in his store. (WRH.)

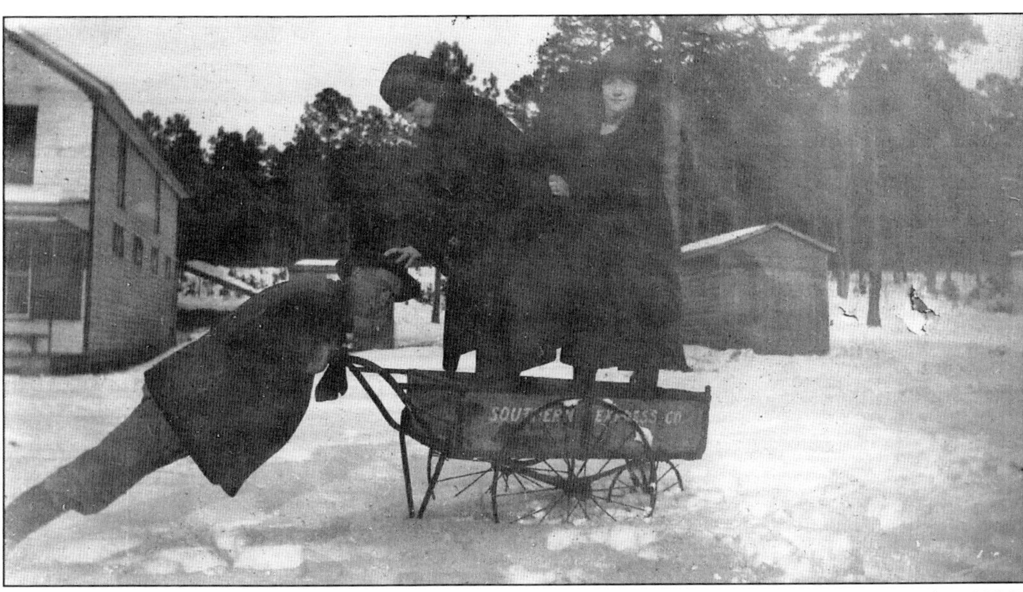

Here is Frank Martin pushing a Southern Railroad mail cart in a snowstorm in the 1920s. Originally the post office was located in the railroad station, but soon Waller T. Bracey built a new post office about a block away. Not wanting to walk in the snow, Cora Graham (left) and Gladys Bracey Bonny are riding to the train station. (WRH.)

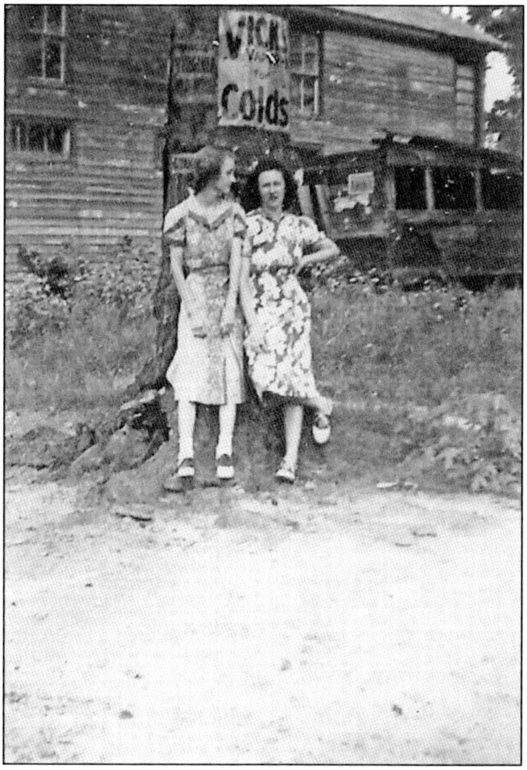

About a block away from the train station toward the country was Nancy Dunn's store. Today the store has been moved about 75 yards and is home to Bracey Mercantile and a barbershop. In this photograph from the 1920s are Margaret Carpenter (left) and Mabel Sims Hite standing near the store. (WRH.)

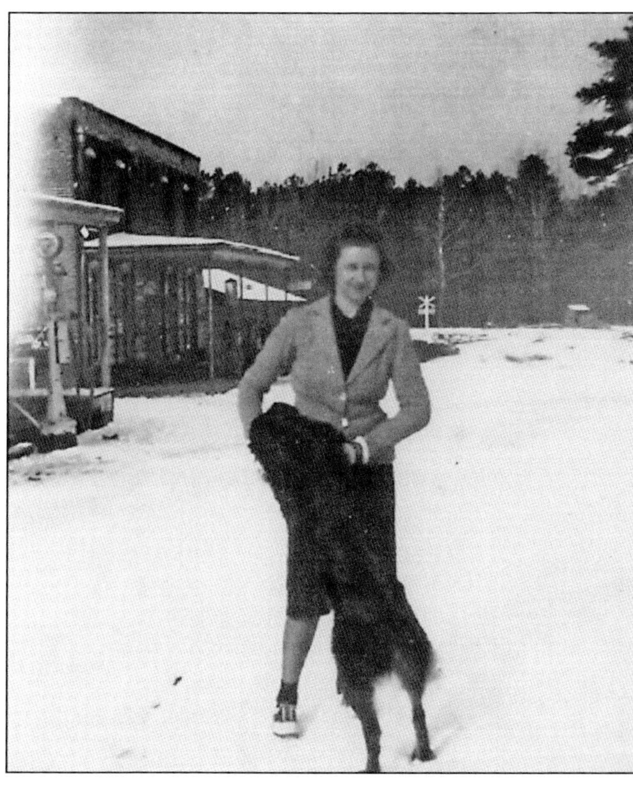

This is Mabel Bracey Sims with Pips in front of the Bracey and Company store (1901) during the later 1920s. Also on the left is a partial view of Mrs. Robbie Fitz Harper's c. 1907 store, and at left in the distance is the railroad depot. (WRH.)

Around 1898, John H. Rideout took over operation of his father's store in the community of St. Tammany. When the railroad stopped short with the new station, Rideout decided to move his store to a more prosperous area in 1905. He moved the store to the new location in downtown Bracey. Standing in front of the store is Mabel Sims Hite. (WRH.)

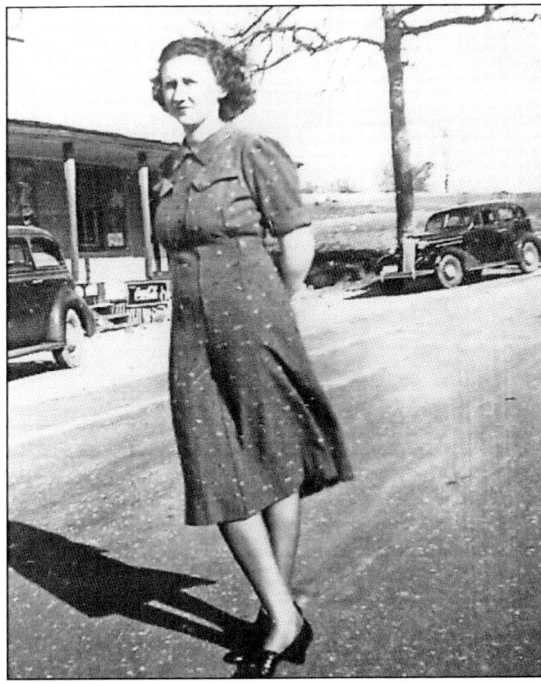

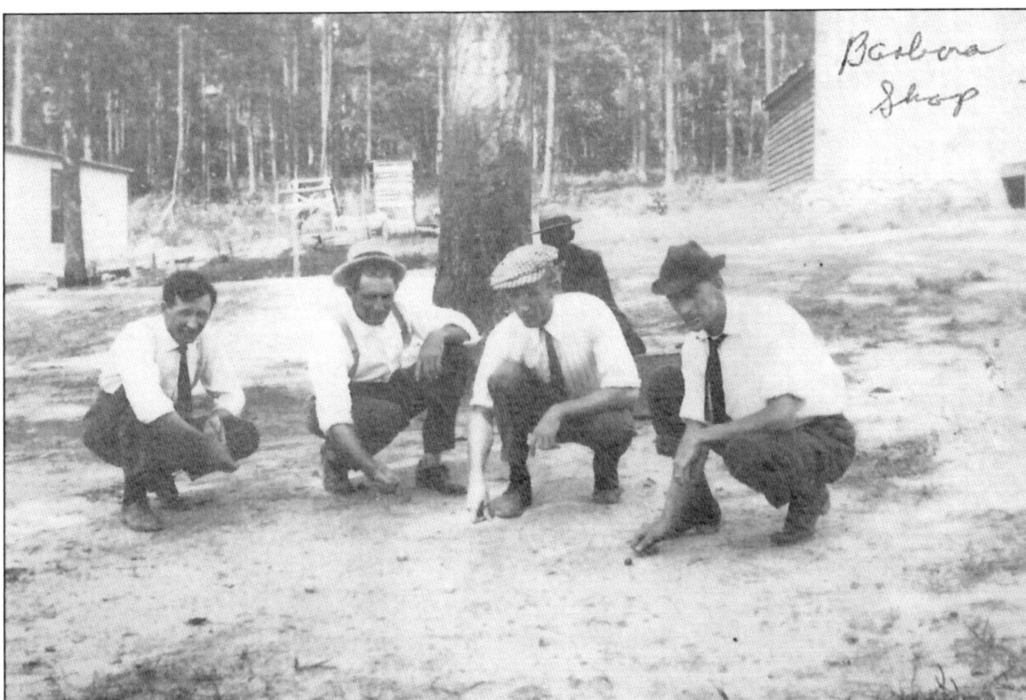

Fierce competition always existed in a good marble match. In the 1920s, there were marble leagues with district, state, and national competitions. Pictured here are most likely the four merchants of Bracey: William T. Harper Jr., John H. Rideout, Waller T. Bracey, and William T. Person (the youngest and the railroad station manager). The building in the background is the Bracey Barber Shop. (WRH.)

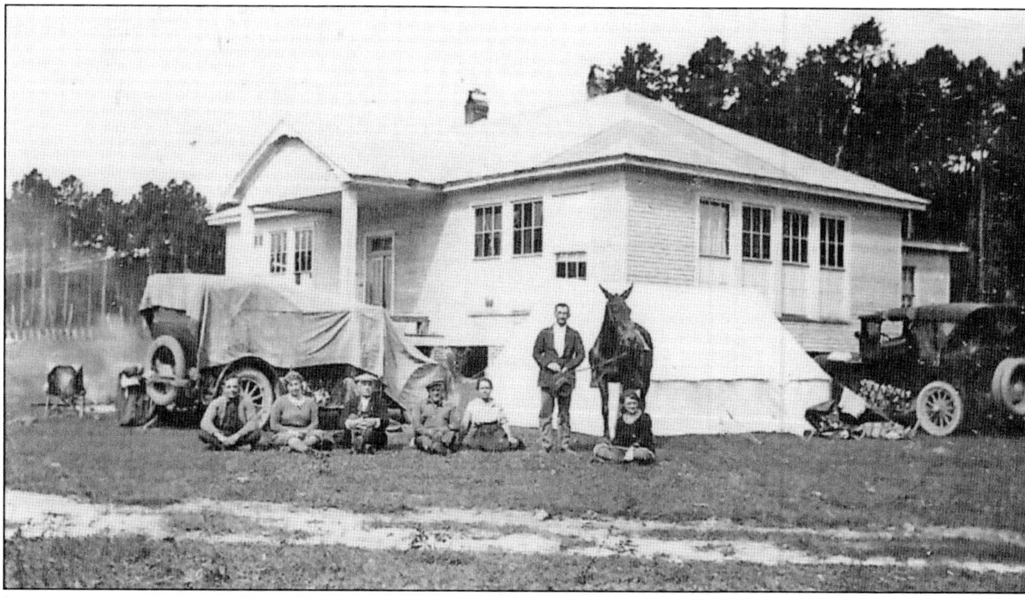

Prior to the commonality of 1920s campgrounds, travelers found school yards a welcome site for overnight stays while waiting for ferries on long trips. Here Waller T. Bracey, still traveling by horseback, is in front of the school with a group of campers. With Bracey's lead, the school opened in 1909. The teachers were Matie Goodman and Mary B. Watkins (boarders in Bracey's home). They were later joined by Wilbur R. Bracey as a new teacher. (WRH.)

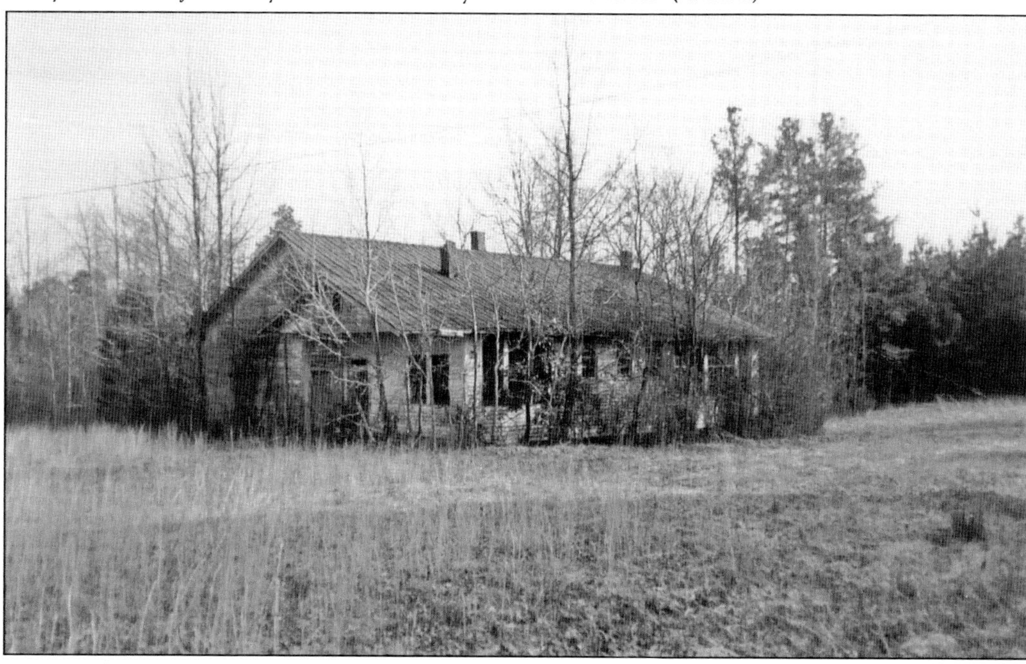

In 1926, the Carroll-Boyd School opened in Bracey for African American children. A Rosenwald school, it began with two classrooms, an industrial arts lab room, and an agriculture room with the initial enrollment of 58 students. The school was begun by Mary Carroll and Nancy Josephine Boyd. The school was next door to the Bracey Episcopal Church, whose minister was Joseph Carroll, husband of Mary. The school operated until consolidation. (JC.)

Four

What Depression?

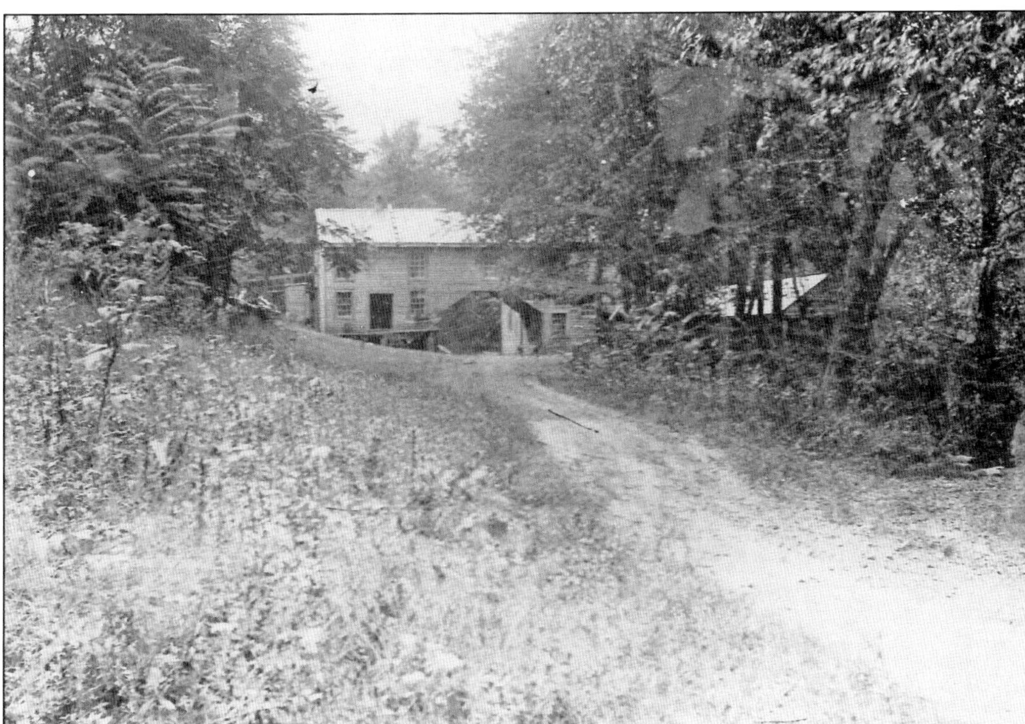

In 1840, John B. Tunstall purchased 400 acres on Allen's Creek about 1 mile from Colonel Stith's gold mine and began to mine for gold along the side of the creek. After several years, he built a dam on the creek and established a milling operation. In this photograph is Tunstall's store, which became the Cedaria Post Office in 1853, with his son John B. Jr. as postmaster. The drive-through has a storage area above with a gristmill to the right. At far right was a sawmill. The post office closed in 1857. (Richard Kinley Dunn.)

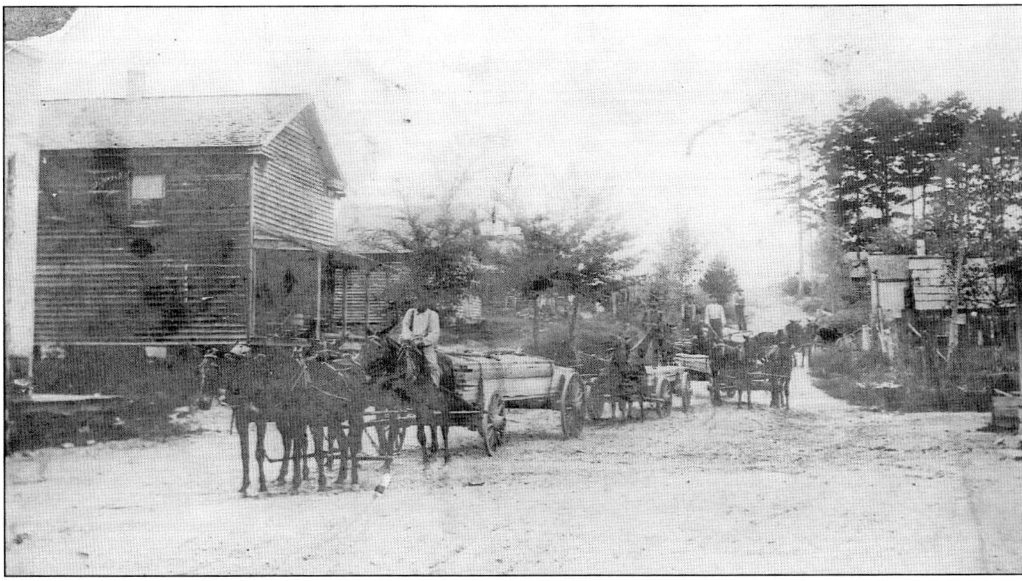

Following the Civil War, Tunstall purchased a parcel of land on the Boydton Plank Road next to John C. Phillips. Both men, along with others, opened businesses to accommodate traffic during the reconstruction. The new community of Cedaria, in this photograph from the 1880s, boasted three mercantiles (which also sold coffins), three saloons (one belonging to Phillips), a dispensary (liquor store) owned by Phillips, and a boardinghouse. Note the teamsters with loads of lumber coming up the highway. (Carol A. Dunn.)

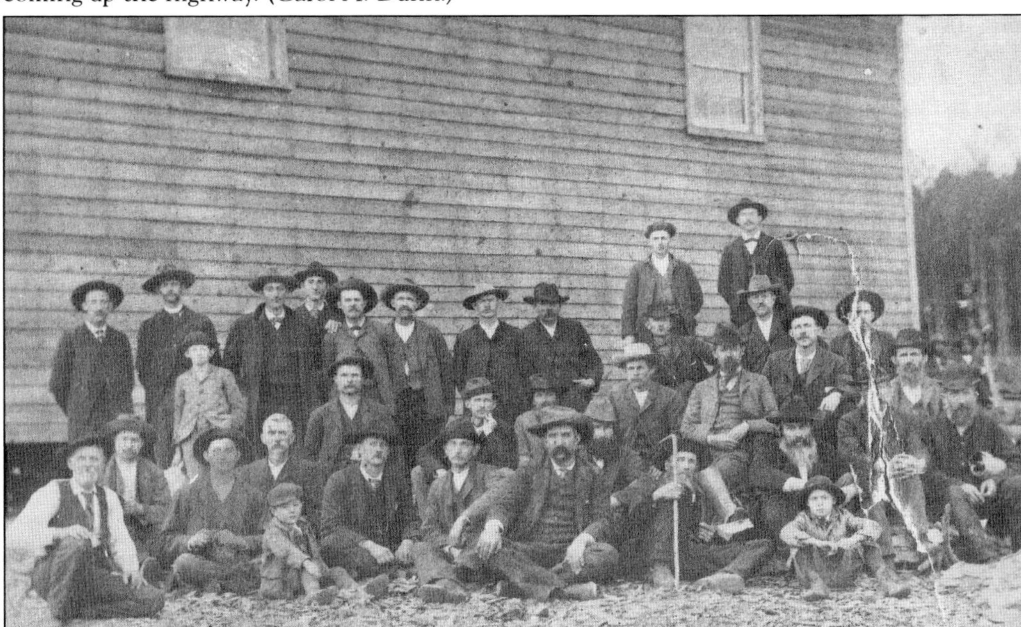

The local farmers united following the Civil War and began the Patrons of Husbandry Society (the "Grange"). Each Saturday, the farmers came to town to collect their orders, and once the Grange was empty it became a social club, sometimes including wives and children. It also served as a community center for political, economic, and social events. Note that all members are dressed the same in this 1880s photograph, even the black farmer in the back. (Joseph Elam Dunn.)

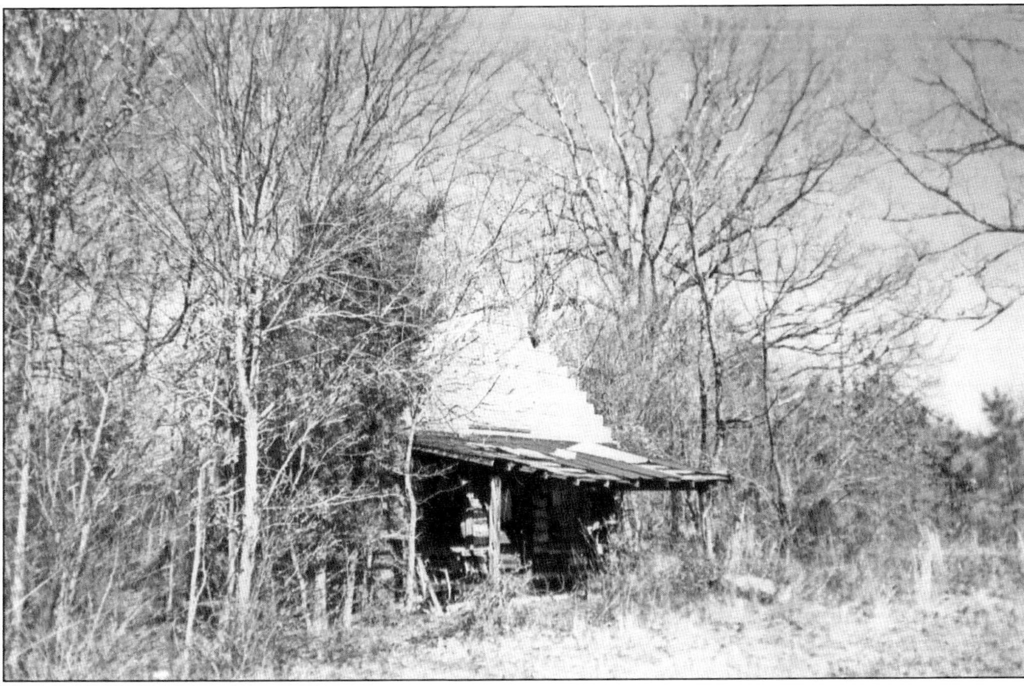

Sterling N. Hutcheson was appointed the first postmaster of the newly renamed Cedaria, now called Baskerville. He built this log store as a post office, a wayside for stagecoaches, and a full livery in the rear. It was situated at the intersection of Boydton Plank Road and Stoney Cross Road. Later, when the railroad station was completed, he moved the post office there, as the mail coaches were no longer needed. (JC.)

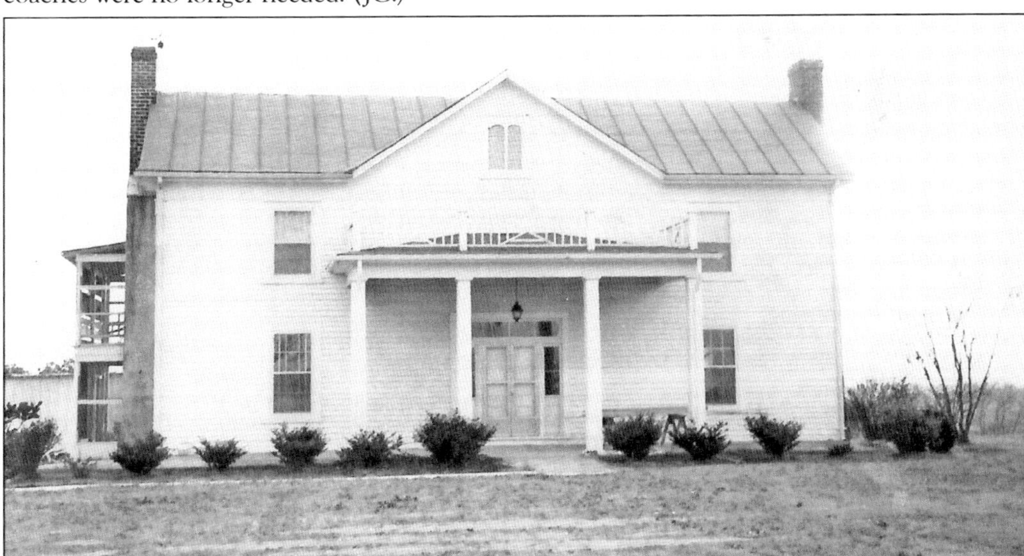

This is the C. S. Dunn family home around 1875. Dunn took over operation of his father's store, C. S. Dunn Hardware, which also sold coffins, in Baskerville in 1891, and in 1892 he married Courtney A. Cole. Around 1909, the old frame store burned, and Dunn contracted with St. Paul's Vocational and Agricultural School in Lawrenceville to build a new and larger department store. (Carol A. Dunn.)

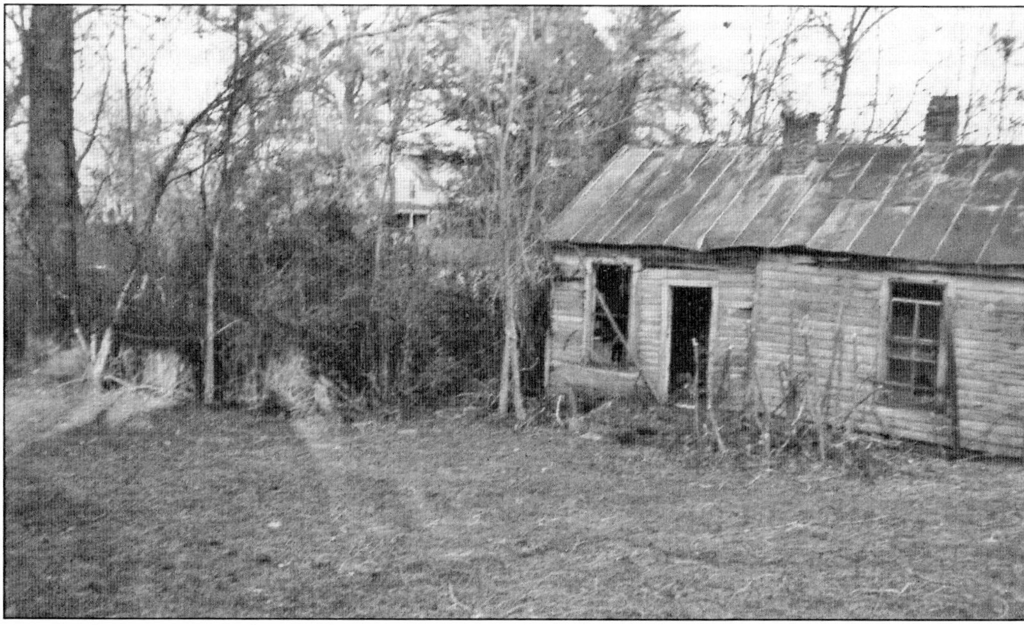

Across the street was the small office (left) of Herbert I. Hutcheson, land surveyor and justice of the peace (with trial day on Saturday), and the general merchandise store of W. G. Cooper. Cooper sold dry goods, clothes, flour, seeds, coffins, and caskets, but being next to the railroad station, his main product was fertilizer, kept in a large backroom, and just out back of his store he had a blacksmith shop. (Martha Dunn Overton.)

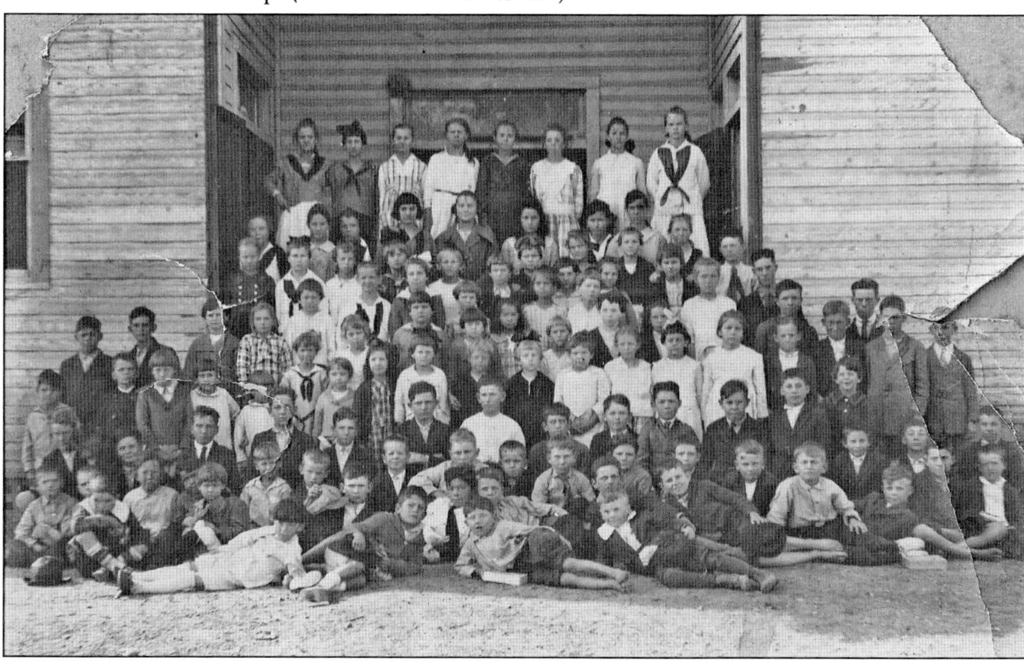

The Hutcheson family founded the Hutcheson School, which opened in 1910 to children ages from 6 to 17. The first teacher was Ginny Dowlings, who not only taught the fundamentals of reading, writing, and arithmetic, but also taught Latin and French. The school closed in 1935 when the students were consolidated into the Boydton School. (Carol A. Dunn.)

The grandson of John B. Tunstall Jr., James M. Tunstall Jr. returned to Baskerville following the Depression and built a new store with a boardinghouse upstairs. This was a prosperous time for Baskerville because the train was coming through town numerous times per day with carloads of gravel from the Baskerville Quarry for construction and roads. In this photograph is James's son Harold (center) with boarders Bee Reese (right) and Ernest Reese (left). (Nettie Andrews Algood.)

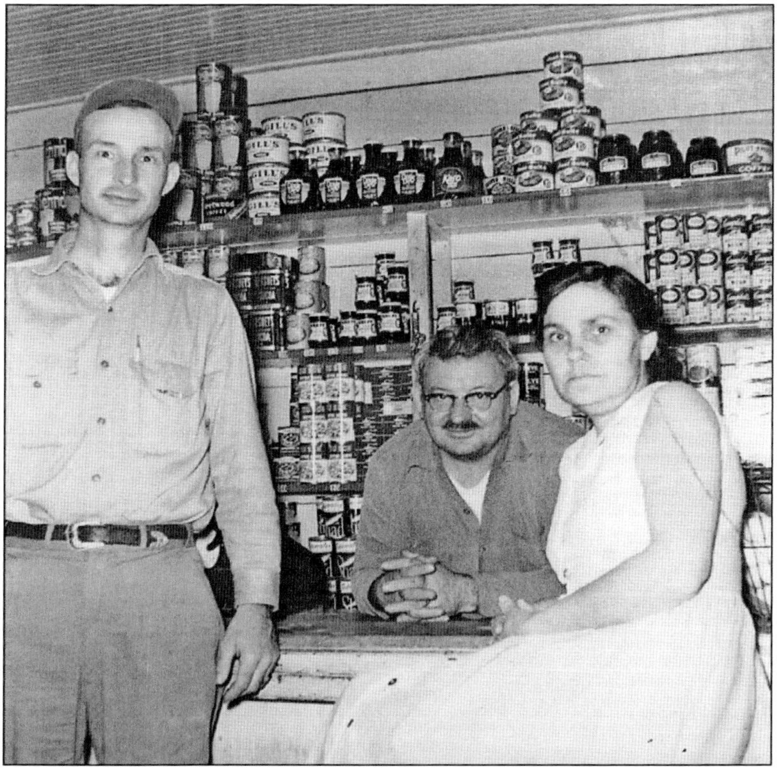

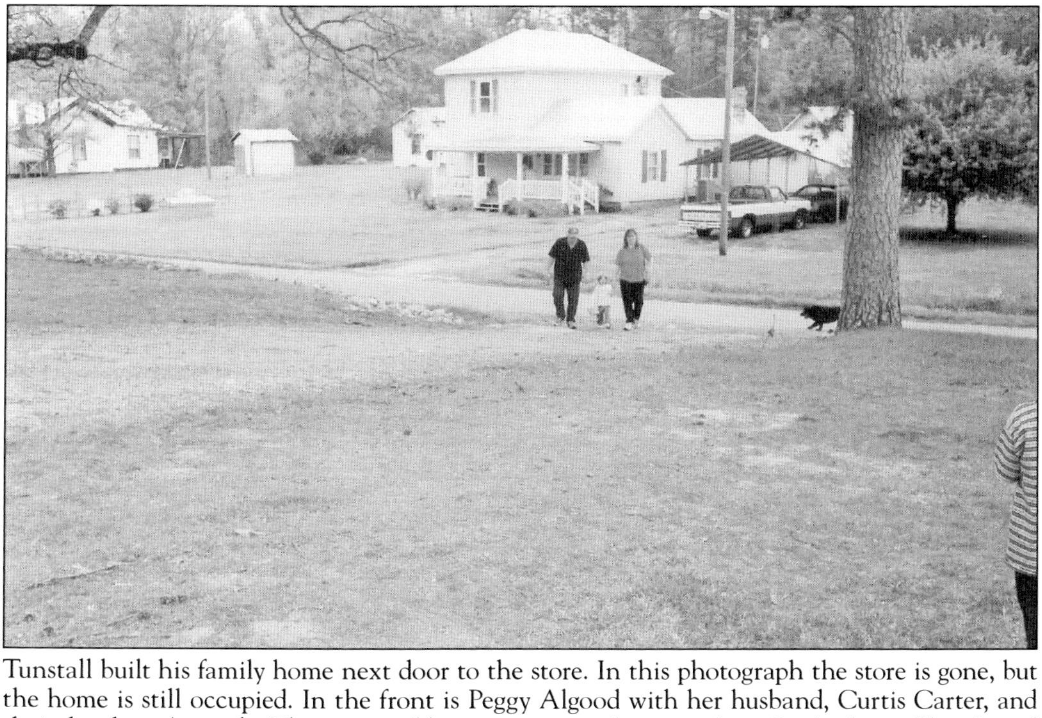

Tunstall built his family home next door to the store. In this photograph the store is gone, but the home is still occupied. In the front is Peggy Algood with her husband, Curtis Carter, and their daughter Amanda. The store and home are across the street from St. Andrews Church and at the bottom of the hill in Baskerville. (Nettie Andrews Algood.)

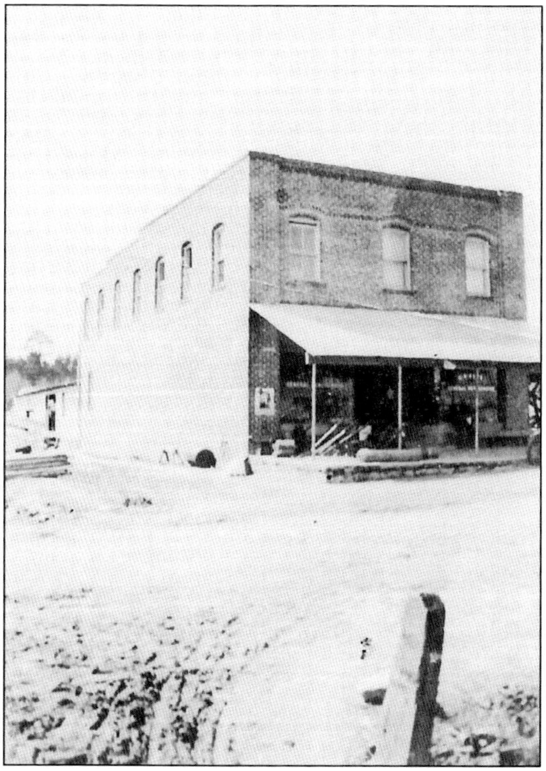

This is the new C. S. Dunn Hardware store, completed in 1910 by a class of students from St. Paul's. In the back of the store Jim Cooper had a shop making tobacco flu pipes. Dunn's store was one of only two flu makers in the county for several years. The store also purchased and sold local produce. Around the potbellied stove inside was the arena for "tall tales, marbles, and checkers." (Carol A. Dunn.)

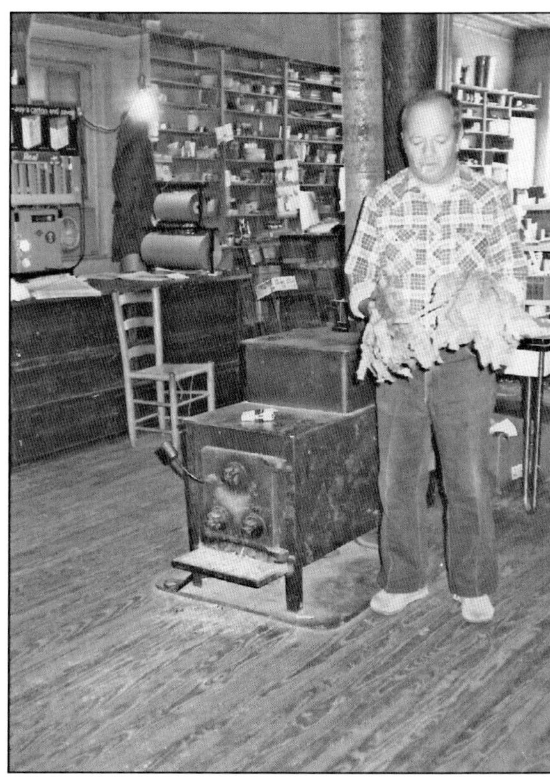

By 1920, the store had a full complement of hardware and building supplies, including roofing and wiring. They also sold cold drinks and tobacco and added gas pumps and oil products to their inventory. In this photograph the stove has been modernized. Standing next to it around 1950 is David Dunn, who is now operating the store. The upstairs of the store was for storage and a display of coffins and caskets. (Martha Dunn Overton.)

In this 1950s photograph is the small tin-roof building between the car and the large structure of the railroad station. The small building is now gone, but for nearly 90 years it stood as a reminder of the Old West. The Cedaria (Baskerville) Saloon was a small establishment to serve drinks and make small talk, not like on television with poker tables and a piano player. (Beth Kinley Dunn.)

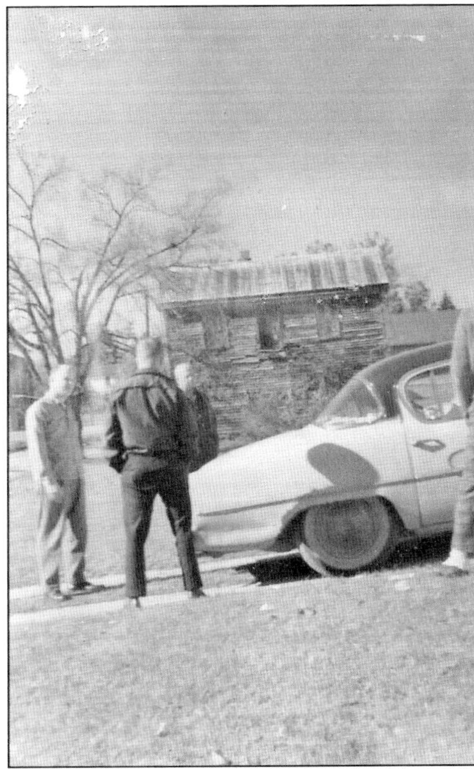

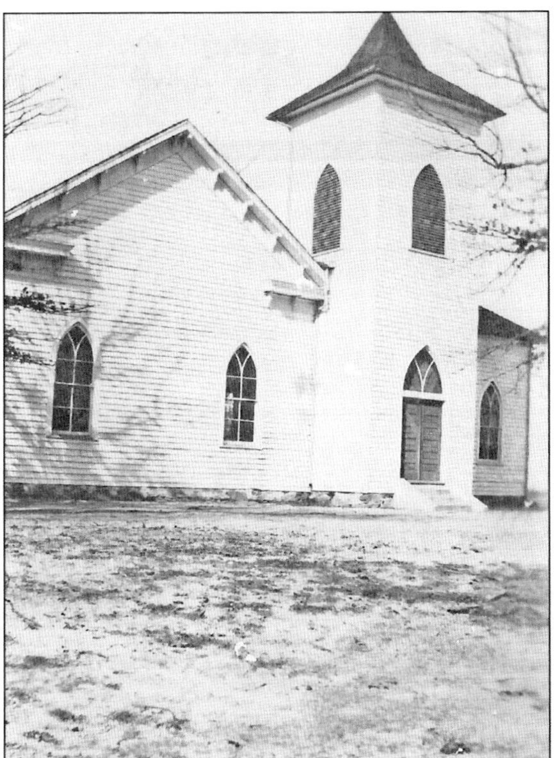

Bethany Baptist Church was dedicated on September 12, 1895, in Baskerville with 26 members. The original organizers were the Elam and Tunstall families. As membership grew, the church was enlarged in 1917, but by 1950 a new church was needed. The old church was sold and moved, and a new church was built and dedicated in 1952. (Beth Kinley Dunn.)

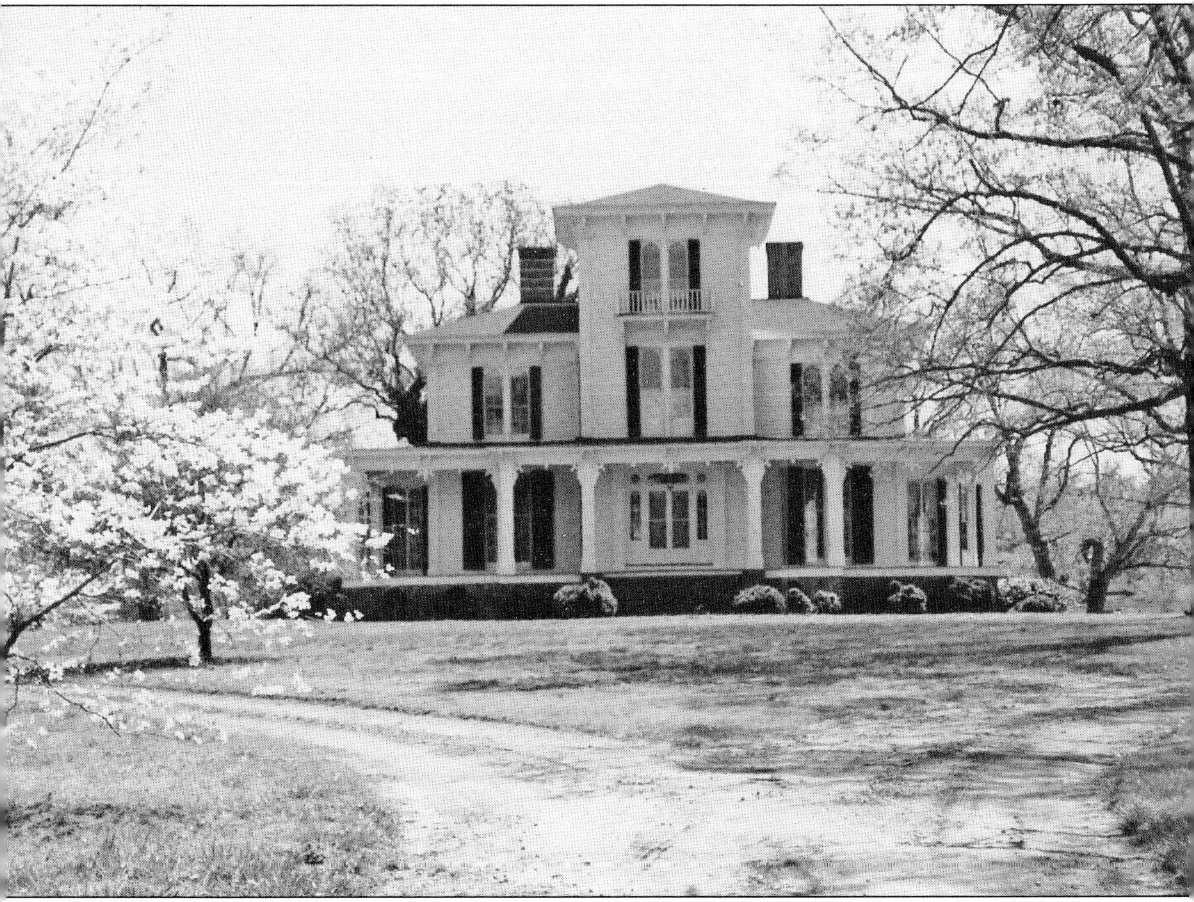

In 1857, William R. Baskervill contracted with famous builder Jacob Holt. At the time, Holt was building numerous structures in Warrenton, North Carolina. Baskervill wanted him to return to Mecklenburg County and build his family home named Eureka. In 1858, the home was completed, and the Baskervill family moved into their new home in Red Lawn near St. Andrews Church. (Carol A. Dunn.)

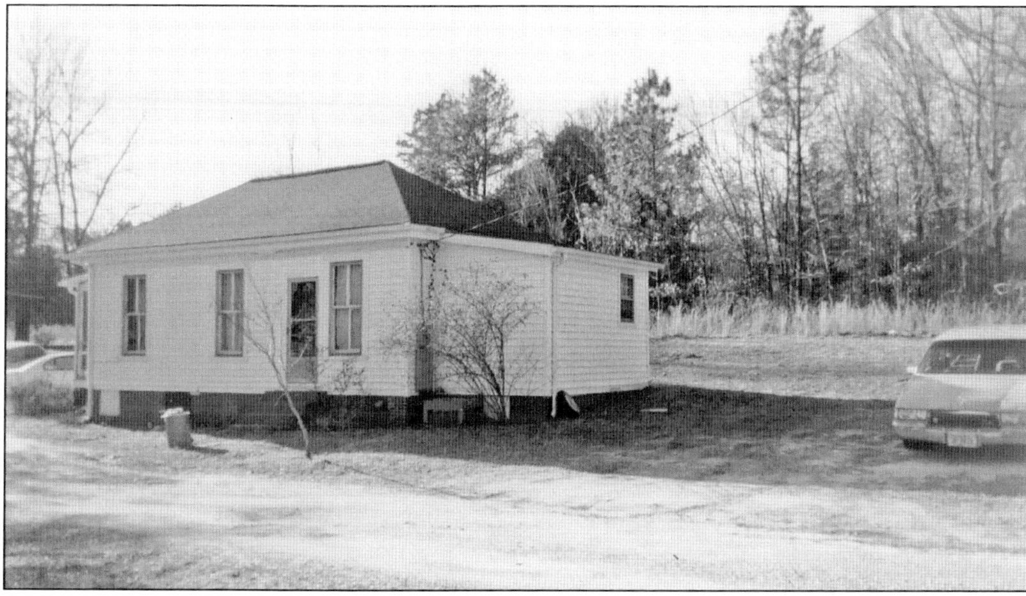

Dr. Ben J. Montgomery left the county to attend the University College of Medicine in Richmond. In 1905, he graduated at the age of 21. He returned to Mecklenburg County and began his practice in Red Lawn in 1905. In 1910, he moved to Baskerville and began his practice at Willard's Store. From there he built this modern three-room clinic from which he practiced medicine until 1943, when he moved to Alberta, Virginia. (JC.)

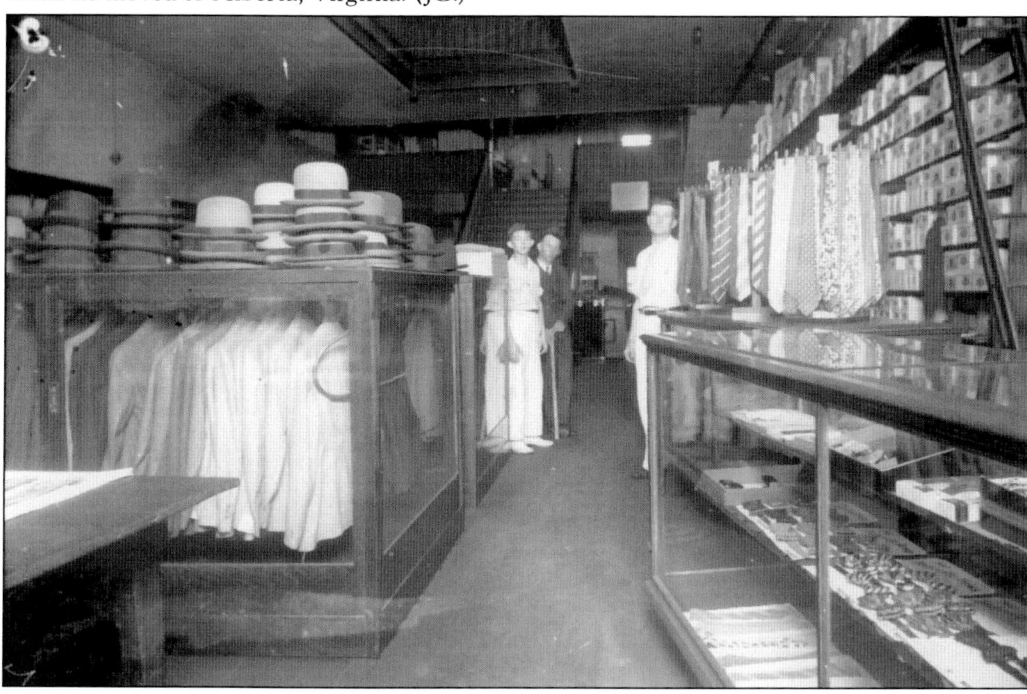

In 1930, C. E. Vasser, an employee of R. E. Yancey's store, purchased the property from Yancey, who was in ill health. This is an interior view of the store during the Depression. Note that the apparel lines are catering to men's ready-to-wear clothing. There was a seamstress available for alterations. (SHC.)

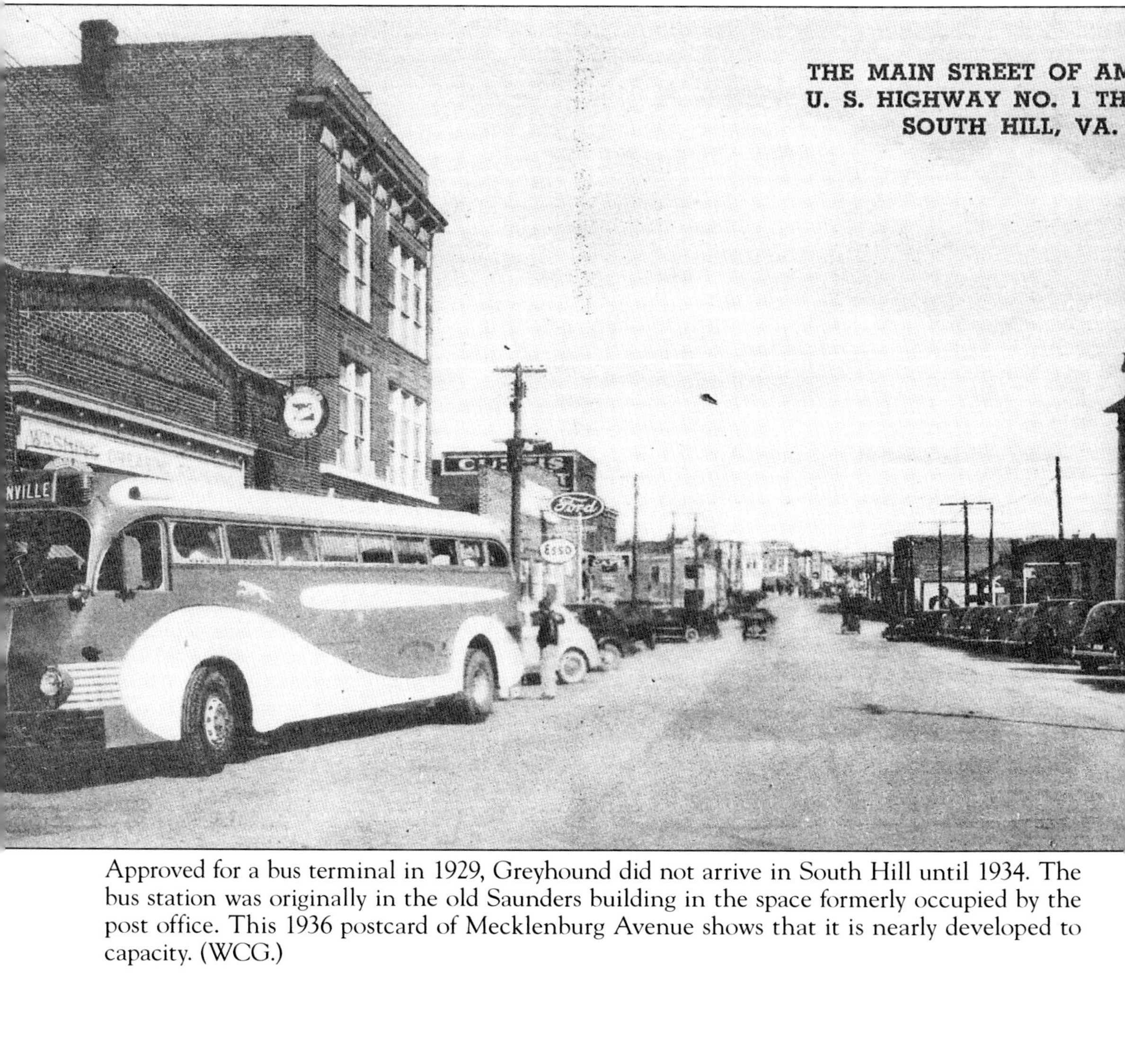

Approved for a bus terminal in 1929, Greyhound did not arrive in South Hill until 1934. The bus station was originally in the old Saunders building in the space formerly occupied by the post office. This 1936 postcard of Mecklenburg Avenue shows that it is nearly developed to capacity. (WCG.)

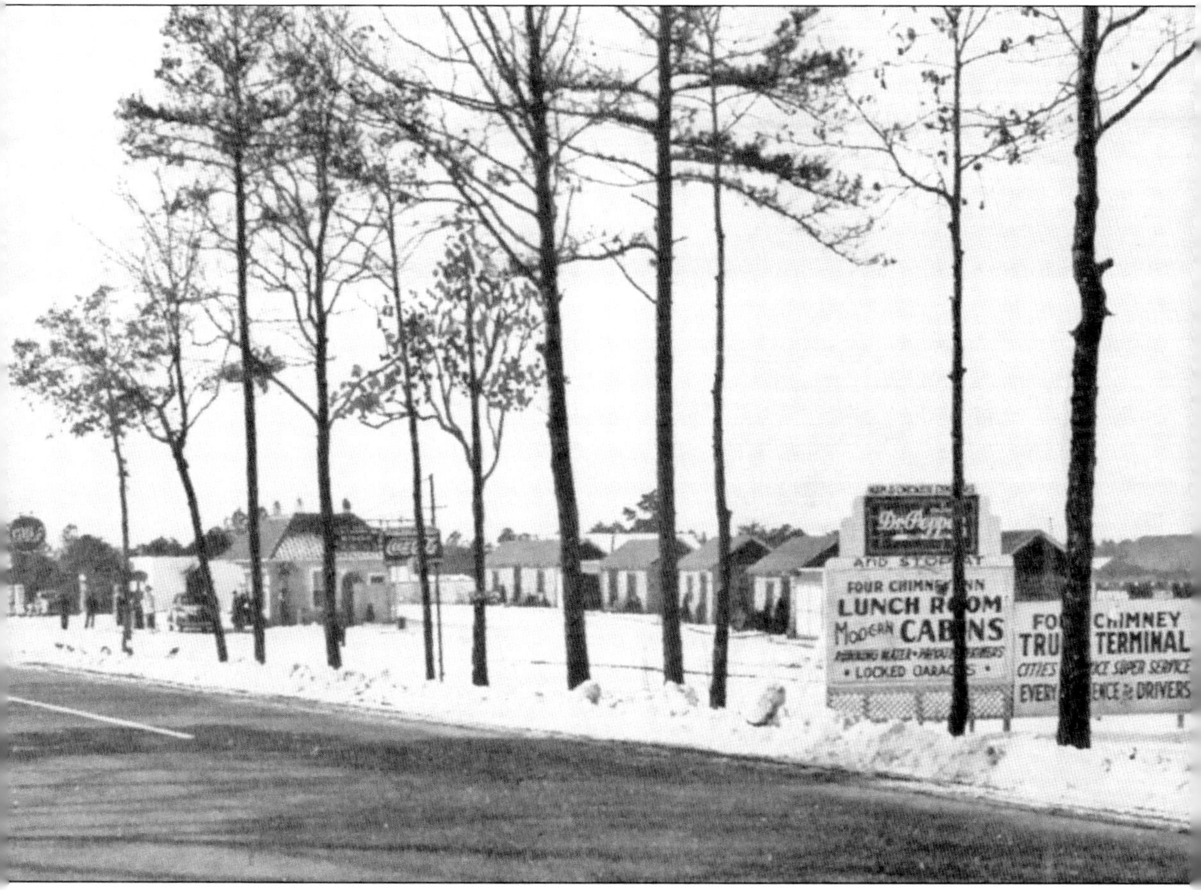

South along U.S. Route 1 continued to develop until the end of the 1930s, with nearly 30 courts, cabins, and eateries. A couple of new marketing strategies were offered by the Four Chimney Inn. Aside from the usual amenities, following the Depression these cabins were advertising "locked garages." They were also advertising a truck terminal with "Cities Service Super Service." (WCG.)

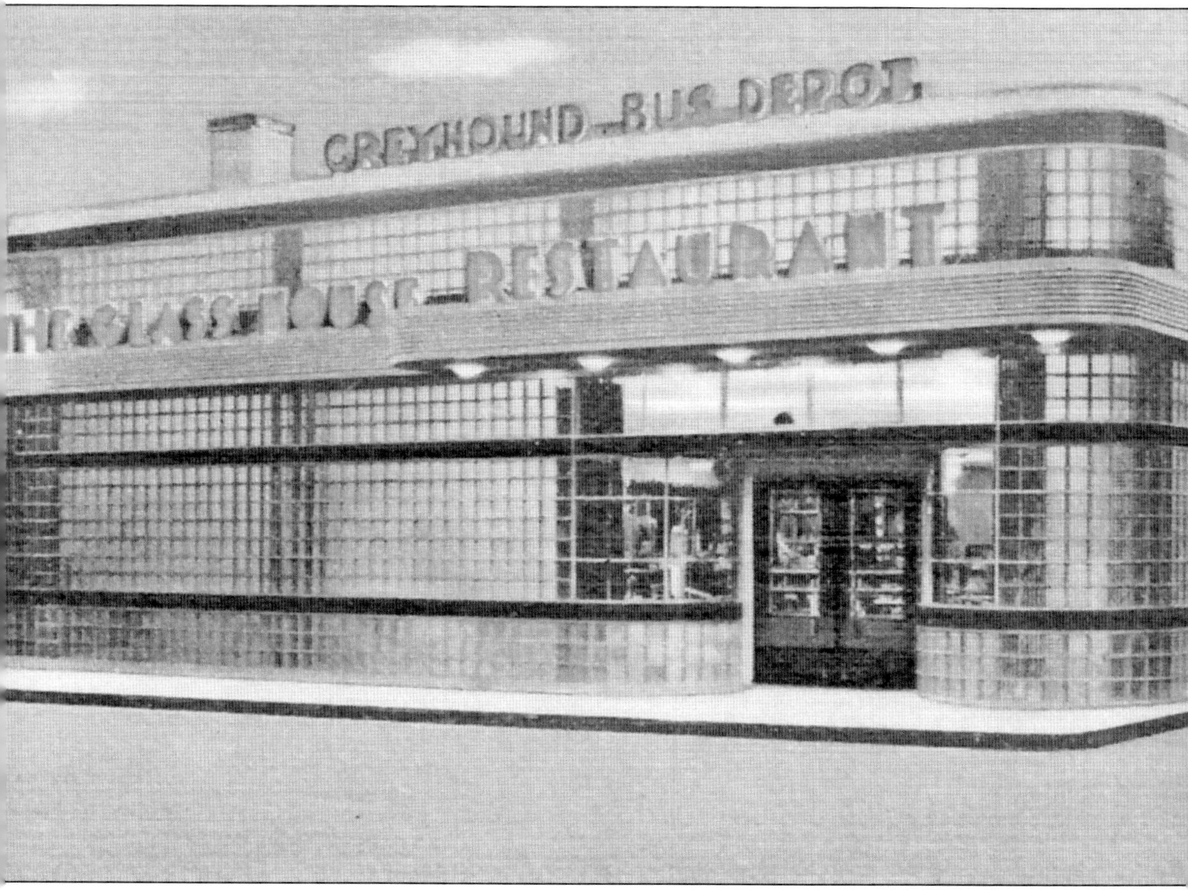

At the intersection of Mecklenburg Avenue and Danville Street, a new restaurant came to South Hill—The Glass House. A chain of highway restaurants, the one in South Hill opened in 1937 and was called "the Building of Tomorrow." It was constructed using Insulux Glass Block masonry with virtuous trim. The building was also fully air-conditioned. Shortly after opening, it housed the Greyhound bus terminal in the rear and to the side. (TJS.)

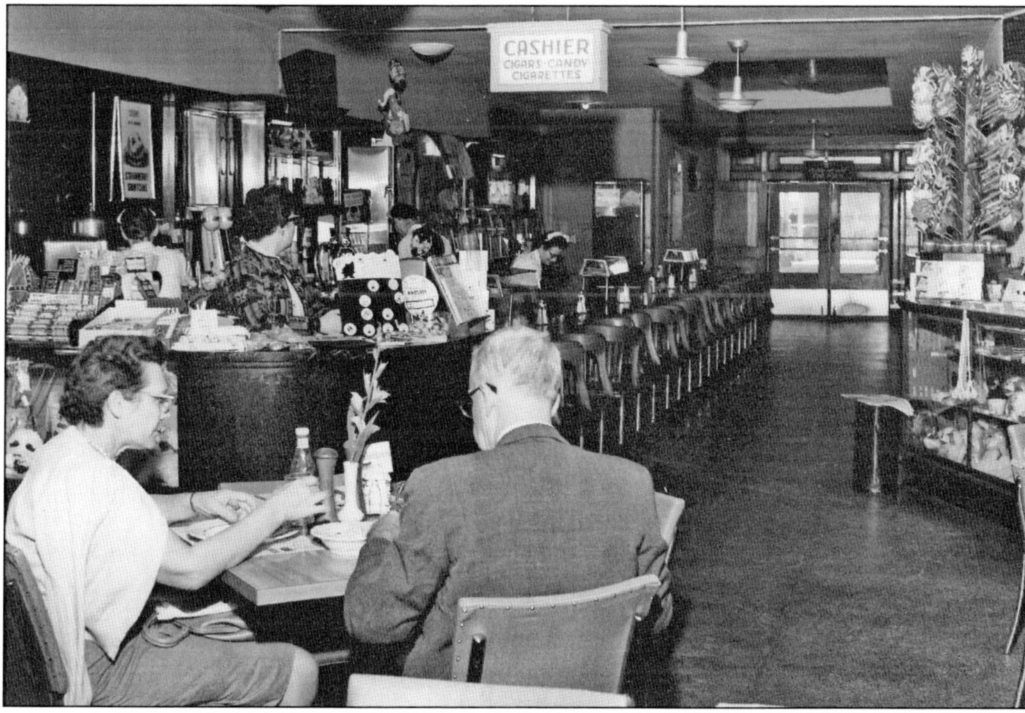

In 1938, there was a pay telephone, and Painter taxi service operated just outside. In 1941, Eddie Cantor and Clara Gabel visited the restaurant. This photograph, taken in the 1960s, shows a large facility with no one suspecting that to the left, on the other side of the wall, was a large bus station. In 1973, when it closed, it became the R. T. Arnold Public Library, but was eventually torn down for a more modern facility. (Photograph by R. L. Harris Sr.)

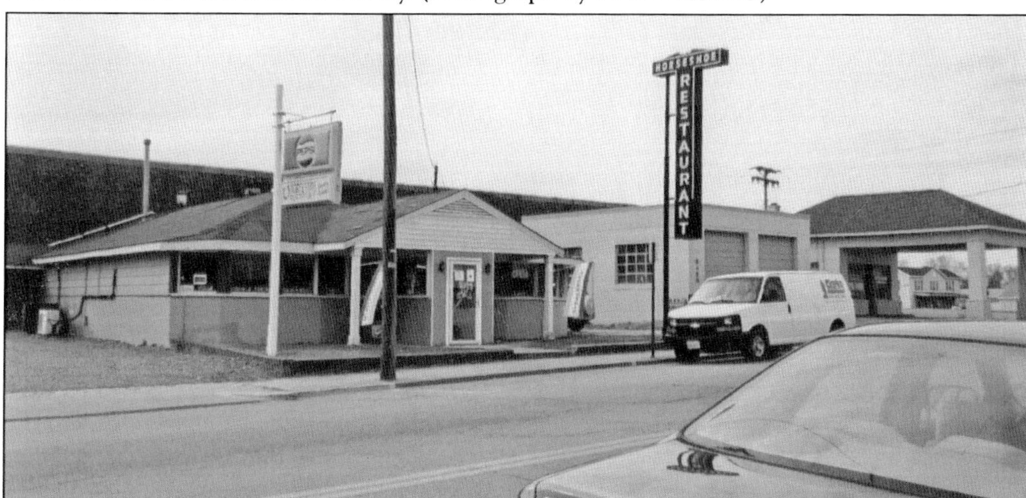

In 1932, the Farmer's Warehouse on Danville Street burned. The land became a used-car dealership. Across the street, the Horseshoe Restaurant opened in 1936. In December 1938, the 20-year-old "Machine Gun" (local lore) Roy Kelley was captured here after he escaped from a North Carolina prison camp. His capture followed a two-month manhunt for Kelley who had been imprisoned for killing a man in a heated gun battle on December 7, 1937. The "capture here was affected quietly and without resistance," according to the *Enterprise*. (JC.)

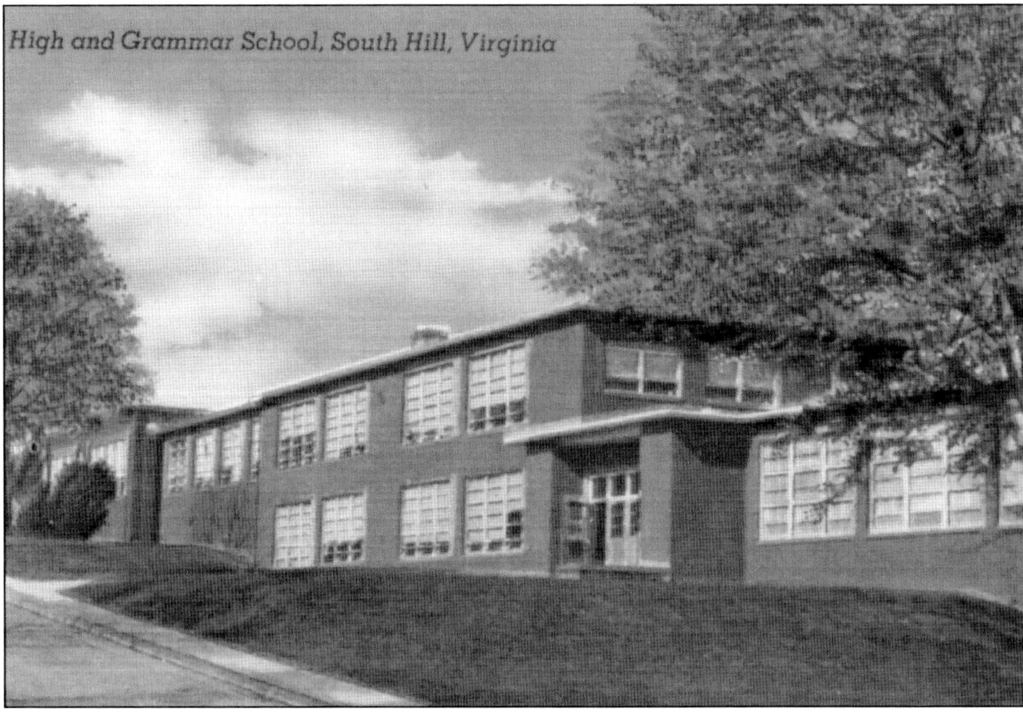

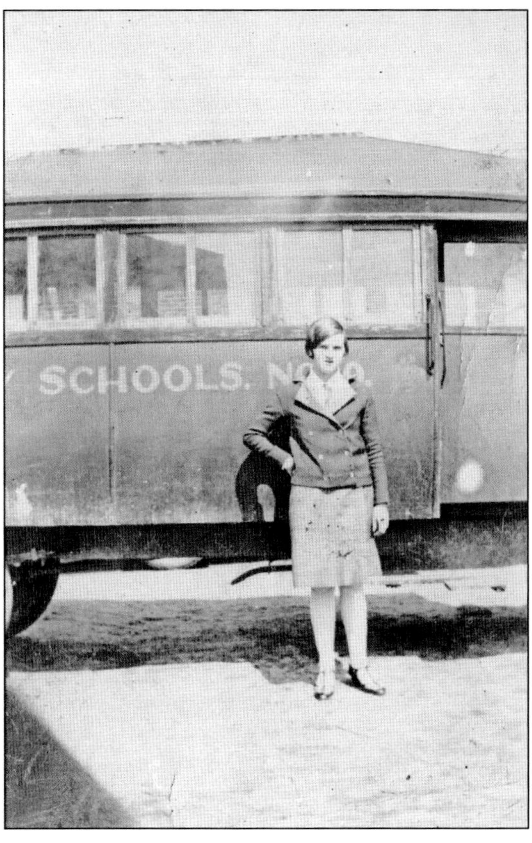

On April 6, 1932, the South Hill School burned, but by October 25, 1932, a new school had been rebuilt. The new school had all the modern improvements over the former 1910 building and had 10 additional classrooms. In 1952, the new school also burned, and the students attended LaCrosse High School until graduation that year. (WCG.)

In 1937, the county school system began a bus service for the newly consolidated students. The buses were, for the most part, privately owned and under contract with the county to provide needed services. One of the first was this bus owned by James Smiley of Big Fork. The driver in front of the bus is unidentified. (Roy and John Wootton.)

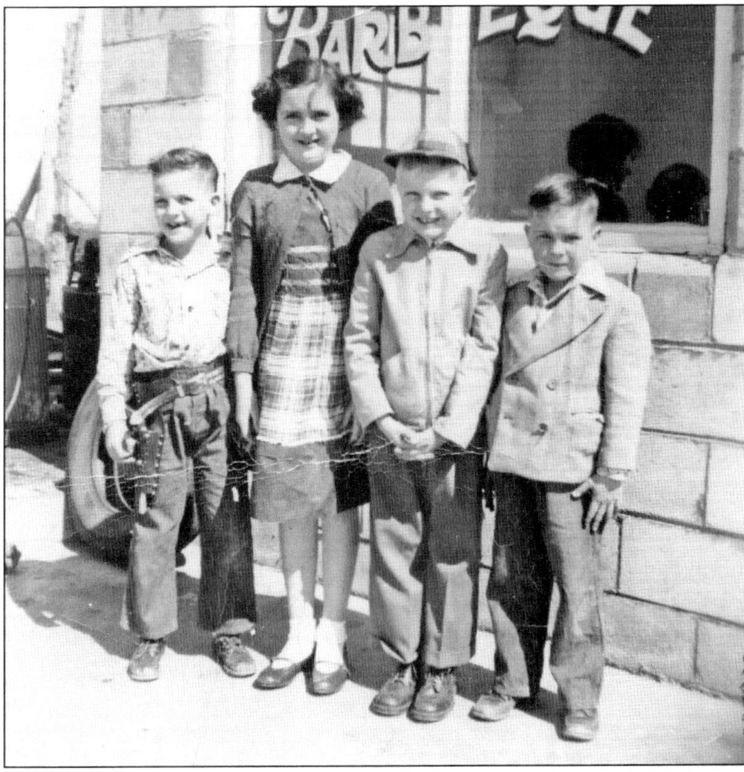

An industrious individual, a farmer by profession for many years, and a musician who entertained, James Smiley also built this Barbeque Restaurant at Big Fork. The children standing in front of the restaurant are, from left to right, Jimmy, Jane, unidentified, and Edna Smiley. (Roy and John Wootton.)

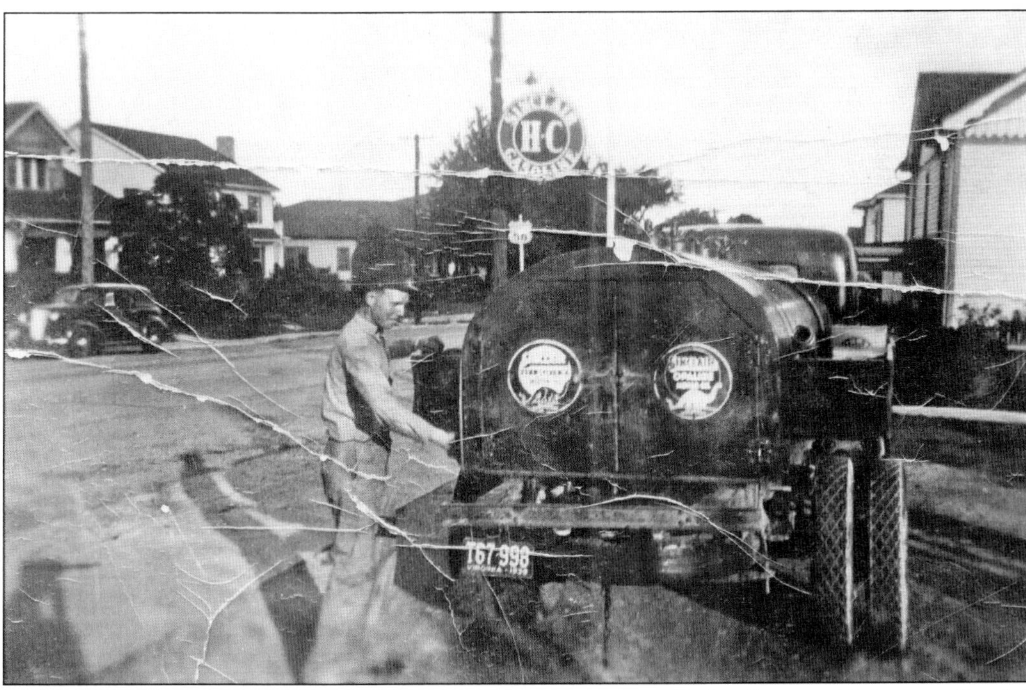

Before World War II, Smiley operated a gas business around Big Fork selling and delivering Sinclair petroleum products for Ed H. Harris. Here Murray Smiley (James's brother) is pictured with his new delivery truck at a nearby station. (Roy and John Wootton.)

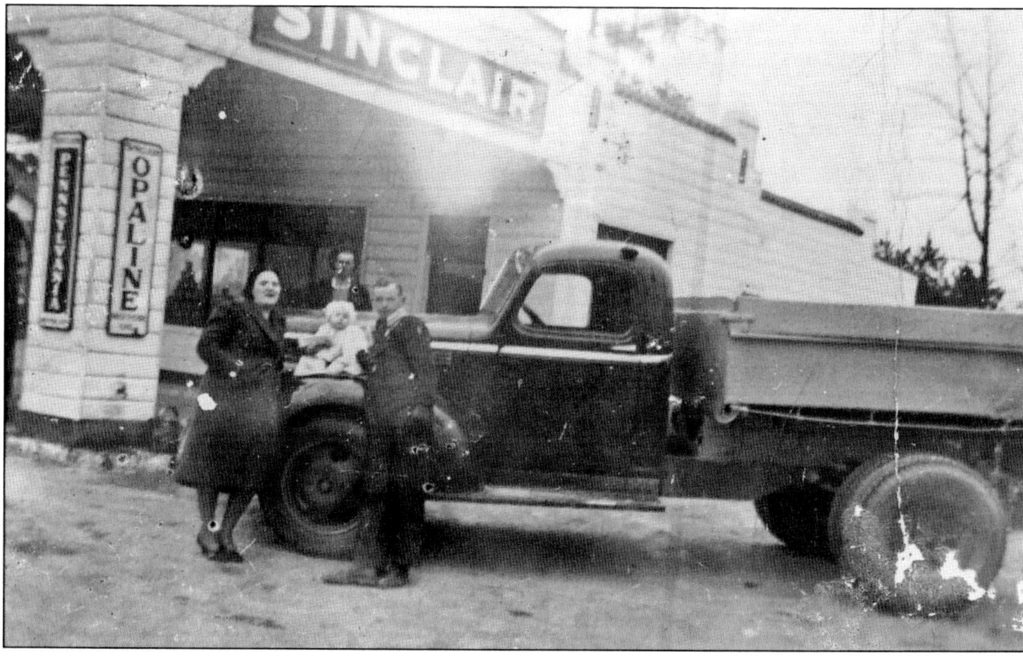

Posing at the Sinclair station for Harris, a family is resting on its new dump truck. The gas station is unique for the day, as it had a drive-through so the customers would have protection from the weather. It burned following a lightning strike in 1948. (Roy and John Wootton.)

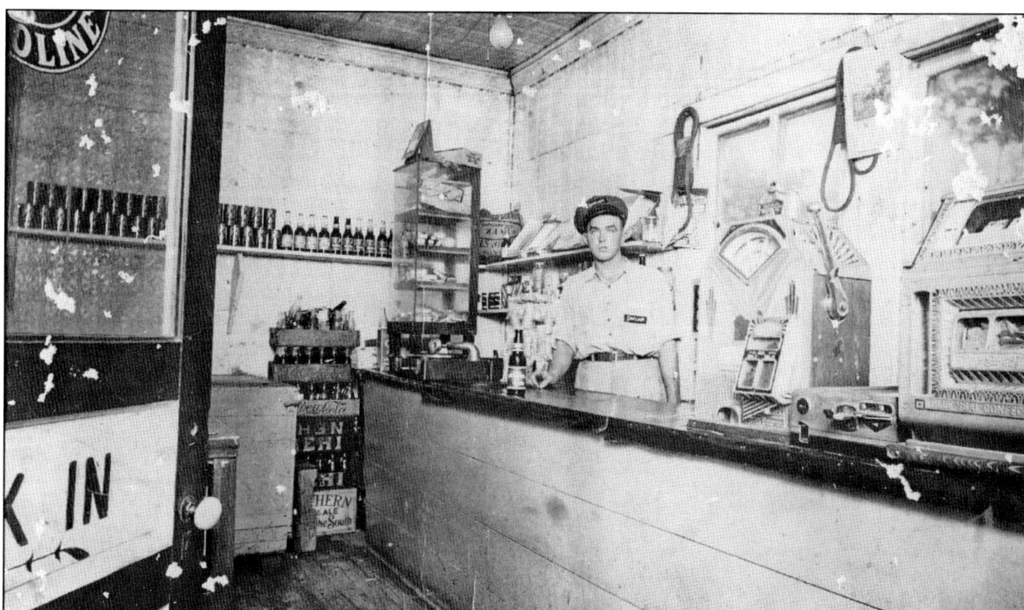

The Smiley family service center also served as a community convenience store selling drinks, beer, and sundries. On the counter is a rare look at a slot machine ("one-armed bandit"). Slot machines were popular and legal in stores from around 1900 until they became illegal in many states following World War II. He also added a wrecker service to the service center. (Roy and John Wootton.)

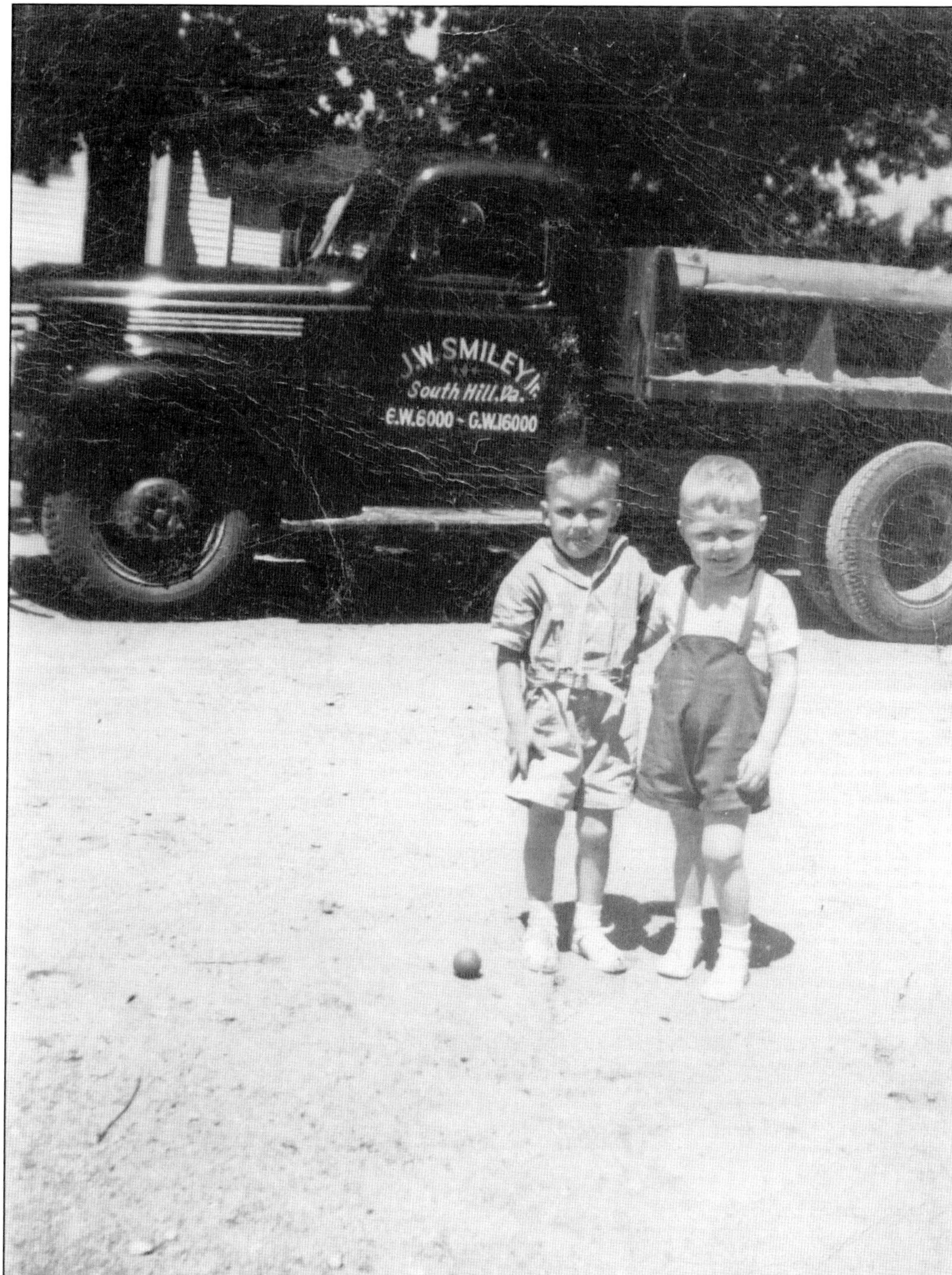

Now the dump truck is official with lettering and license. Following the war, a concerted effort was made to catch up on graveling the county roads that had sat idle for almost five years. Homeowners were beginning to have their driveways graveled, and many road repairs were "quick-fixed" by gravel placement until a tar truck could be scheduled. The children pictured here are unidentified. (Roy and John Wootton.)

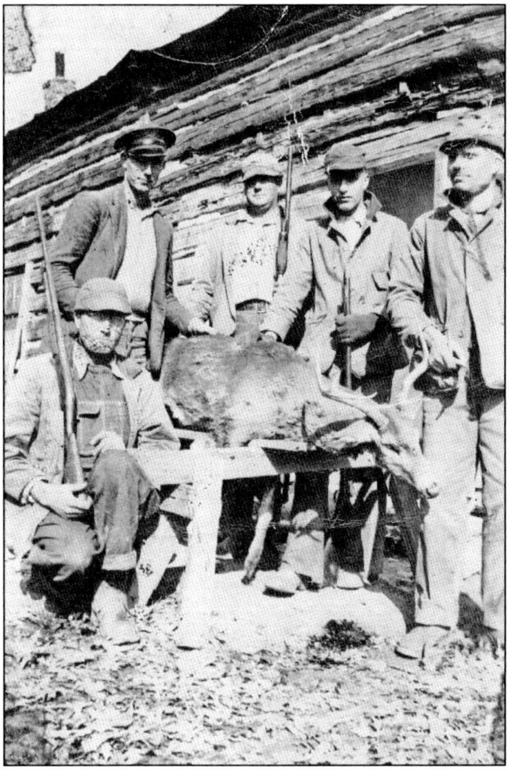

Of course the primary meat for the table, smokehouse, and icebox was the white-tailed deer. Jack Smiley (kneeling) had a good day with the family hunt, harvesting this nine-point buck (about 50 pounds of meat for the table). Standing behind him are, from left to right, Ralph Thompson, Roy P. Wootton, and two unidentified men. (Roy and John Wootton.)

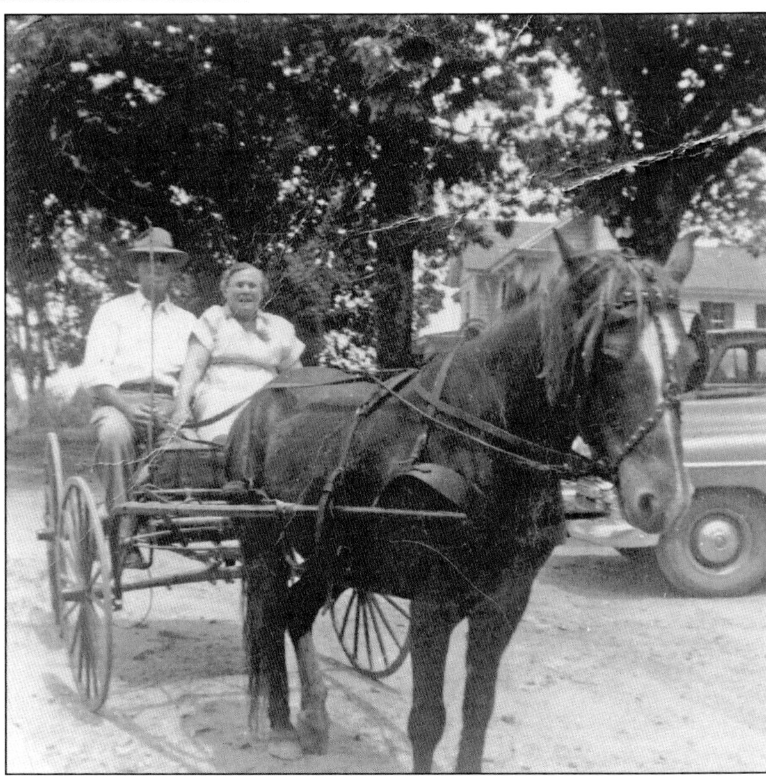

Jack Smiley Sr. and his wife, Florence Murray Smiley, still enjoyed going for a buggy ride (in this case a doctor's wagon with a small seat) on Sunday afternoons, probably reflecting on the days gone by. This photograph, taken in their front yard, suggests they were about to tour the fields and crops to ensure things were going as planned. (Roy and John Wootton.)

Pictured here is Ben Homes, who worked with the C. R. Dunn store in Baskerville for over 30 years. Taken in the early 1920s, he was proud of his new "tin tub" washbasin in this photograph. It appears he is preparing a wash. The boy in the background is Dick Dunn. Homes passed away in January 1929. (Martha Dunn Overton.)

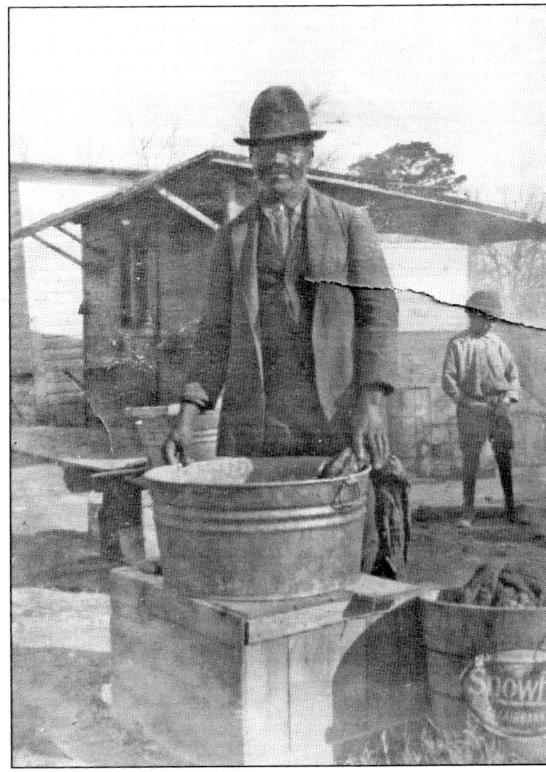

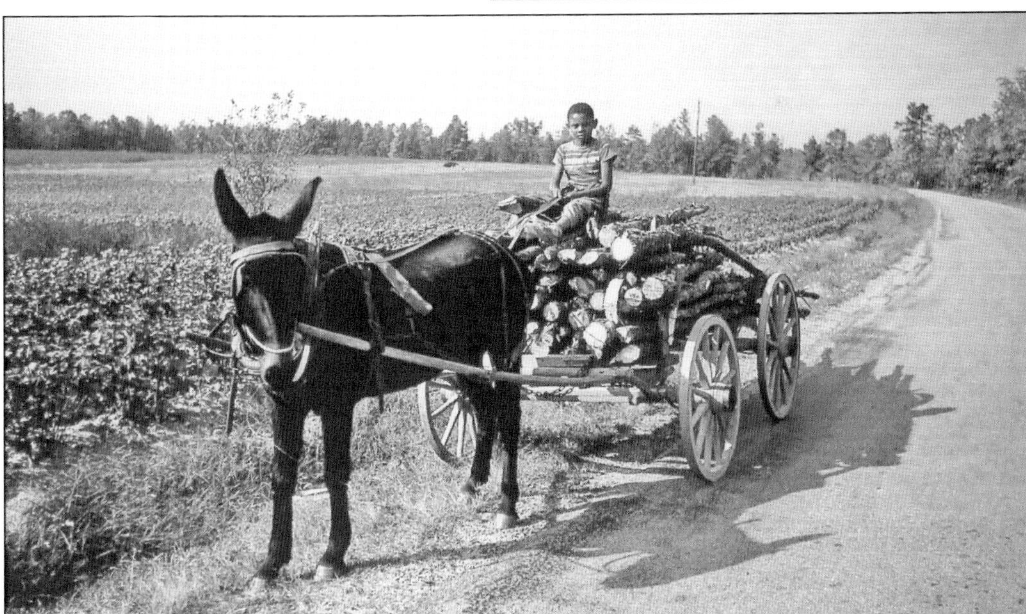

For centuries, logging, timber, and lumber have been the backbone of Mecklenburg County's economy. Once a tree is cut, it is topped when the circumference becomes too small for pulp. The tops were left in the woods, though today they are piled and burned once they dry. Many families will, even today, go to the woods and limb the tops, load them onto a wagon, and bring them home, primarily for firewood. (PMA.)

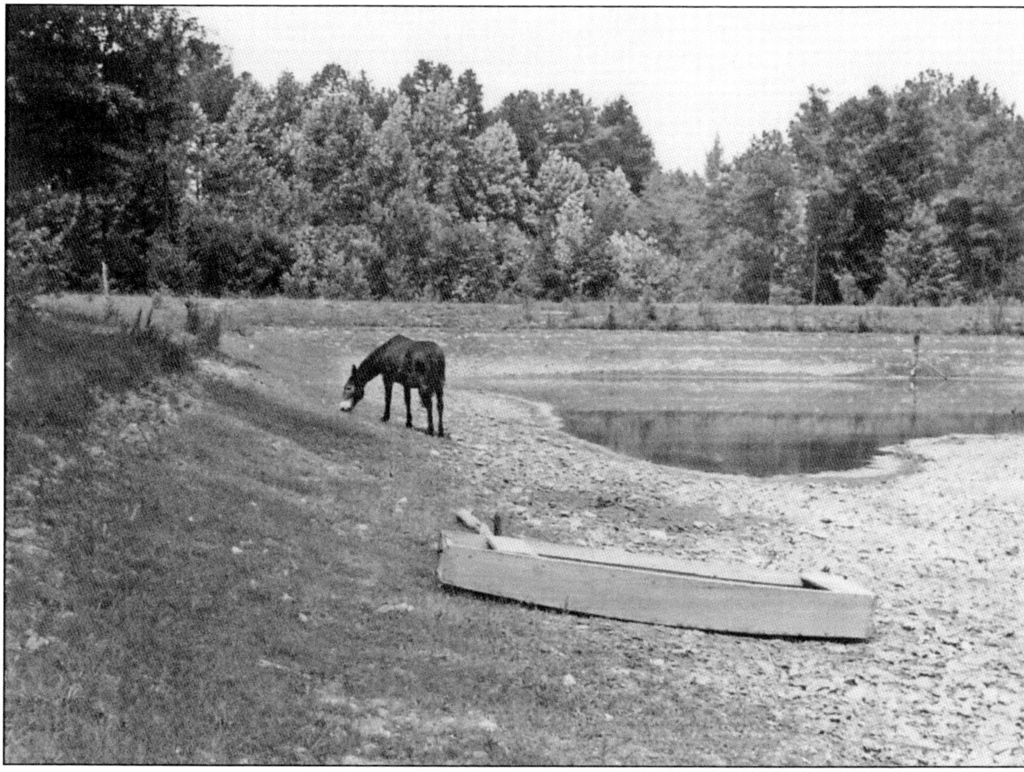

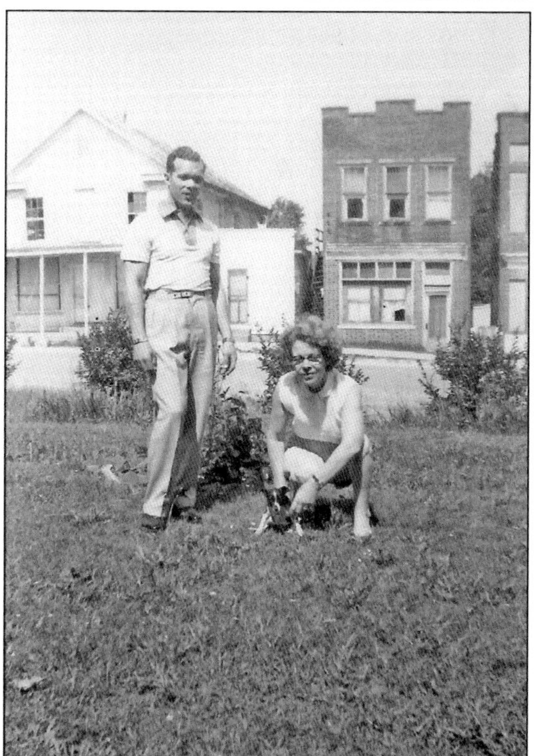

Aside from the Depression, the drought of 1932 proved to be one of the worst in over 50 years. Once a very large body of water, notice the now-tiny pool and the distance of the shoreline, about 10 to 15 feet in front of the mule's face. The mule is grazing on grass and weeds that are growing where the water once was. Needless to say, there was a serious crop failure that year, and many farmers literally had to pay to sell their tobacco. (Photograph by R. L. Harris Sr.)

The white building to the back left began in 1890 as W. Simmons fertilizer and grain store. When Simmons constructed a new store near the railroad station, this building was the Village Pool Hall managed by James Carroll. Following the Depression, Peter Bennett leased it as a dance hall for African Americans of Union Level. He added the small store to the side of the building and sold his produce on Saturdays, followed by a dance. In front are Clara Thompson, her son C. W. Johnson, and dog Bonny. (CST.)

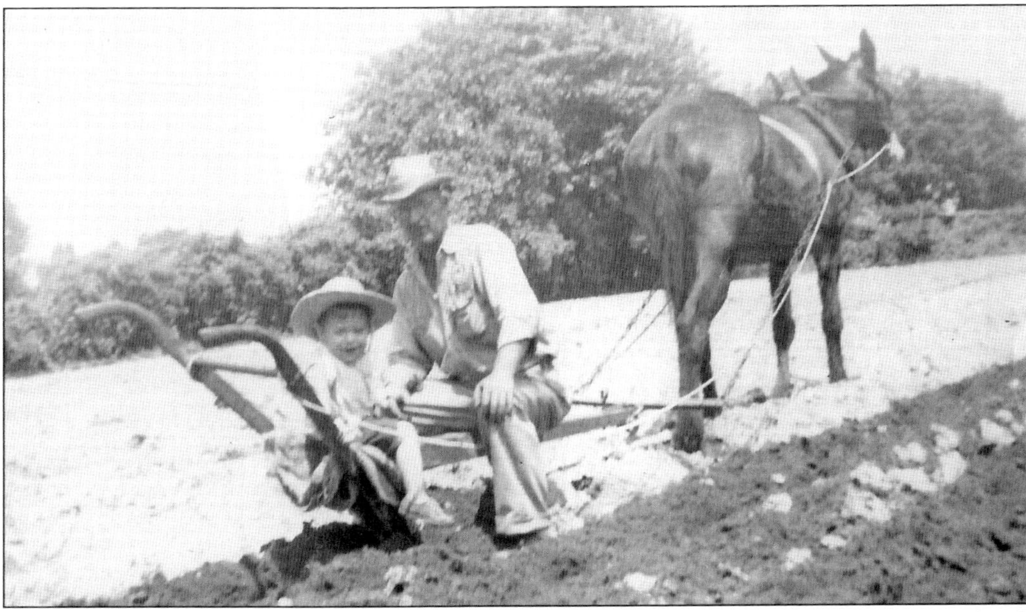

Generally an older mule is put out to pasture (and called a "plug" when they retire). To earn family care and keep, a mule still had to perform chores like pulling a wagon or buggy to town for a visit and taking care of the family garden. Garden season always brought out the mule and plow to break the ground and ready it for planting. In 1951, Spot Thompson (the mule) was preparing the home garden when it was time for a break. Little Jimmy climbed on the plow for a photograph with his dad to remember the day. (CST.)

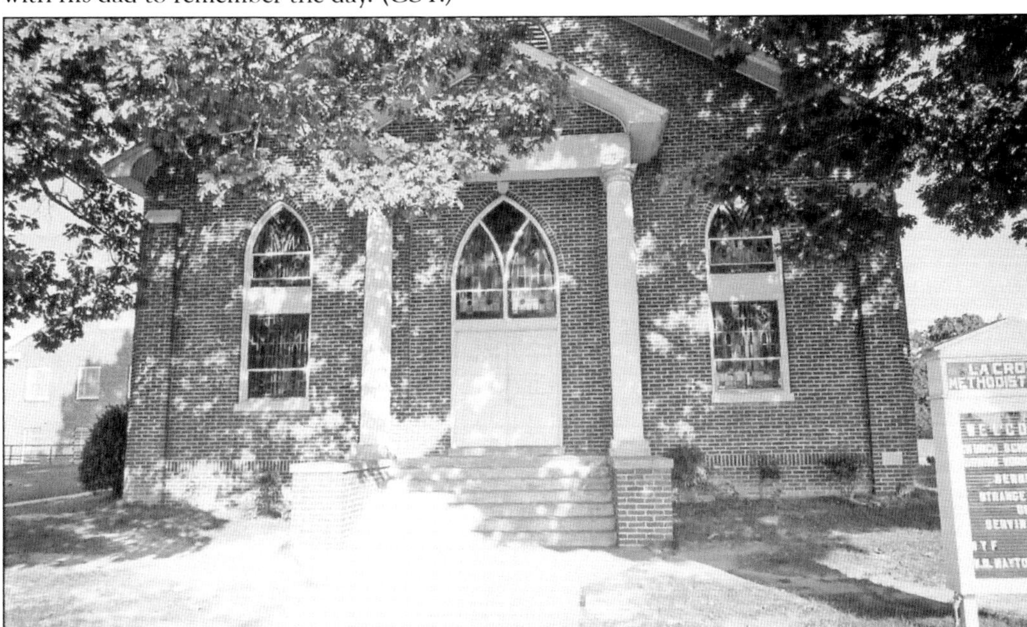

By 1909, the Methodist Church of Lacrosse needed a larger facility than their one-room building. They tore down the building and erected a new six-room sanctuary. In 1936, this structure was also torn down, and this new brick facility was built with an auditorium, a balcony, and nine Sunday school rooms. A parsonage was built next door in 1926. (PMA.)

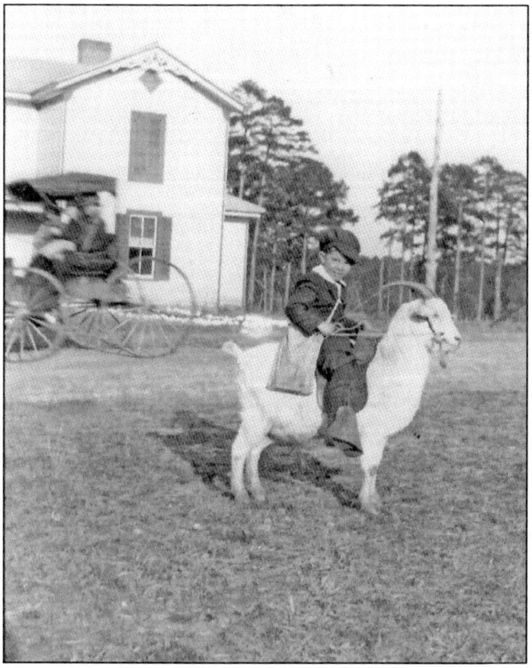

Hillsman Warren, sporting his new tick schoolbag, is riding his goat to school. Warren was a firm believer in education and strongly encouraged his son Charles to complete law school. Charles is presiding Mecklenburg County General District Court judge. In the buggy are Frank and Maude Rose Martin in front of the E. W. Rose home in Bracey. The photographer was William Perkins, who had recently arrived from North Carolina with his family to start a new business around 1910. (Waller Randolph Hite, great-grandson of Waller T. Bracey.)

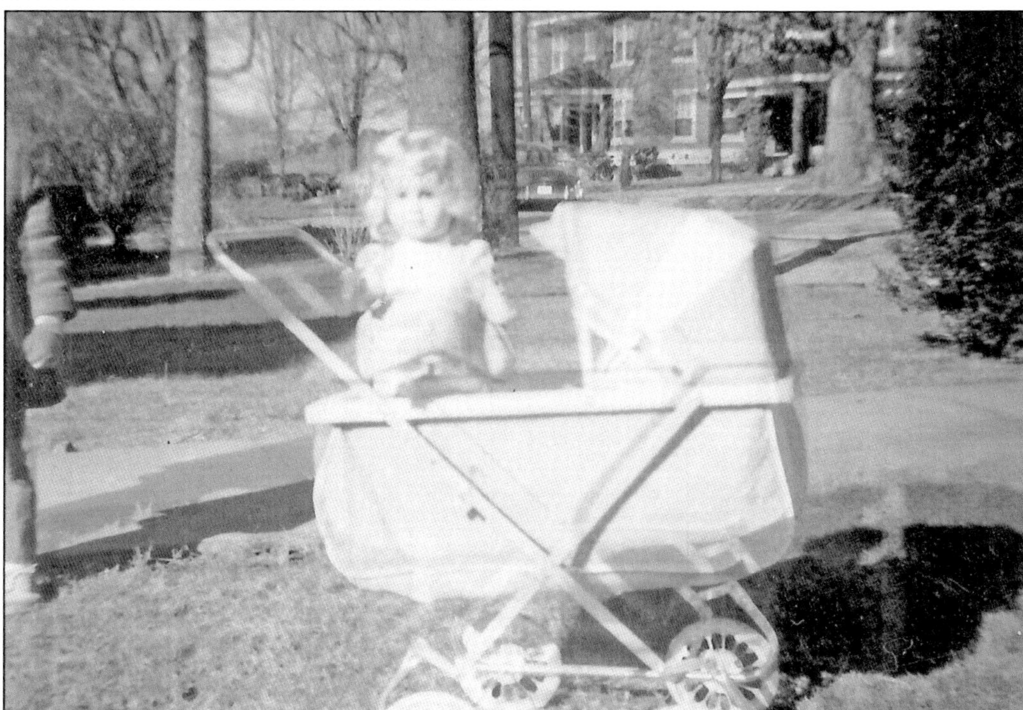

Dr. Wilkerson's practice continued to thrive in Lacrosse, but he and his wife had a handicapped son. Across the street from their home, Dr. Wilkerson built this large brick home. The rooms were situated so that no matter which room the Wilkerson's were in, they would have their son in the next room and would be able to observe him. In the foreground is Betty Axson taking her new Christmas doll and stroller for a tour of the town. (Page Cook Axson McGaughy.)

Five

Floods and Wars

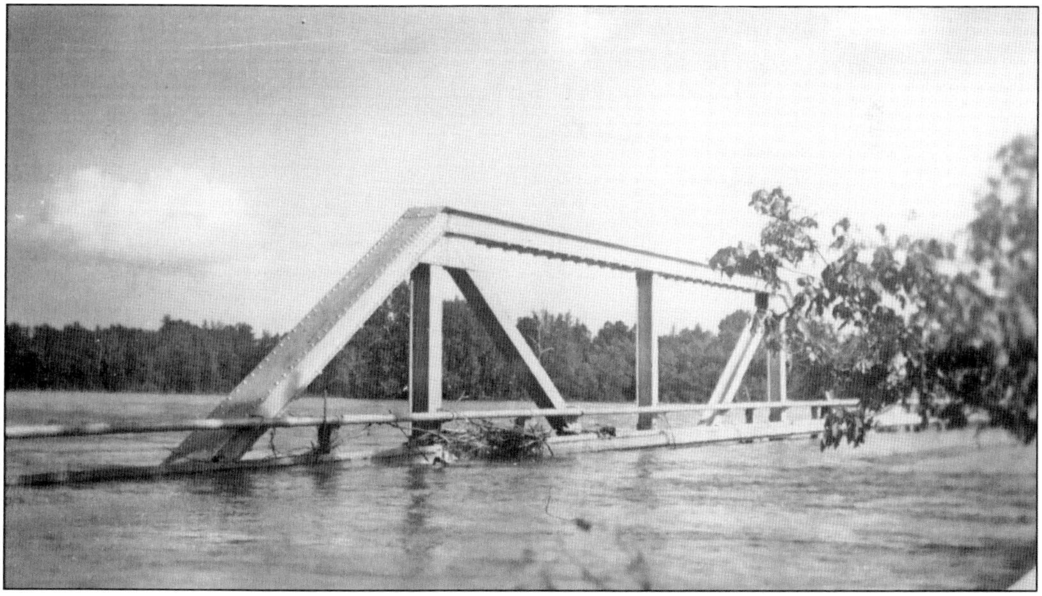

An excellent crop year, precipitation was plentiful in 1940, beginning with unusual snowstorms that saturated the land. Then between August 10 and August 17, a rainstorm followed by a hurricane deposited over 15 inches water. The Roanoke River rose to over 27 feet out of its banks, flooding over 8,000 square miles from Danville, Virginia, to Rocky Mount, North Carolina. Note the top rail of the steel bridge on U.S. Route 1. (James E. G. Taylor.)

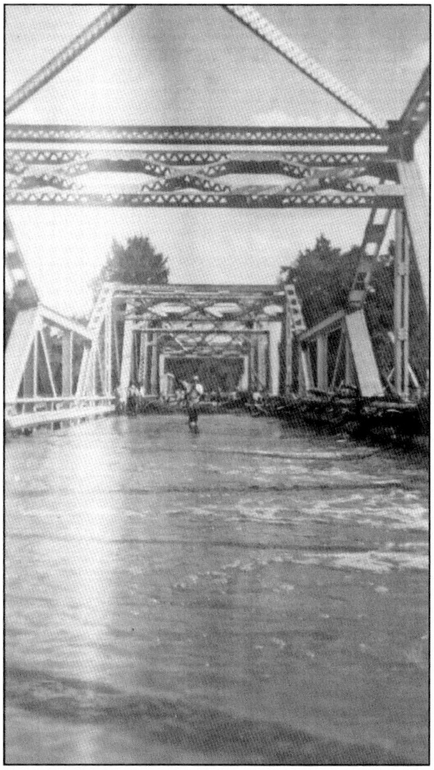

During the worst storm recorded in 225 years crops ready for harvest were washed away. Families were displaced, and thousands of people were out of work for months. Within a few days, cleanup began, but the waters were slow to recede. Note in this photograph that the steel bridge still has almost 2 feet of water across U.S. Route 1. The bridge also served as a trap for trees and debris coming downstream. (James E. G. Taylor.)

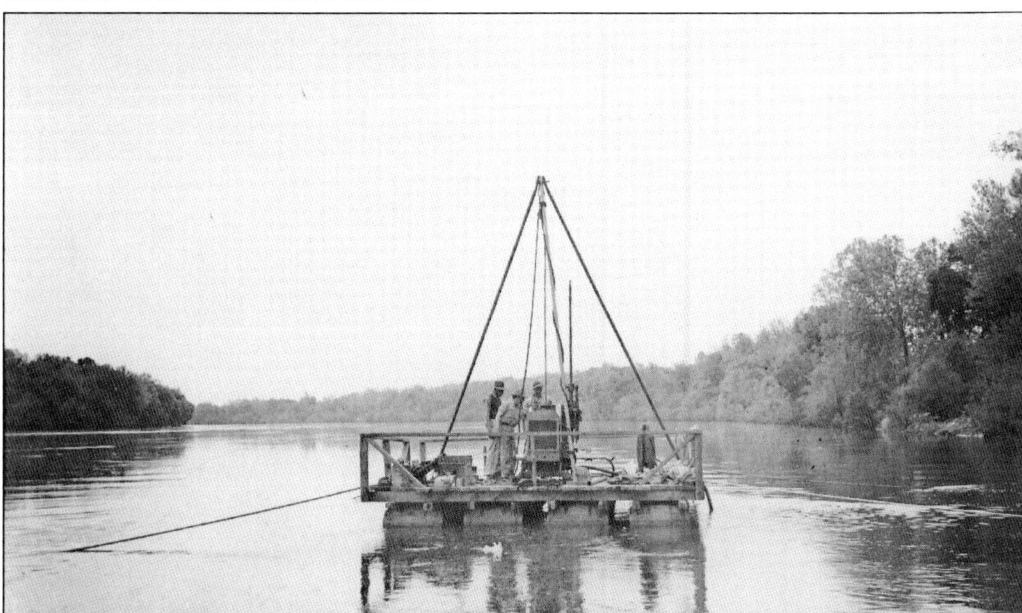

Congress approved the development of the Roanoke River Basin in 1944, but it was not funded until after World War II. Once funds were approved, core drilling began in the river to find a suitable location for a dam site. This photograph was taken on April 24, 1946, of rig No. 4 conducting water pressure tests in the river. (COE.)

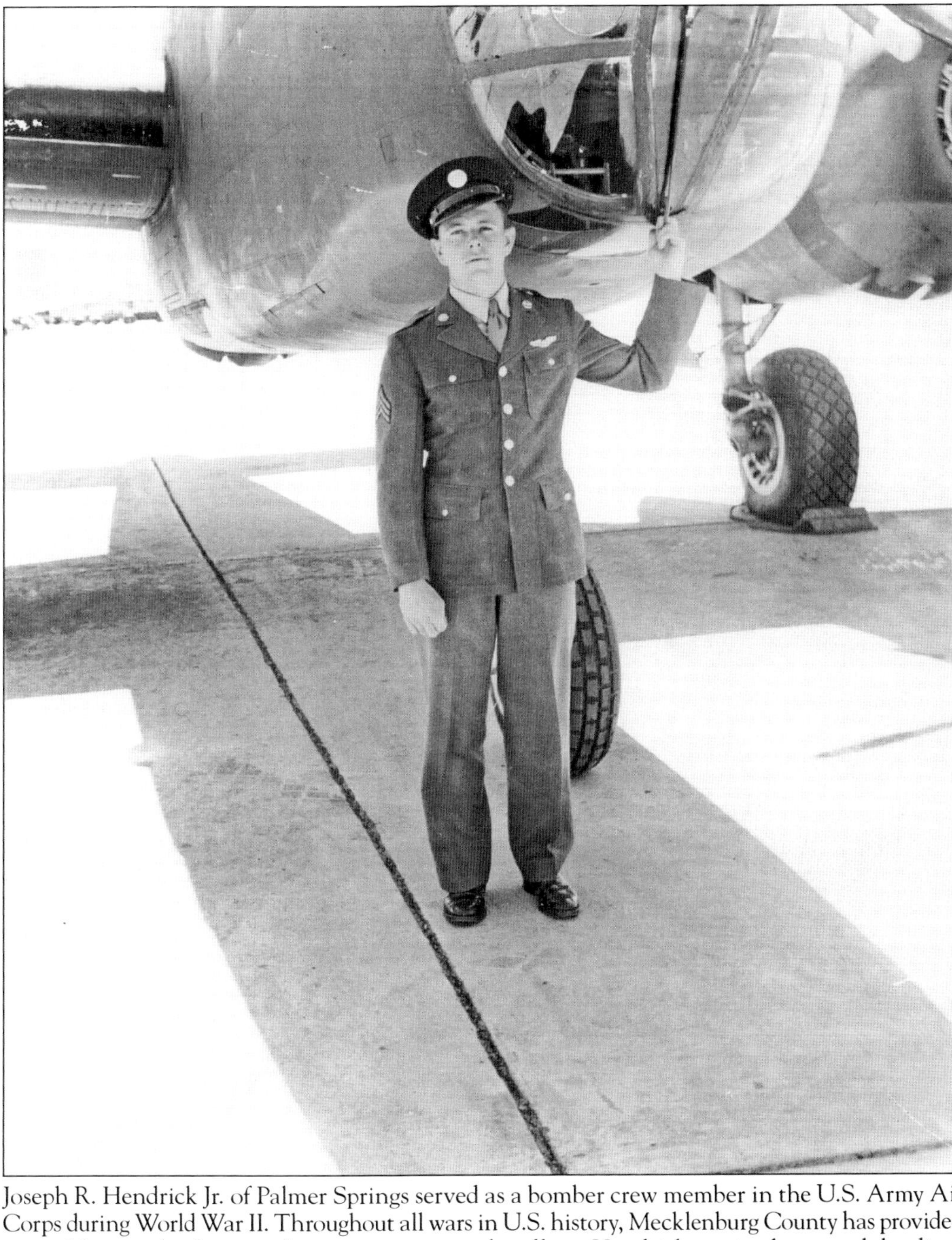

Joseph R. Hendrick Jr. of Palmer Springs served as a bomber crew member in the U.S. Army Air Corps during World War II. Throughout all wars in U.S. history, Mecklenburg County has provided tens of thousands of men and women to support the efforts. Hendrick survived two crash landings as a tail gunner and flight engineer of this Martin B-26 Marauder. (Hendrick Motorsports.)

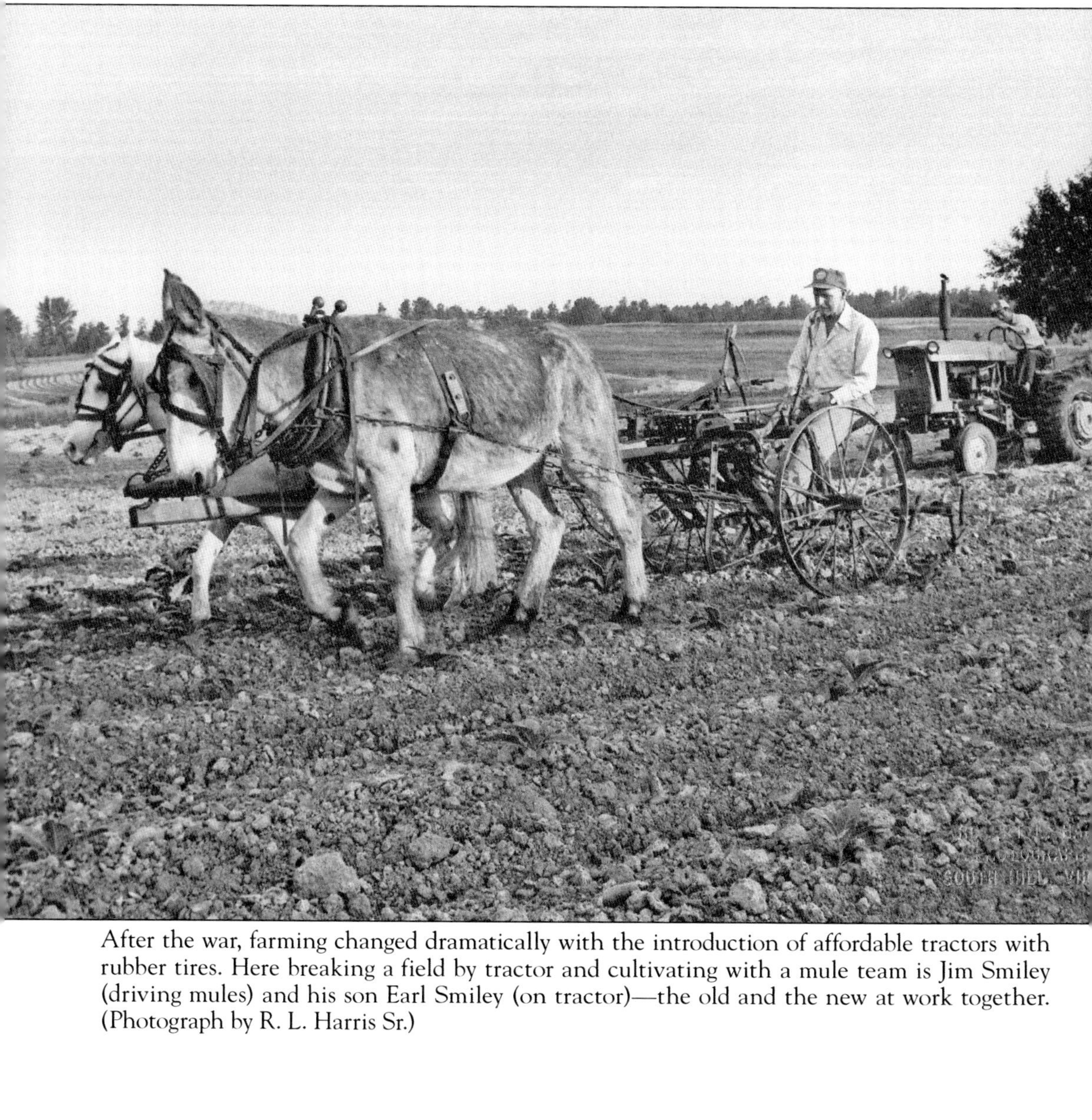

After the war, farming changed dramatically with the introduction of affordable tractors with rubber tires. Here breaking a field by tractor and cultivating with a mule team is Jim Smiley (driving mules) and his son Earl Smiley (on tractor)—the old and the new at work together. (Photograph by R. L. Harris Sr.)

Too young to serve in the war, 14-year-old Dwight Moody Jr. of Lacrosse, with the help of talented family members, learned to play the guitar. Through the years, Mecklenburg County has been host to numerous talented musicians who have gone on to become recording artists. After the guitar, Moody learned to play the fiddle and in 1945 appeared with the Virginia Playboys on WHNC radio in Henderson, North Carolina. (Dwight Moody Jr.)

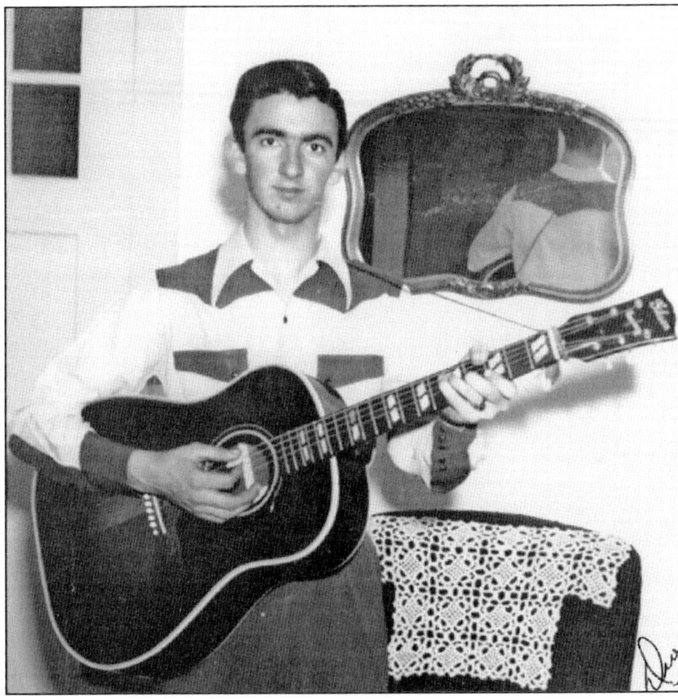

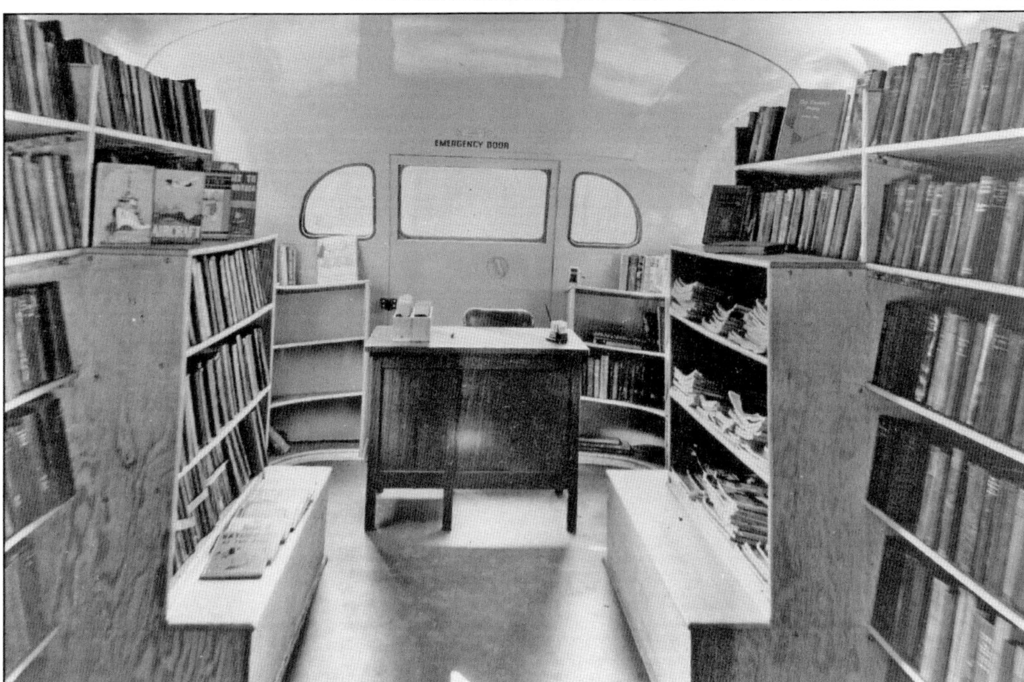

Following World War II, the United States began a literacy program, which gave impetus to bookmobiles. In October 1946, at the South Central Fair in Chase City, the South Side Regional Library unveiled their regional bookmobile. It served South Hill until they established a library in 1974. This photograph shows the vast numbers of books that had to be checked, loaded, and unloaded on a frequent basis. (South Side Regional Library, vertical files.)

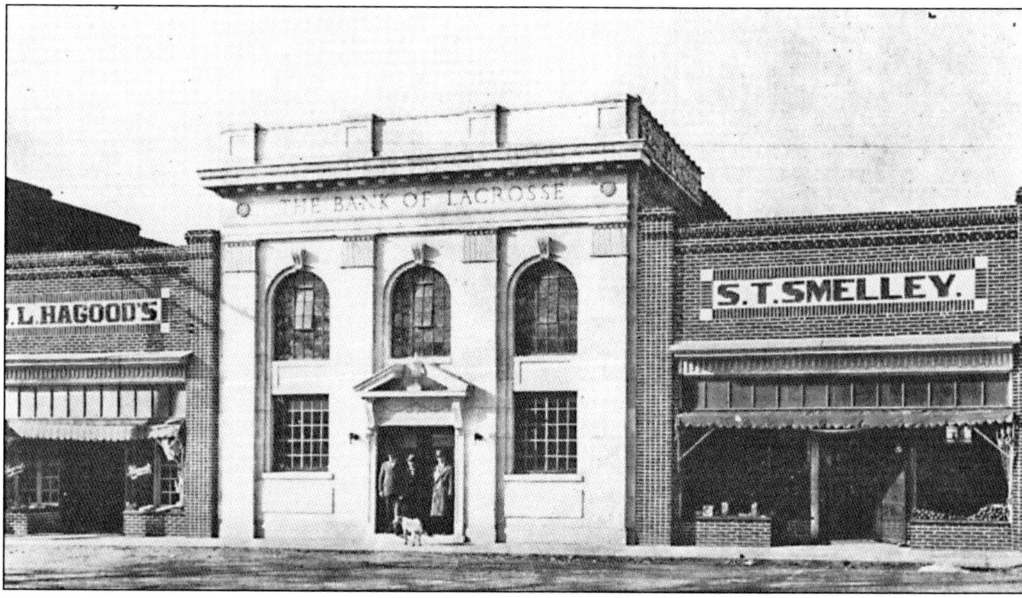

This postcard shows a face-lift for downtown Lacrosse. The individuals in front of the bank are unidentified. To the left is the J. L. (Joe) Hagood's shoe store, which began as a heel factory, with shoe repair and sales added later. To the right of the bank is S. T. Smelly's grocery store, which also bought and sold local produce. (H. Ryland Rash.)

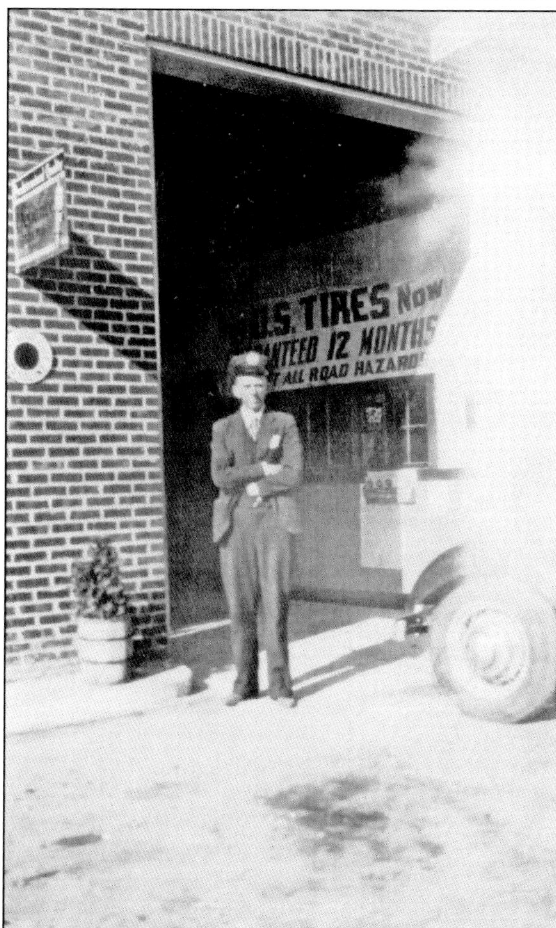

An important automobile component and the sale of which had been forbidden or severely rationed during the war, tires returned to consumers in 1946. Every garage carried a line of new and recapped tires for automobiles and trucks. New tires also began to be sold with a guarantee that year. Standing in front of this garage is mechanic Joseph R. Hendrick Sr. (Hendrick Motorsports.)

Relaxing on the front porch of Mrs. Robbie Fitz Harper and Myles Coles's general merchandise store in Bracey is Buster Perkinson. A new horse-drawn hay mower is on the porch beside him, and the sale flyers on the window shutter are of tobacco products in the store. (WRH.)

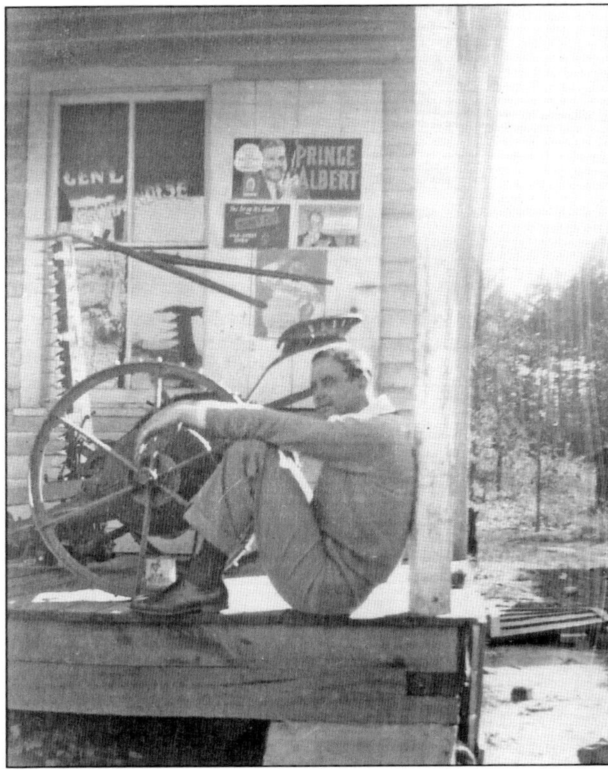

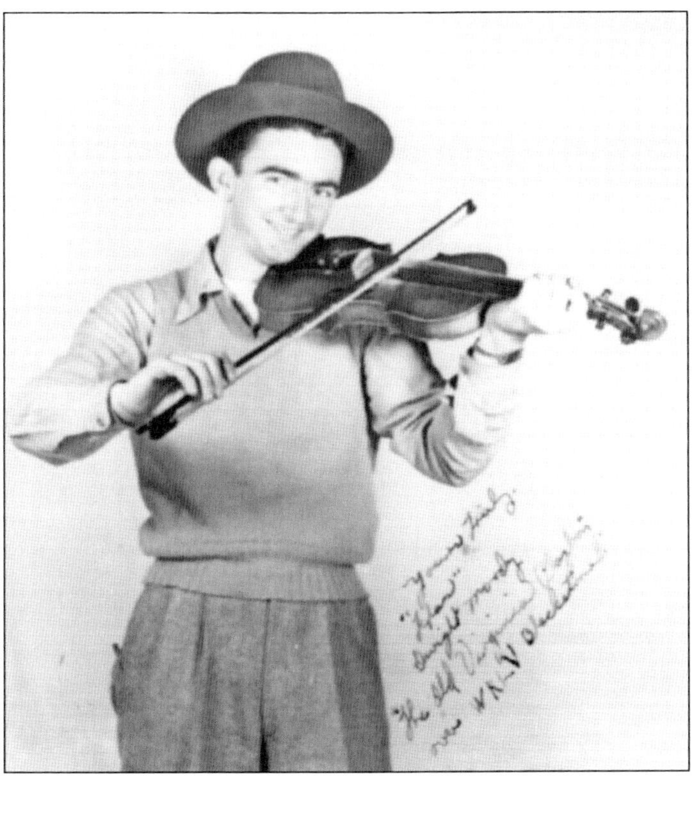

By 1946, the Virginia Playboys group was appearing all over south Virginia and northern North Carolina. This photograph is of "Fiddlin' " Dwight Moody Jr., age 16, appearing on WKLV Blackstone radio station. (Dwight Moody Jr.)

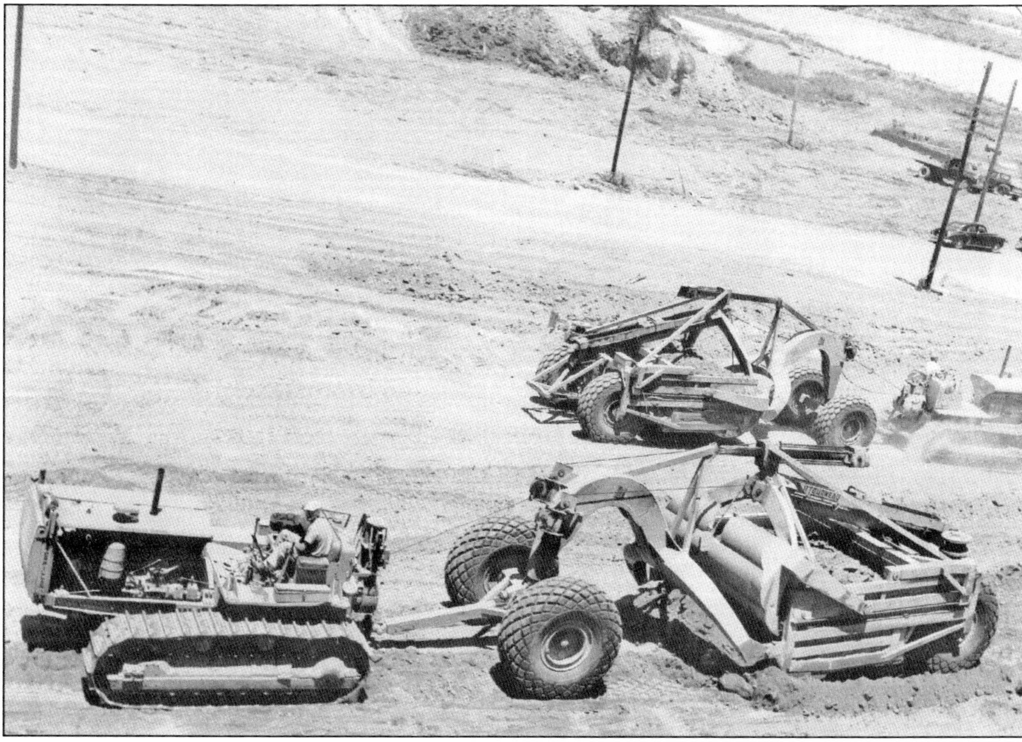

During the clearing phase of constructing a dam, the U.S. Army Corps of Engineers purchased 115,000 acres of land along the Roanoke and Dan Rivers. Excavation included the dam site, work site, a site for Kerr Village (office center), Castle Heights (living accommodations), and a highway (Route 4). Many homes and outbuildings were moved or destroyed. (COE.)

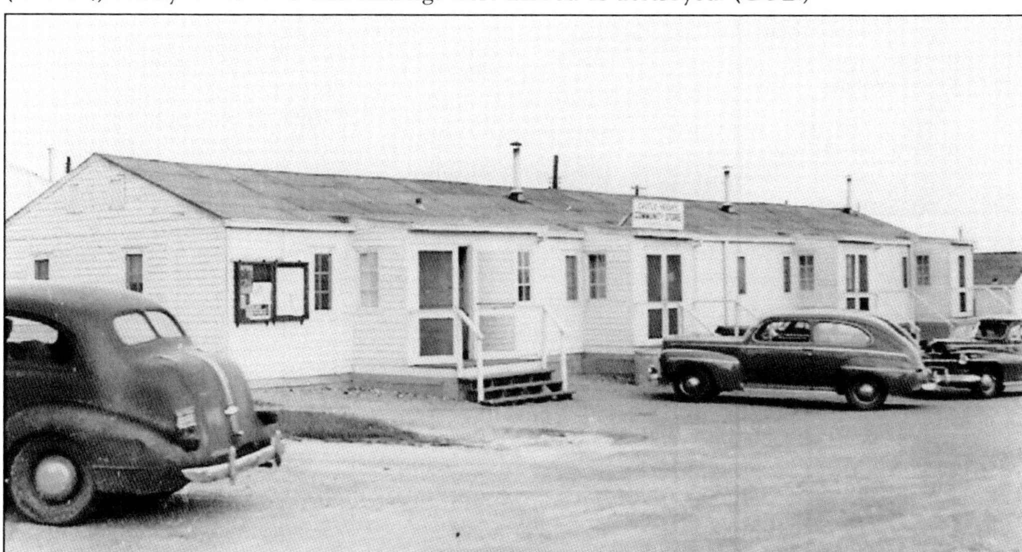

This was a community center with a meeting room, community general store, and offices located at the entrance to Castle Heights and built during 1946 and 1947. The total cost of the dam was $92 million, 54 cemeteries were moved (2,100 graves), 304 families were displaced, and in Mecklenburg County 15 percent of the land acreage was under water. (COE.)

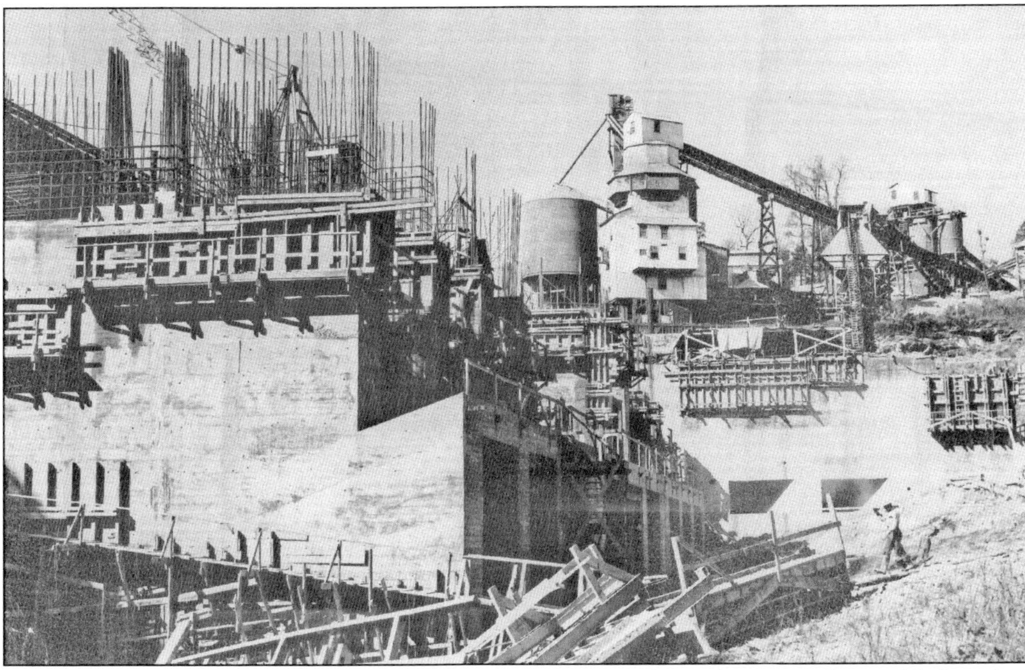

One of the first pieces of equipment that needed to be brought to the site and assembled in place was this nine-story cement mixer. Kerr Village was located just behind it to the left. The mixer was installed in 1949 once the railroad tracks were securely in place. The last pour from the mixer to complete the dam was on October 27, 1951. (COE.)

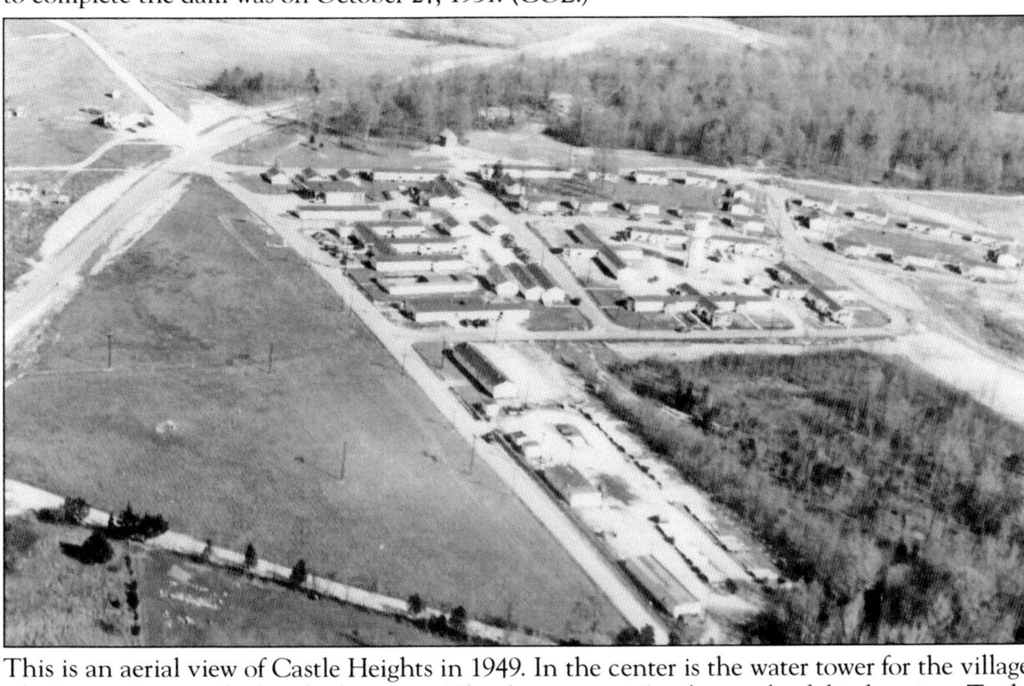

This is an aerial view of Castle Heights in 1949. In the center is the water tower for the village, which was also supplied with electricity. The dam was a 1.5 miles south of this location. To the left in this photograph, near the intersection of the two roads, is the Baskerville quarry, where most of the stone came from for the dam construction. (COE.)

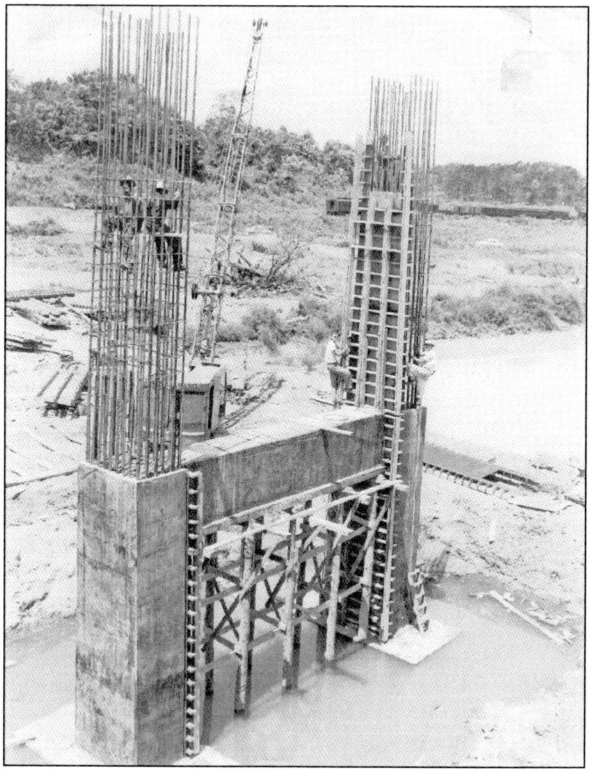

The materials used for the dam, powerhouse, and switchyard included 650,000 cubic yards of concrete, 570,000 barrels of cement, 1.1 million tons of crushed stone, and 5,400 tons of reinforcing steel, with 7,200 tons of miscellaneous metal piping, castings, and the like. Progress was initially slow and tedious as indicated in this photograph in 1949. (COE.)

This aerial view from 1950 shows the big picture of the operation. At front and center is the cofferdam on the Roanoke River, then Kerr Village is above, and following the road to near top center is Castle Heights. To the side of the photograph, along the river in the distance (left side), is Elm Hill Plantation, and the island in the river is "Bugg's Island," the local namesake for the lake, which has over 800 miles of shoreline. (COE.)

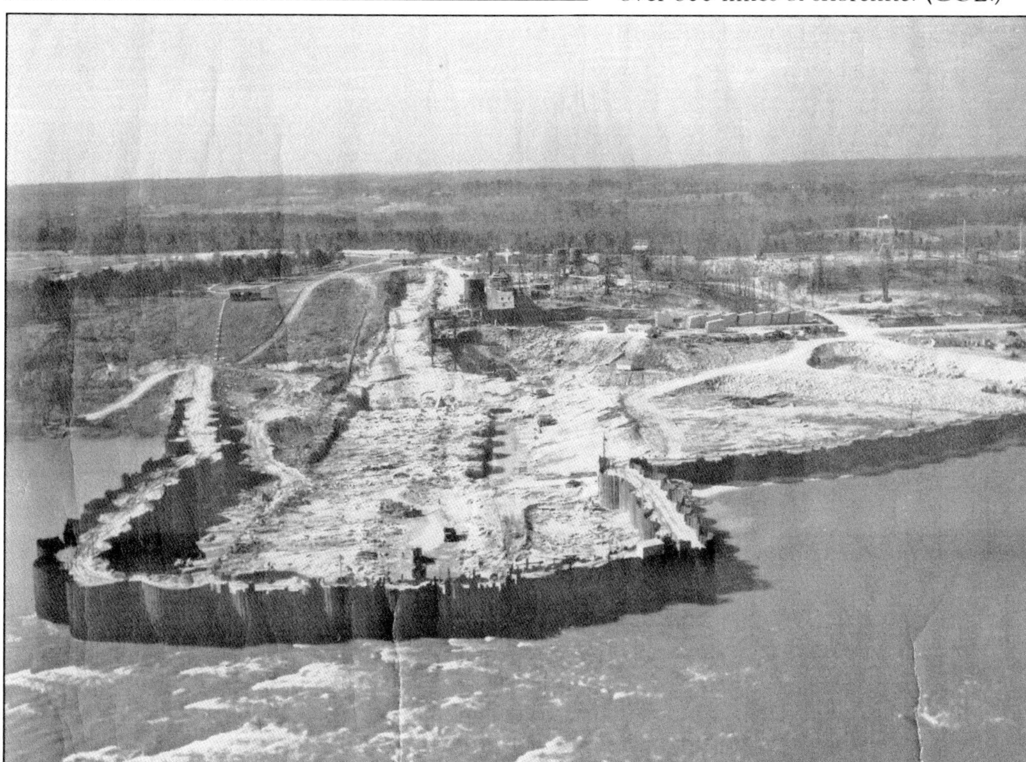

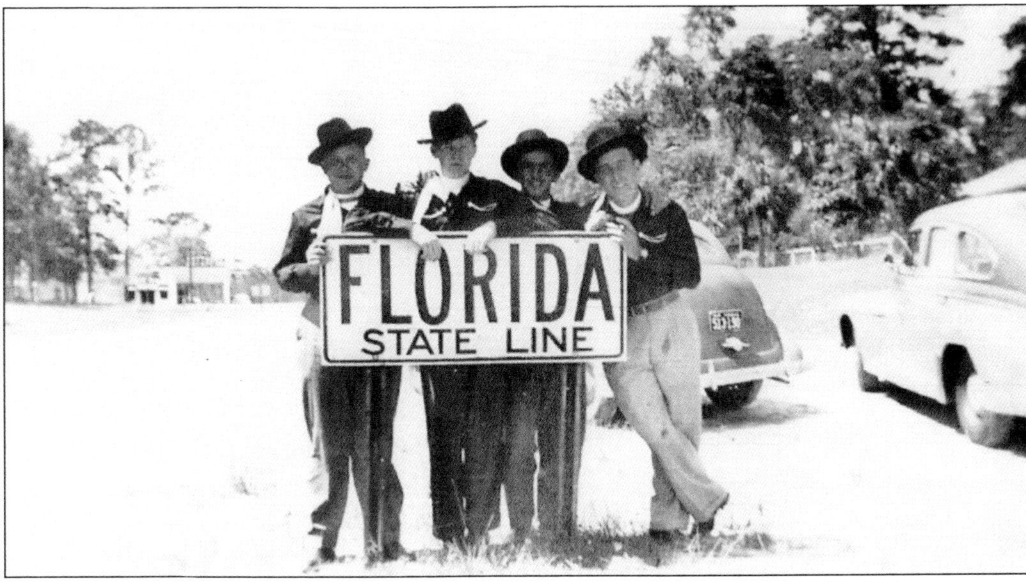

Following high school graduation, Moody and the Virginia Playboys toured Florida for a year, and then Moody joined the Wheeler Band. Moody also attended Smithdeal-Massey Business School and enlisted in the U.S. Army after graduation to serve in the Korean War (1951). After discharge he joined the Cleo and Lucille Burner Band and later joined up with Homer Briarhopper for a TV show in Durham, North Carolina. (Dwight Moody Jr.)

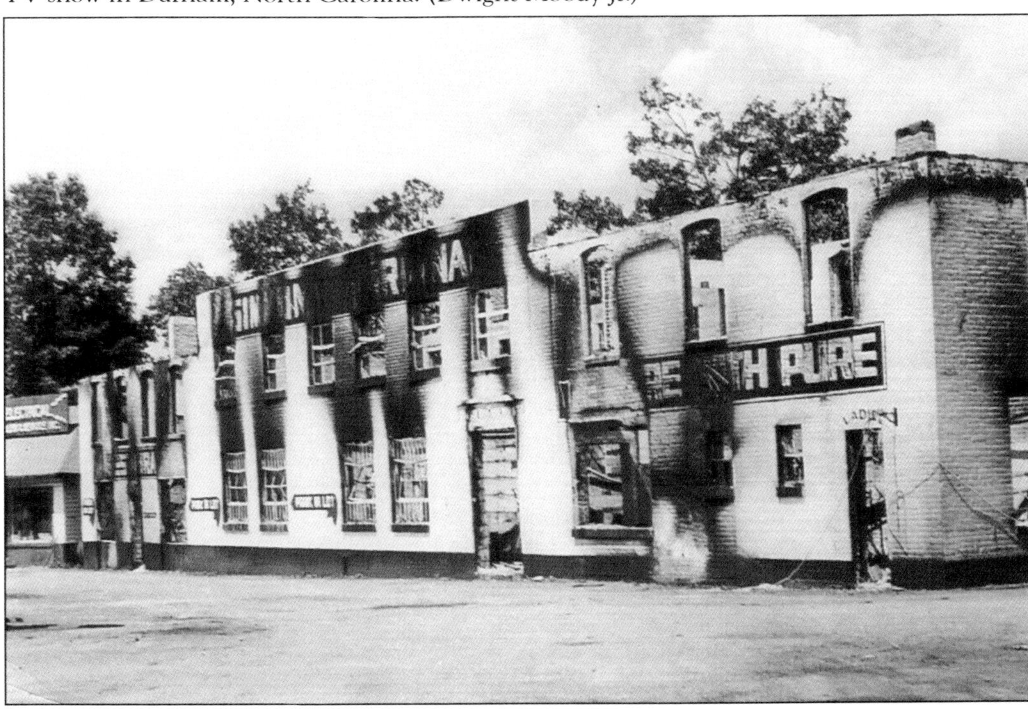

On July 16, 1949, South Hill was still plagued with fires when Simmon's Terminal on U.S. Route 1 burned. The terminal housed a service center and a restaurant with a store, and corporate offices for Parker Oil Company were upstairs. No one was injured. The terminal was quickly rebuilt and is still in operation today. (Parker Oil Company, Inc.)

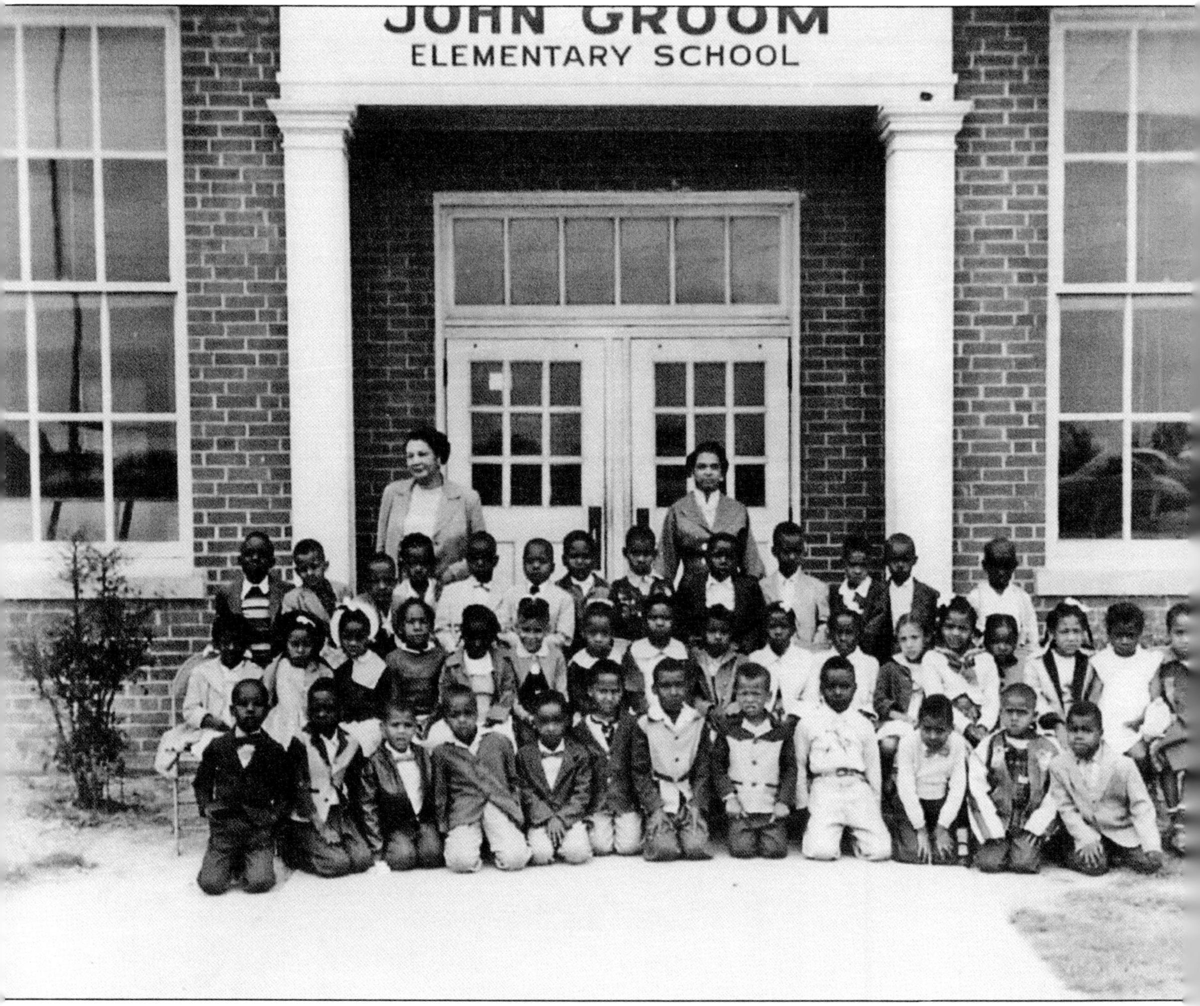

John Groom lived on Clay Street in South Hill, and when he died in 1946 there was a will. In his will he stipulated that $10,000 was to be set aside to "improve conditions of African American students in South Hill." When the new public elementary school was opened in 1948, it was named the John Groom Elementary School in his honor. (SHC.)

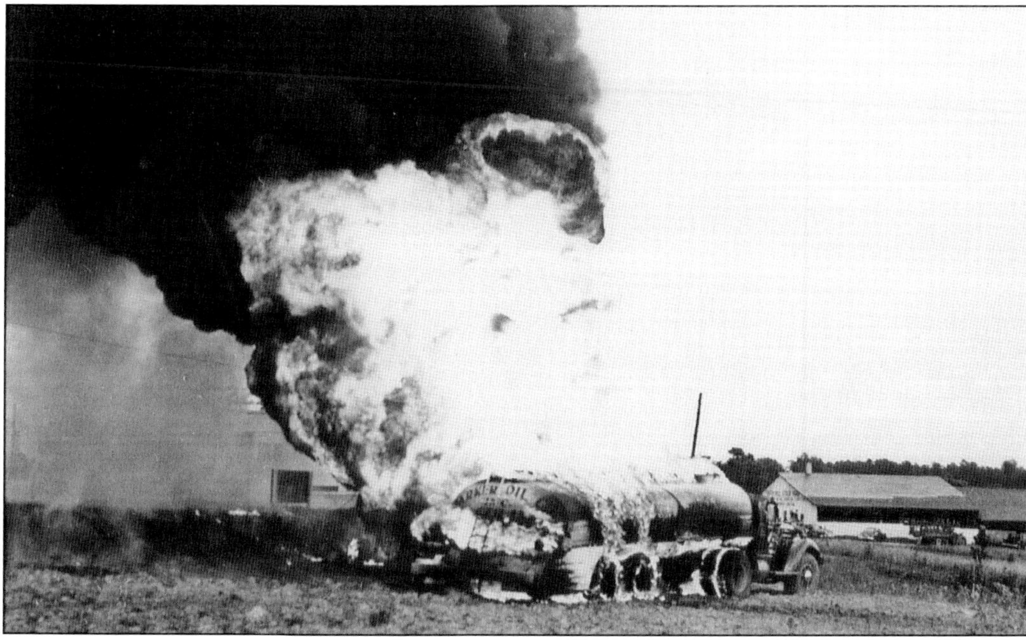

Tragedy again struck South Hill with yet another fire and this time a fatality. A fire engulfed a Parker Oil truck on March 25, 1950, and spread rapidly. The transport driver was Woodrow Evans. His son was still in the cab when it burst into flames. Across the street was a storage/warehouse building. (Parker Oil Company, Inc.)

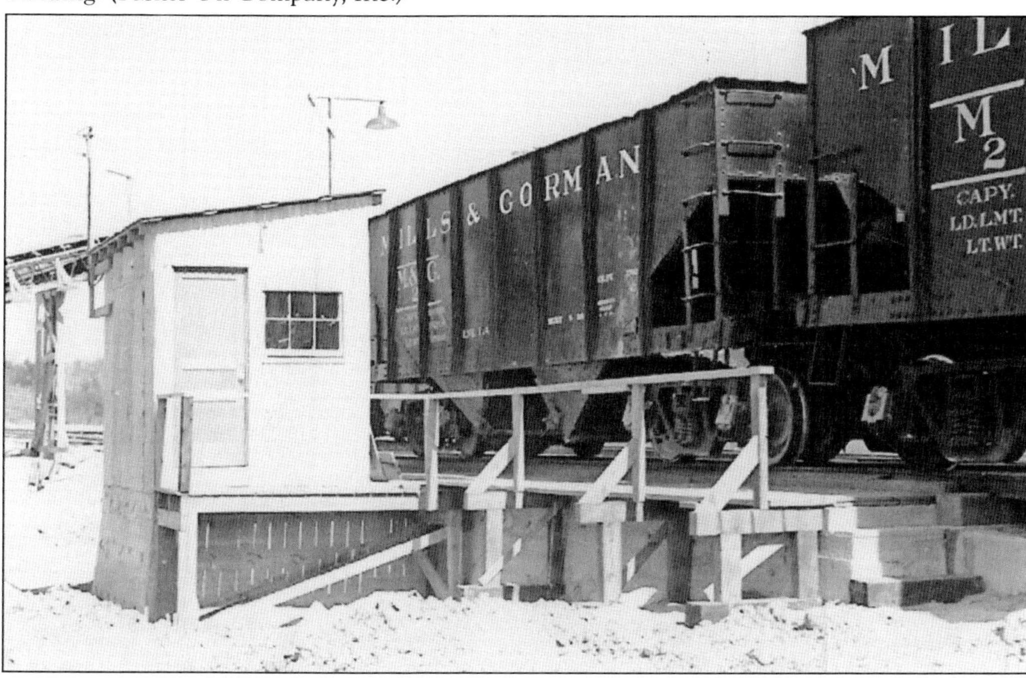

To transport the stone and gravel from the quarry to the dam site required miles of railroad track to be installed. Hauling monstrous equipment, cranes, and tons of stone often led to tragedy, including collisions and trains overturning along the 5-mile route. During the five years of operation there was only one fatality. (COE.)

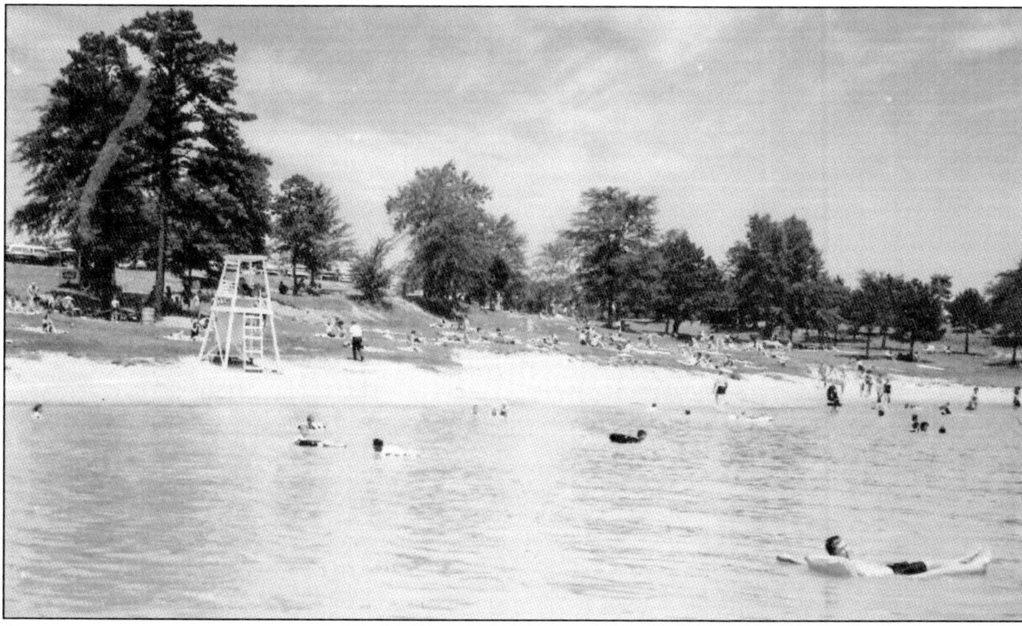

The campgrounds and marina overlooking the dam were North Bend (named for the former plantation). North Bend attracts thousands of tourists annually. Services include campsites with electric hookups, bathhouses, toilet facilities, a large beach area, boat launch ramps, and ample parking. The lake covers over 48,900 acres of land. This photograph was taken in October 1958. (COE.)

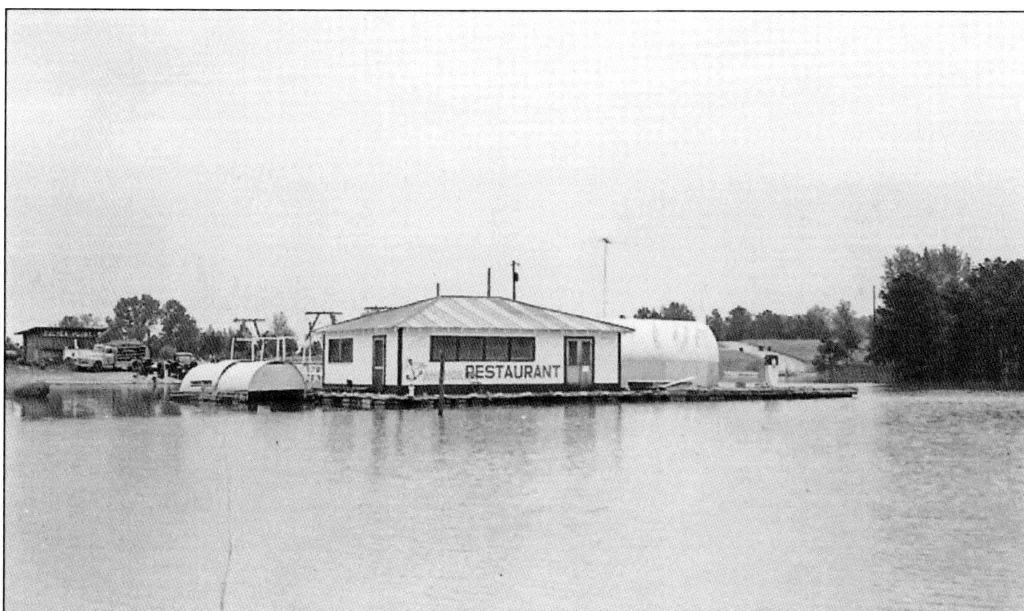

Across the lake was a flotilla restaurant with a marina at Palmer Point. The flotilla had been established and was also operational by 1958. Shoreline management was taken over by the U.S. Army Corps of Engineers in 1974. Of the 28 marinas, only two remain, and there are no restaurants on the lake in Virginia. The lake has over 800 miles of shoreline and spans through five counties. (COE.)

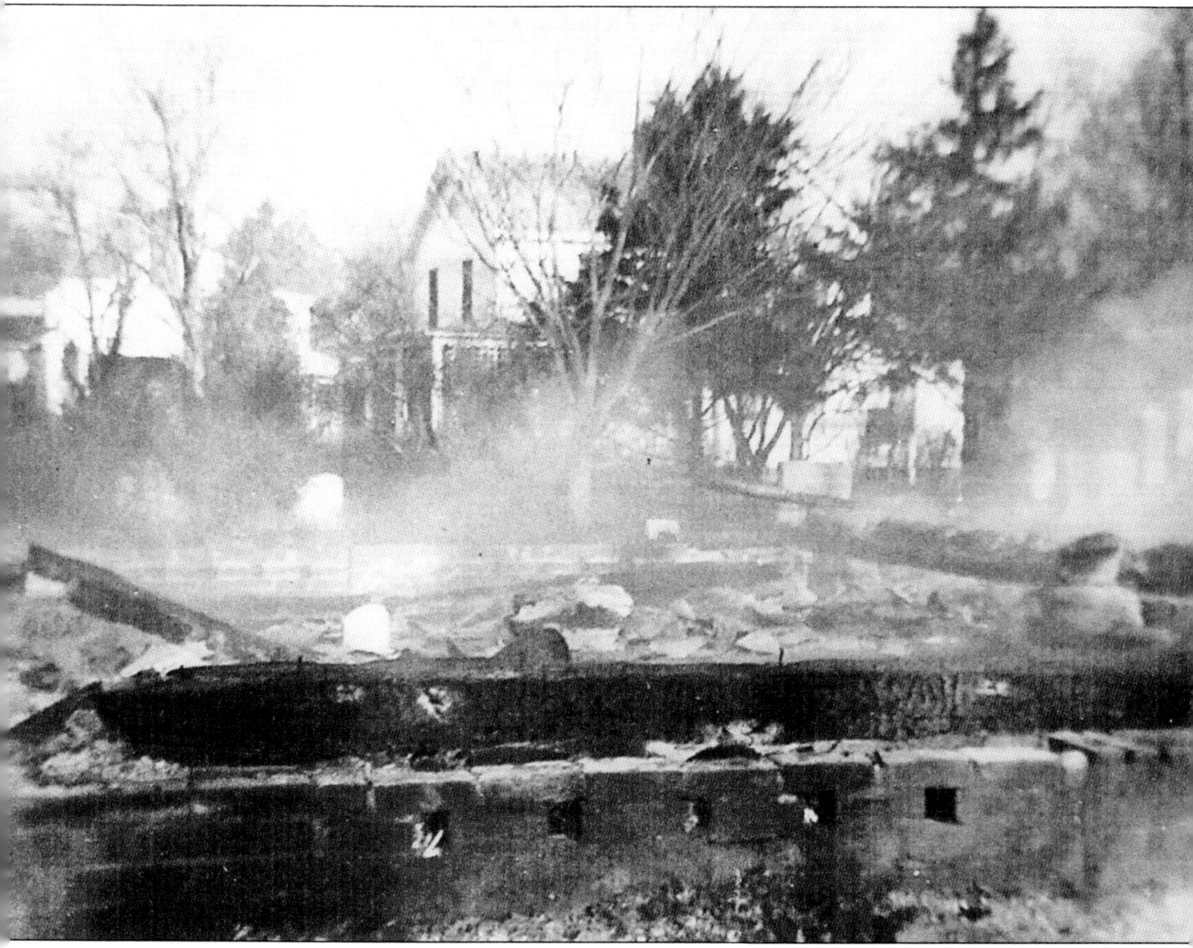

St. Andrews Church served Baskerville continuously and was enlarged on two occasions. In 1896, a cemetery was added. The sanctuary burned in February 1952. A new brick building with modern electric and plumbing was dedicated in October 1953. This photograph was taken shortly after the fire, as the ashes were still smoldering. (St. Andrews Church.)

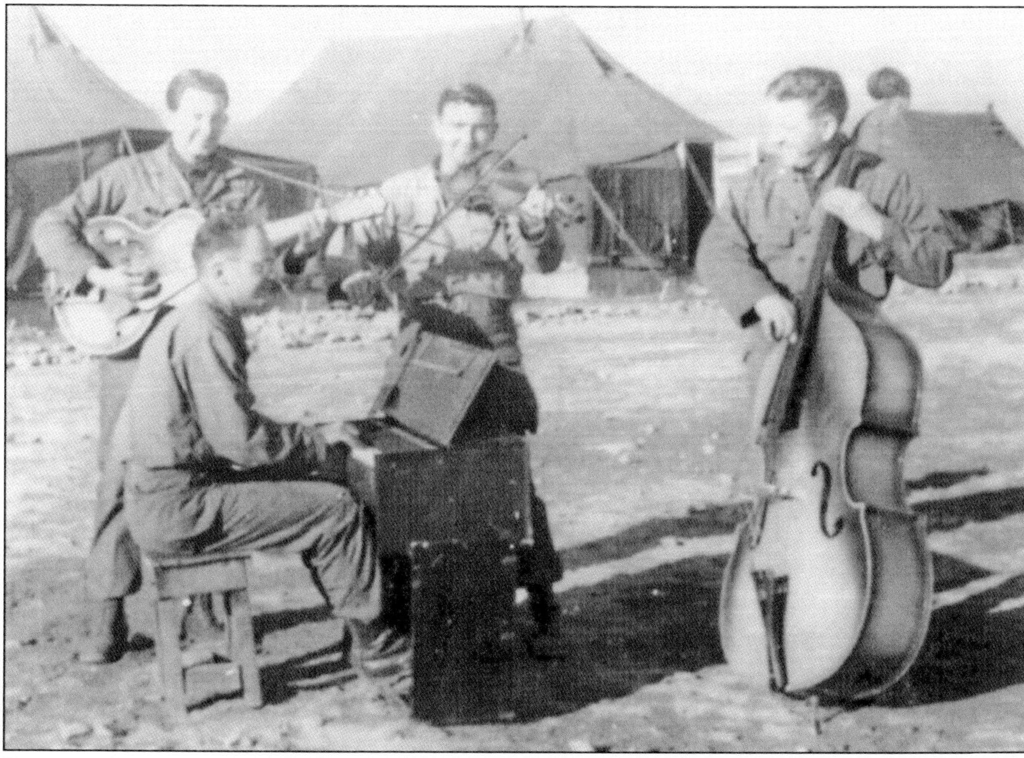

During military service Dwight Moody Jr. generally carried his rifle, but with his fiddle close by. A rehearsal in Inge, North Korea, is pictured here in 1952 just outside a MASH unit where the fellows would be entertaining in short order. Reverend Hoffman is on guitar, Dirkson is on keys, Moody is on fiddle, and Carnes is on bass fiddle. (Dwight Moody Jr.)

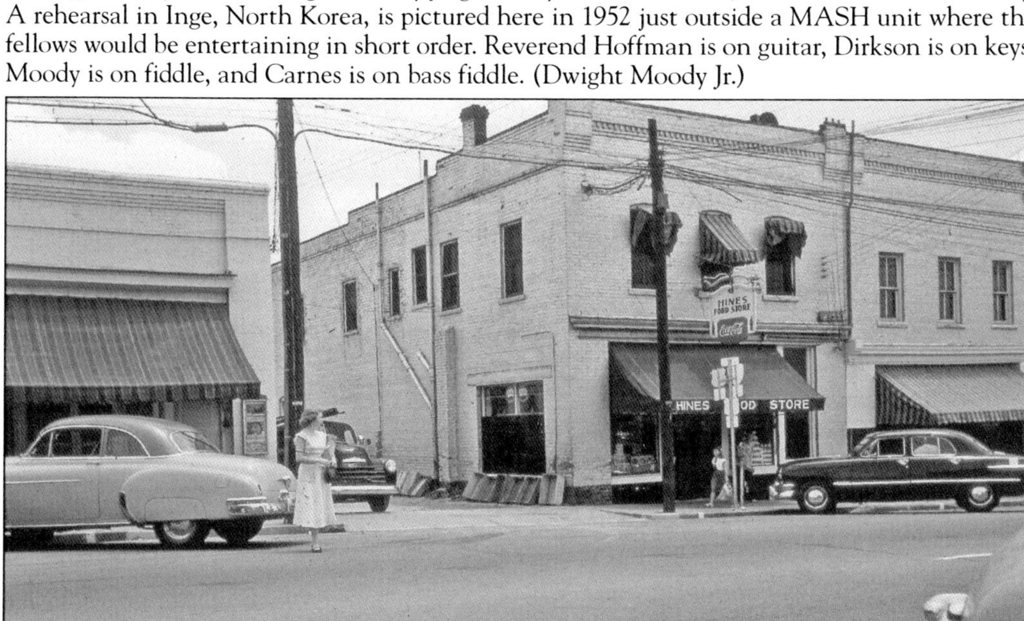

The stores on South Mecklenburg Avenue have new owners but are still standing in 1952, despite all the fires throughout the town. Here Thomas B. and Robert Lee Hines began a grocery store in the old Wall Building on September 16, 1938. In this photograph it has been expanded to a supermarket and is now operated by T. B. and his wife, Earline Hines. (PMA.)

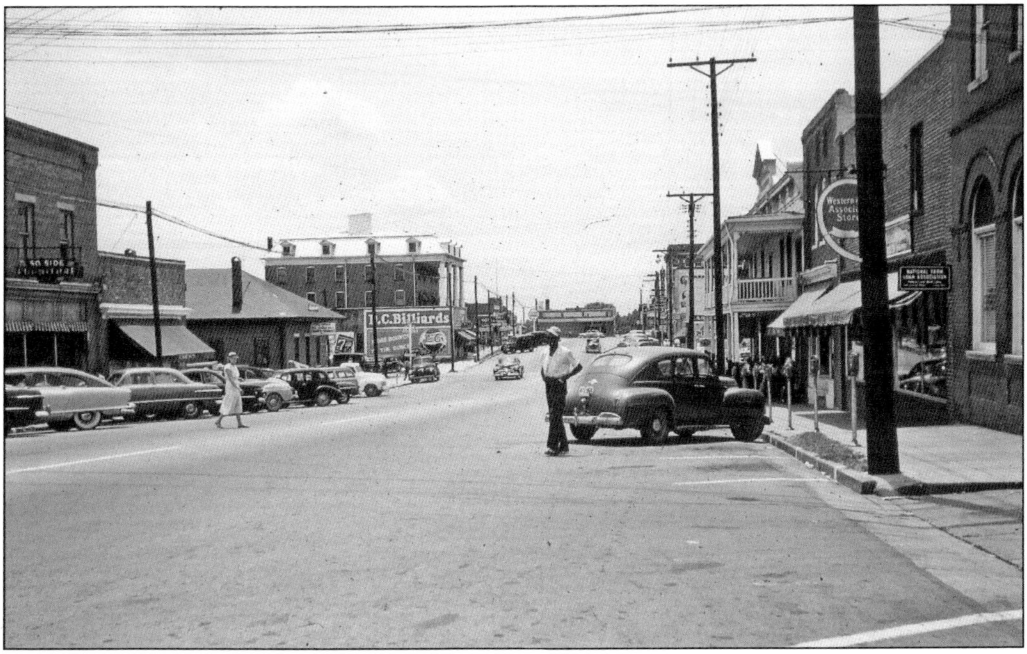

In this photograph from 1954 are, to the left, Crew's Funeral Home (established January 10, 1941), the railroad station, D. C. Billiard parlor, the Nordan Hotel, and at the end of Mecklenburg Avenue is the Glass House Restaurant and bus station. On the right is the Western Auto, and the awning/balcony is Crowder and Sons Department Store. (PMA.)

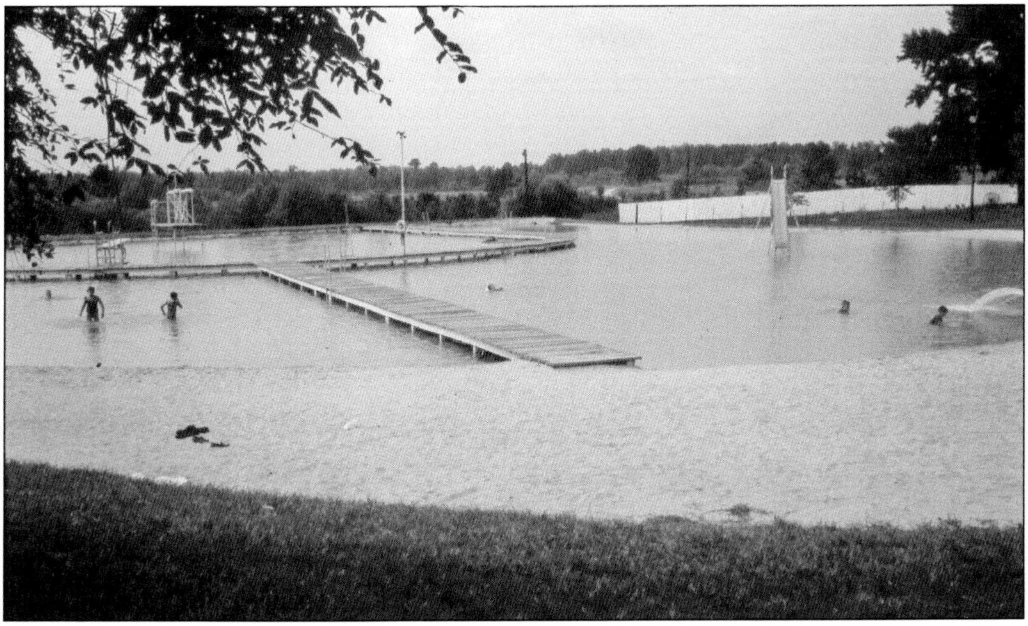

"Pine Lake" (part of the Butterworth farm) was built as a farm pond in 1947. T. E. Allen sponsored teen dances on Friday and Saturday nights starting on June 5, 1948, and the lake was one of only a few areas where Bermuda shorts were allowed in public. By adding ground cover, docking, a diving board, a pavilion with jukebox for dancing, a parking lot, food, and so on, the pond became a successful getaway. This photograph was taken in front of the clubhouse. It closed in 1970. (PMA.)

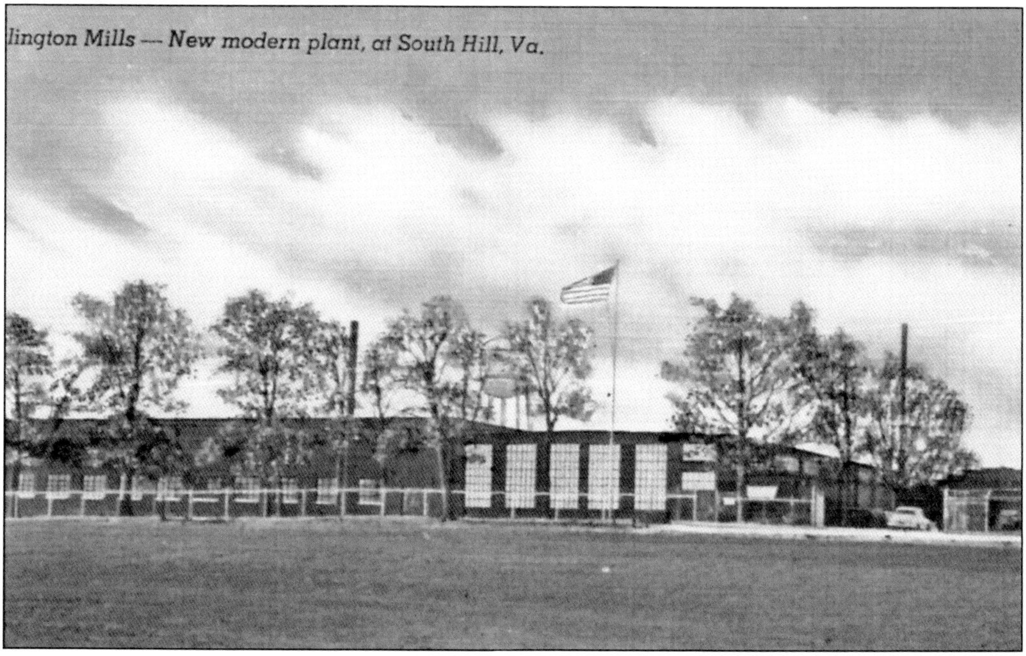

In June 1939, the South Hill Ribbon Mill (a locally owned stockholders business) began operation with 40 looms and 51 employees. In August 1945, it was sold to Burlington Industries to make cloth. In 1953, it was modernized and expanded to produce men's sportswear. (TJS.)

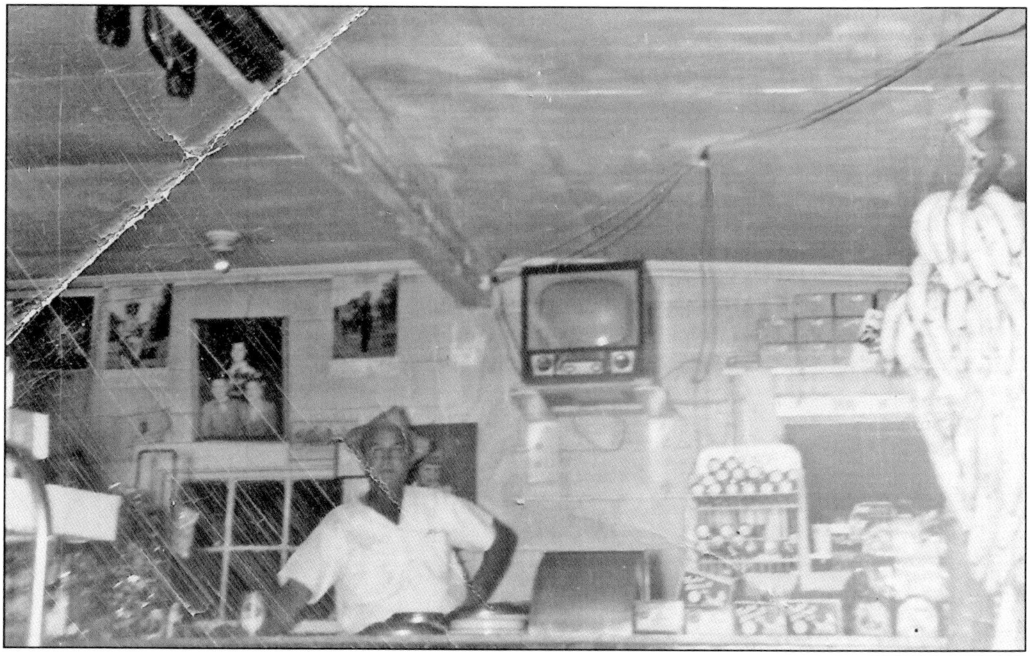

Following the 1948 fire that burned the Harris Sinclair Station, Jim Smiley purchased the property and built a new cement-block station and service center. He opened it as a community store and barbecue restaurant. He hired others to operate his dump truck and wrecker/garage business. Inside the new store, pictured above, bananas hang from the ceiling, and there is no slot machine. (Jimmy Smiley Jr.)

Six

HIGHWAYS COME, HIGHWAYS GO

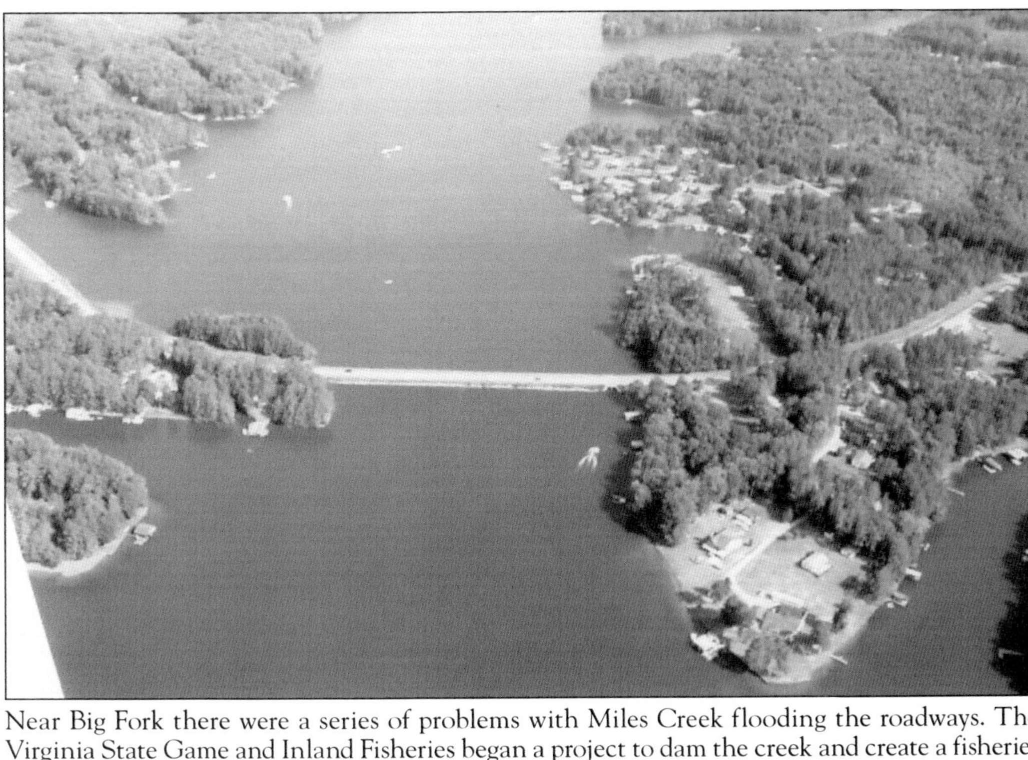

Near Big Fork there were a series of problems with Miles Creek flooding the roadways. The Virginia State Game and Inland Fisheries began a project to dam the creek and create a fisheries lake. The grand opening of Lake Gordon (seen in this aerial view) was June 6, 1950, and it was reported that by 3:00 p.m. over 1,000 fish had been caught. The town of South Hill had been having trouble with their well-water system and petitioned to use the lake, but they were denied. (Joe Noah, Lakeside Flight.)

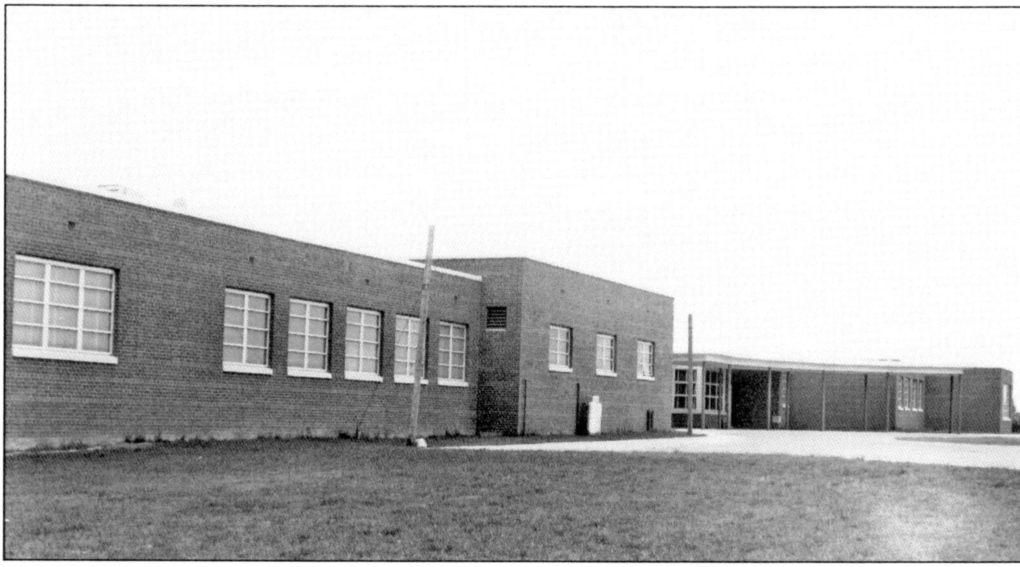

On December 2, 1947, a public meeting was held and a board of trustees was elected to build a community hospital. Fund-raising over $460,000 on June 30, 1950, Community Memorial Hospital was registered as a nonprofit corporation. The 48-bed hospital opened in June 1954 with Thomas Leggett as the first administrator and Dr. Altamont Bracey Jr. as the chief of staff. (Community Memorial Health Center.)

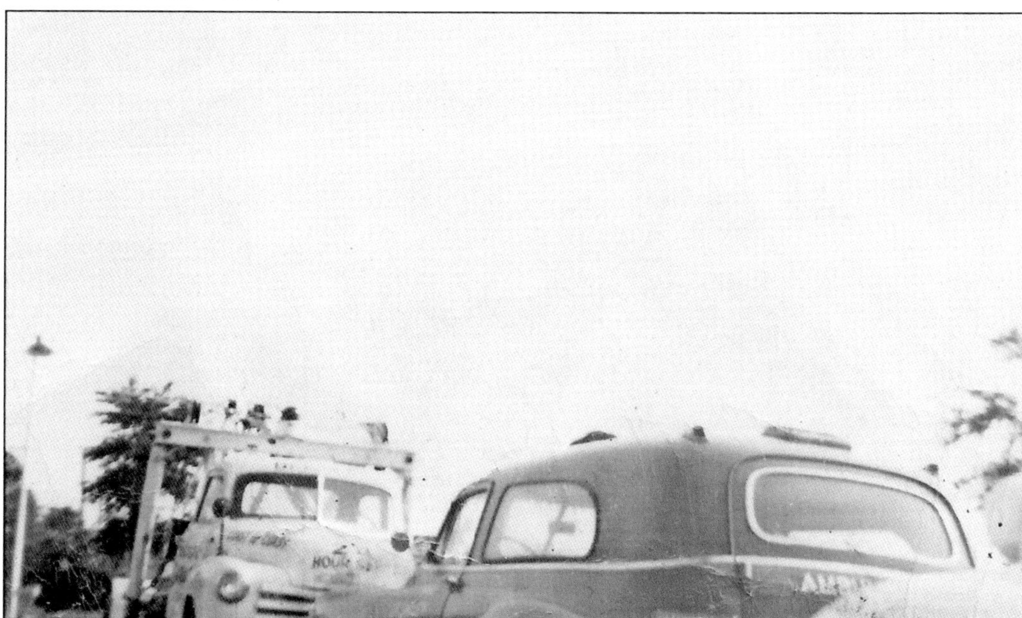

Jim Smiley, having been in the wrecker business for years and working U.S. Routes 1 and 58, had seen his share of tragedy. With no hospital or ambulance service in the county, he decided to add an ambulance to his fleet in 1951. Each time he was called for wrecker service for a serious crash, the ambulance went with him. If there was a serious injury, he would drive the victim(s) to Richmond as quickly as possible. A few of them actually returned to Big Fork and paid him. (Jimmy Smiley Jr.)

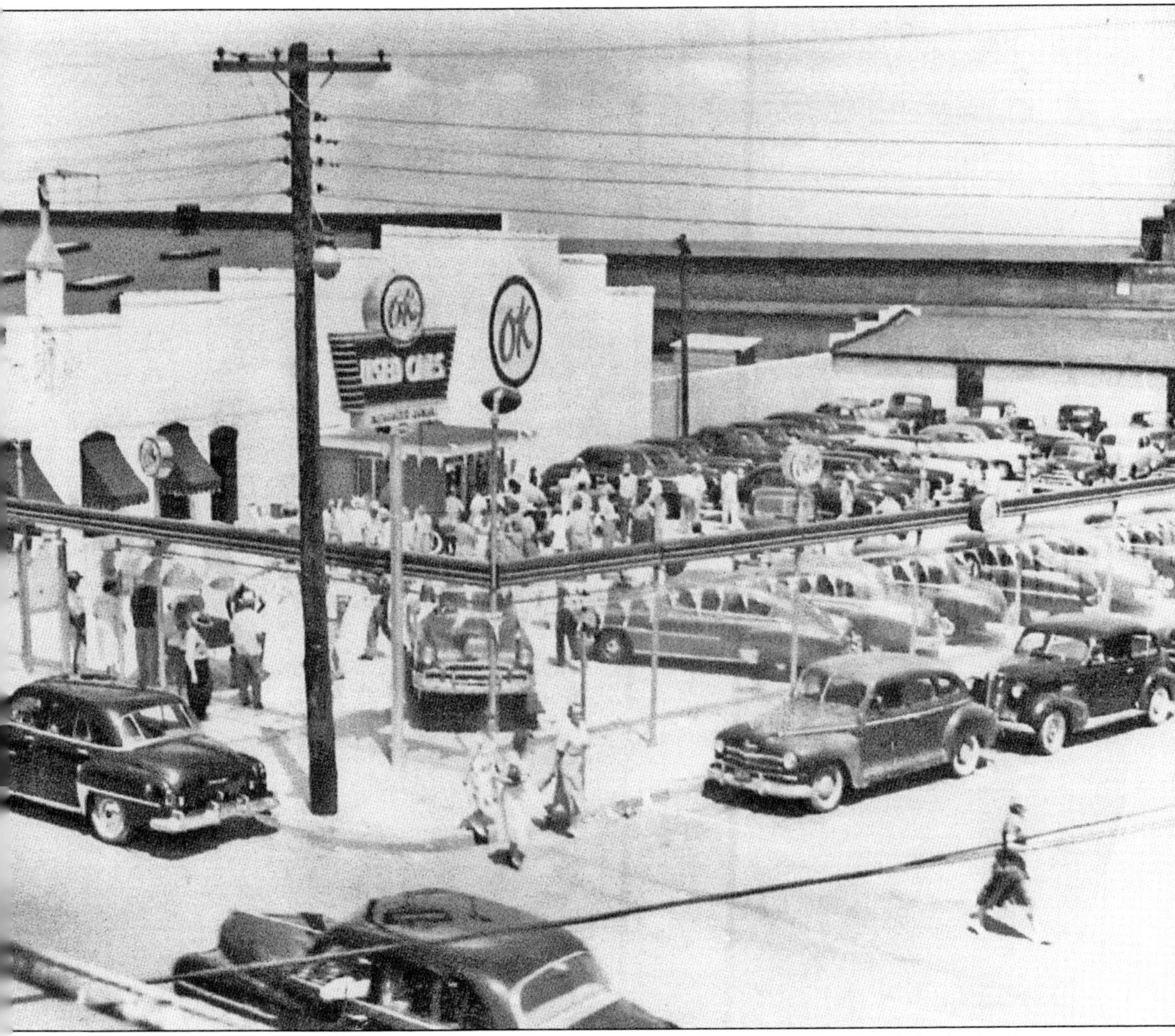

In 1951, Fred E. Watkins, chairman of the hospital board, expanded his automobile dealership to establish a used-car lot on the site of the former Farmers Warehouse. When it opened on Danville Street it was the first used-car dealership in town. (SHC.)

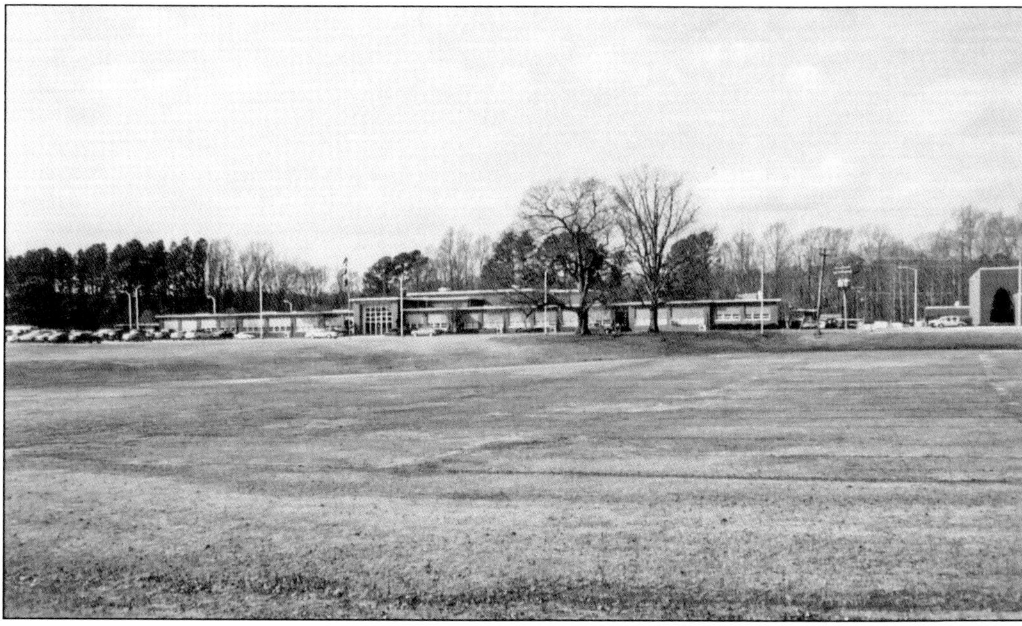

On September 12, 1955, Park View High School opened as the east Mecklenburg County consolidated high school on U.S. Route 1, four miles south of South Hill. In this photograph, the field in front of the school has become usable, but when the school was built, and for many years, this field was a swamp. (JC.)

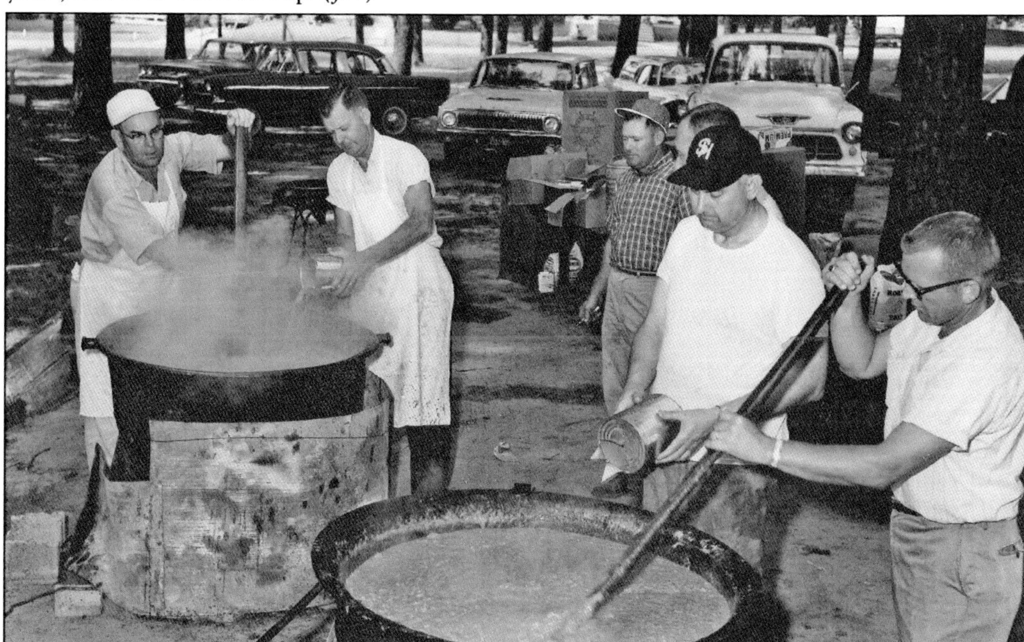

One of the most popular fund-raisers in the county and neighboring counties is a Brunswick stew. Cooked and stirred all night, it is sold by the bowl or quart. Pictured here in 1964 are, from left to right, E. H. Cox, deputy sheriff; W. B. Bryson; Bo Murphy, South Hill Police Department officer; G. R. Holbert, police chief; Paul Jeffreys, owner of the Exchange Warehouse; and "Dookie" Creedle, with the paddle. (Photograph by R. L. Harris Sr.)

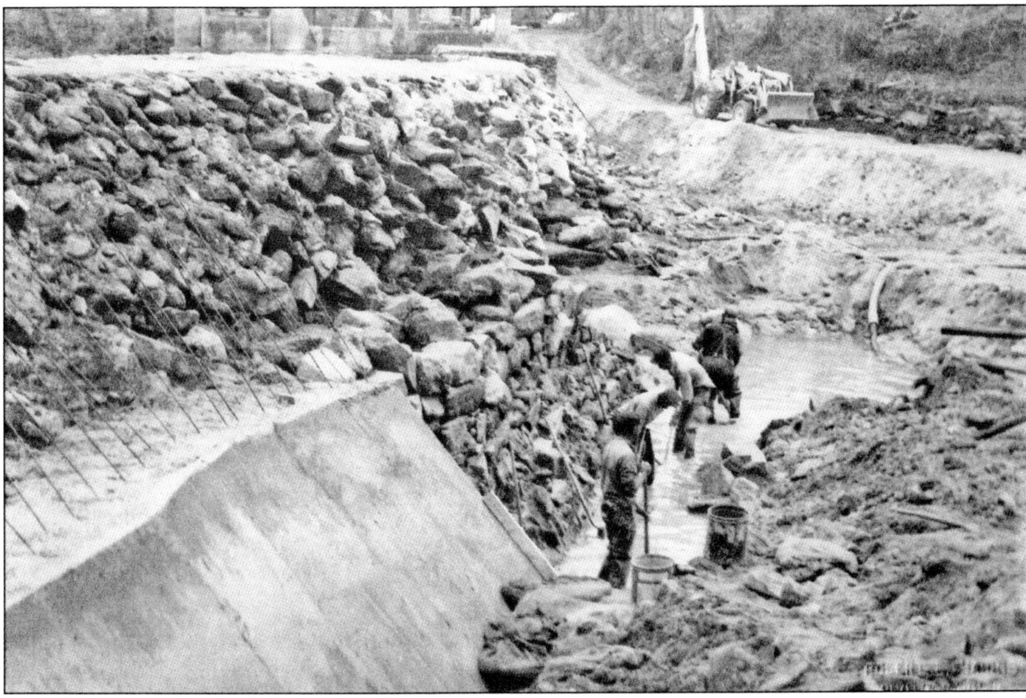

On September 4, 1951, South Hill appropriated funds to build a pumping station and filtration plant at Whittle's Mill on the Meherrin River for town water. In 1963, a breach occurred in the dam. In August 1963, the Town of South Hill purchased 34.5 acres and built a new dam. Today it is a silt-sand community park for fishing and picnicking. (Photograph by R. L. Harris Sr.)

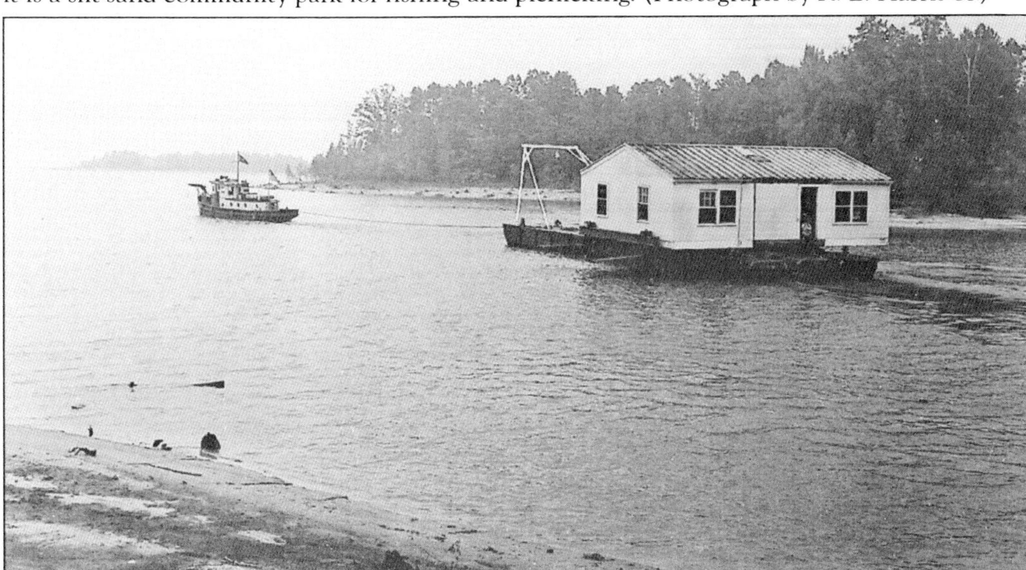

Following the opening of John H. Kerr Dam in 1952, Kerr Village and Castle Heights were dismantled. Most of the usable homes and offices were sold at public auction, but they had to be moved. Most were trailered away by house movers, but some were taken to North Bend Park, loaded onto the barge, and escorted by tugboat *Dan* to a new destination, mostly in Virginia but some to North Carolina at Satterwhite Point. (COE.)

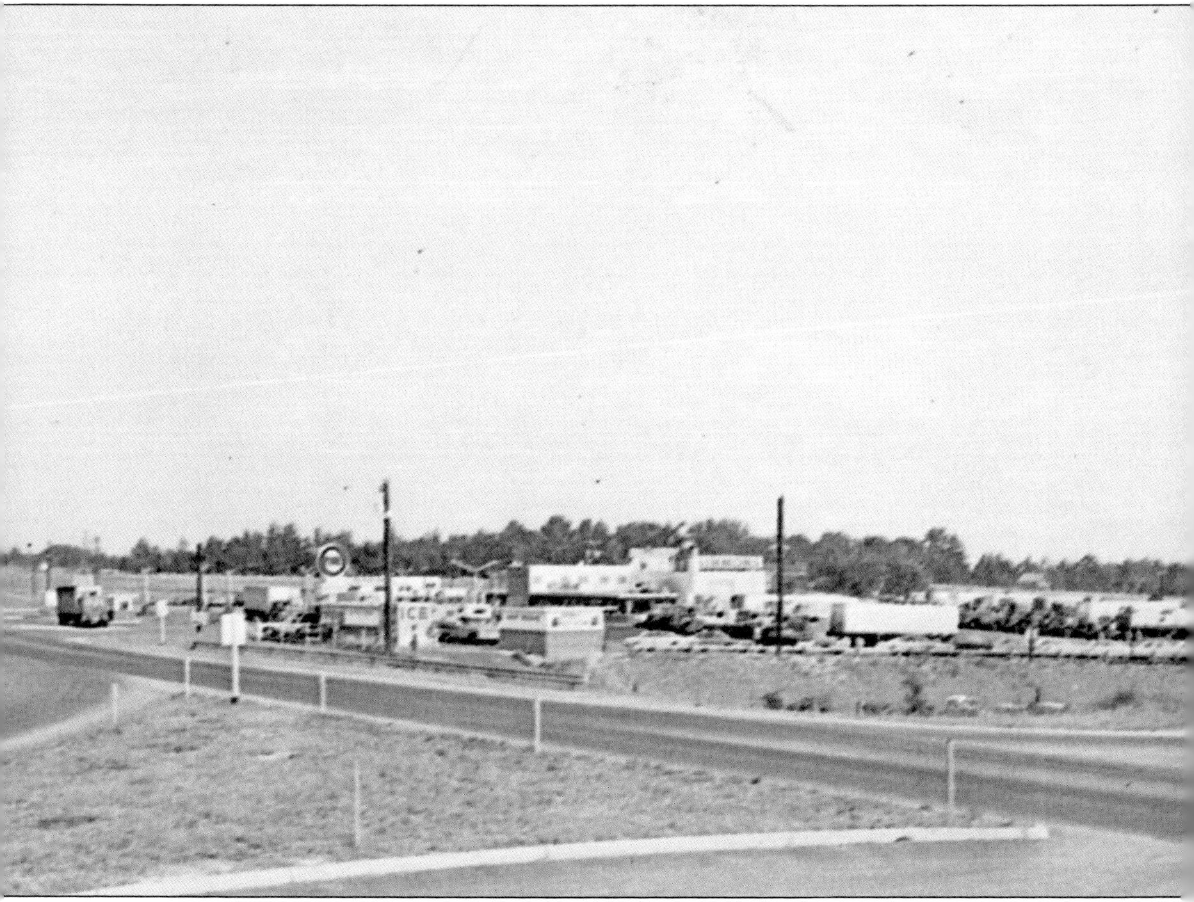

During the construction of Interstate I-85, Parker Oil Company, Inc., purchased property at the first Virginia exit, Bracey, in 1963. There they built a new modern trucking terminal with a service center and restaurant. The truck stop was in a perfect location, as it also sits at the exit for Lake Gaston. The Gaston Dam was completed along the Roanoke River in 1963 as part of the ongoing flood control project. (TJS.)

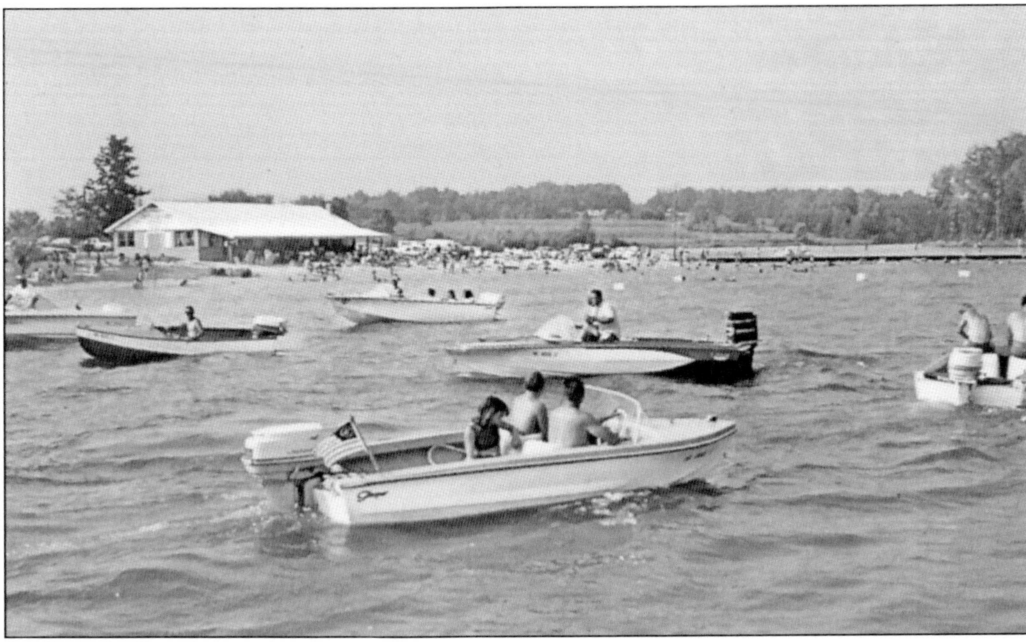

With a controlled lake level, permanent structures could be built along the water's edge. Lake Gaston has three Virginia state records for largemouth bass. Much of Lake Gaston runs along the edges of Mecklenburg and Brunswick Counties in Virginia and Vance County in North Carolina. This postcard is from Delbridge Recreation Area in Gasburg, Virginia. (TJS.)

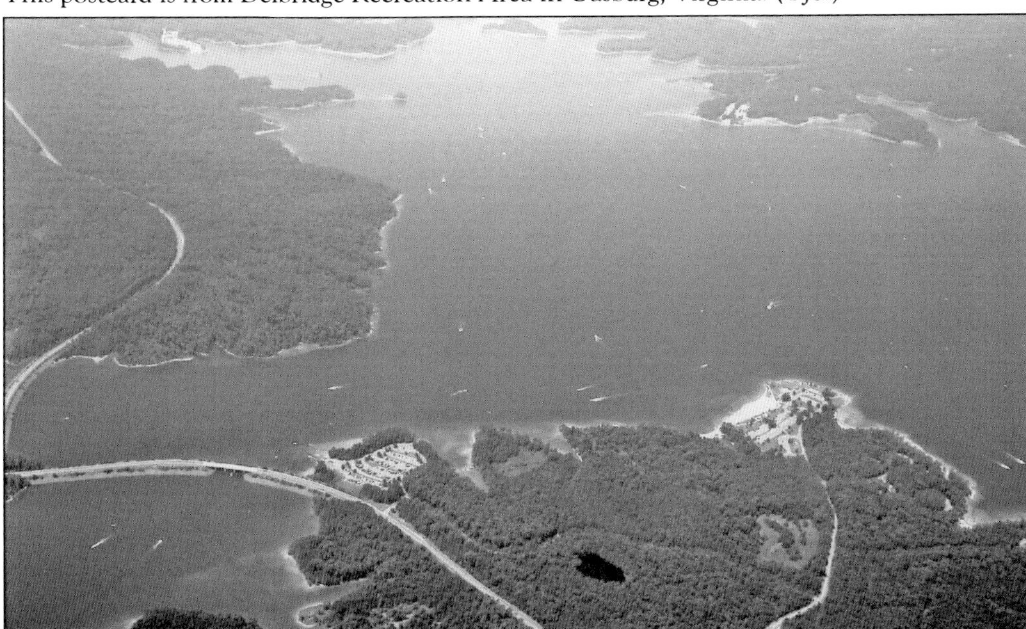

Lake Gaston, with more than 350 miles of shoreline, has become a destination because of the controlled water table. Kerr Dam releases water into the lake, and when it gets too high, Gaston Dam releases it downstream into the Albemarle Sound. This aerial shows the complexity of the lake, in that it is not one solid body of water, but more of a spiderweb of fingerlings. (Joe Noah, Lakeside Flight.)

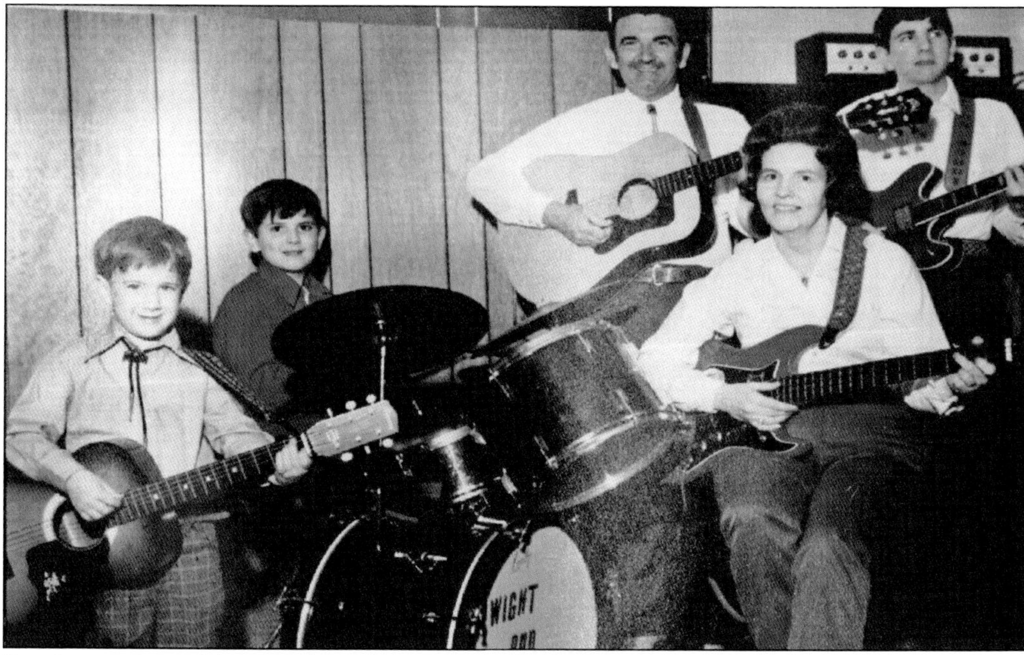

Family members of the Dwight and Kathy Moody Show, pictured above from left to right, Trent, Dwight, Kathy, and David have toured the world fund-raising for Ruritan Club International and working with Disney International. The group created Lamon Records with headquarters in Charlotte, North Carolina. They've jointly and individually received about every country, bluegrass, and gospel music award there is, including eight Grammy Award nominations. (Dwight L. Moody Jr.)

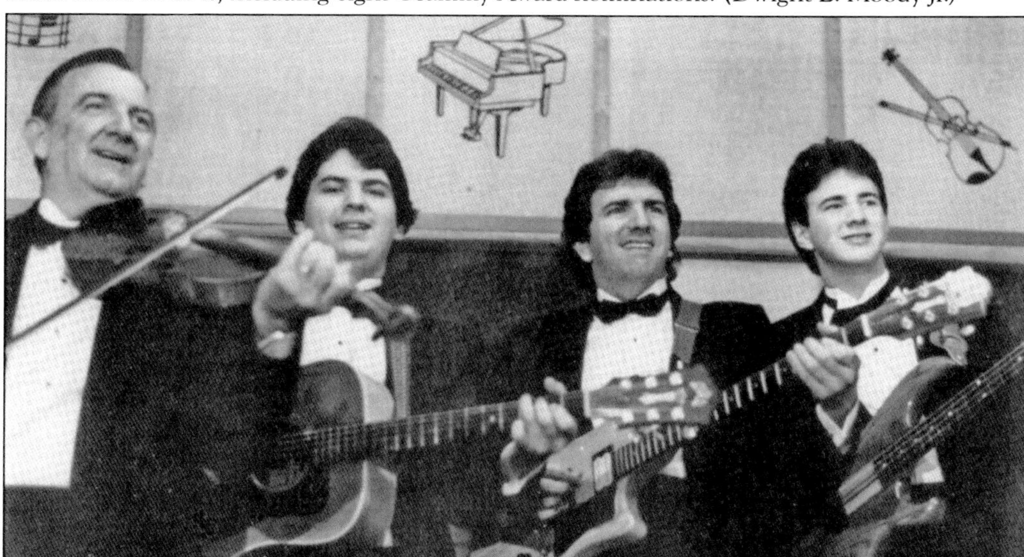

The three Moody sons have been employed by Disney International for many years, and one is retired from there. They serve as producers, directors, and performers for Disney U.S. and Disney Europe. Much of their time has been spent in Paris. When in the United States they perform at the Grand Ole Opry with dad. Now the Moody group has two new members—grandson Joshua and granddaughter Rebecca. Pictured above in this c. 1980 image are, from left to right, Dwight Moody Jr., Carlton, David, and Trent. (Dwight L. Moody Jr.)

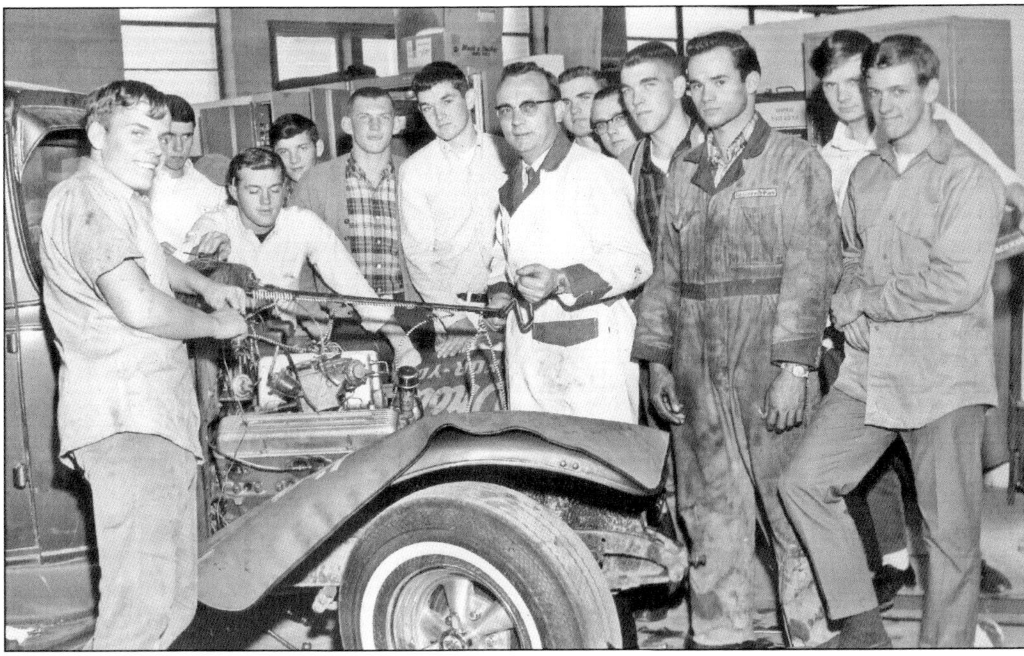

Eight-time NASCAR Sprint Cup championship race team owner Rick Hendrick (front left) is pictured with his Park View High School class in 1967. They are, from left to right, Rick Hendrick, Wade Crowder, John Ballard Clark, Jimmy Newman, Charles Mooney, Allen Bing, Charles Clary, Johnny Walker, Wade Creedle, Harry Creedle, Tre Winn, Larrie Matthews, and unidentified. The first power mechanics class at the school was taught by Elmer Pixley (white coat). The class is rebuilding Rick's 1931 Chevy, the car that inspired Hendrick Motorsports. (Hendrick Motorsports.)

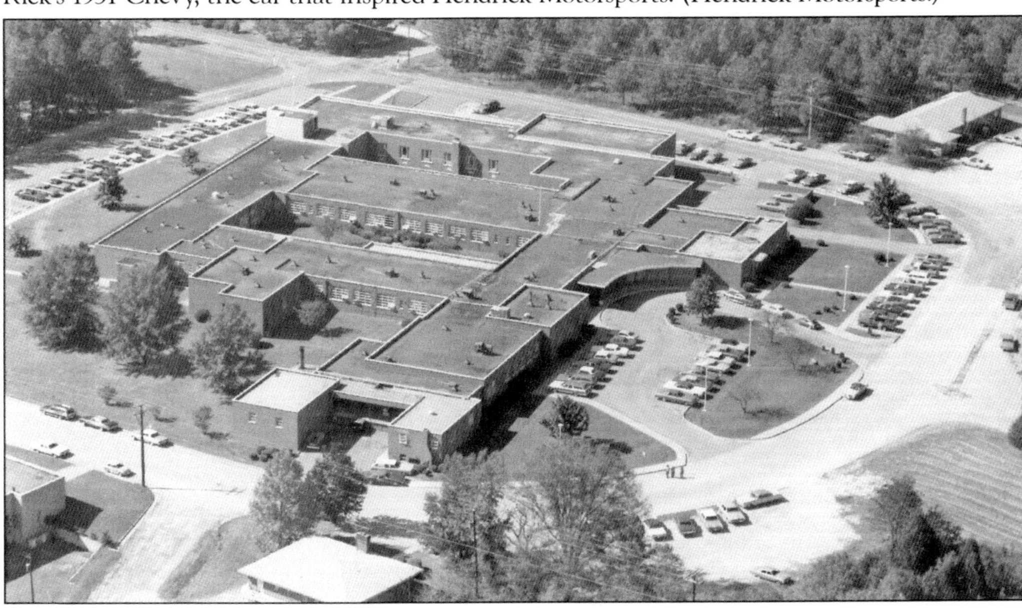

A 38-room south wing was completed at Community Memorial Hospital in 1960, an x-ray and lab department in 1962, obstetrical department in 1967, and in this photograph in August 1972, a million-dollar cardiac intensive-care center is being added. It was dedicated in July 1973. In October 1977, a 140-bed extended-care facility was added. (Community Memorial Health Care.)

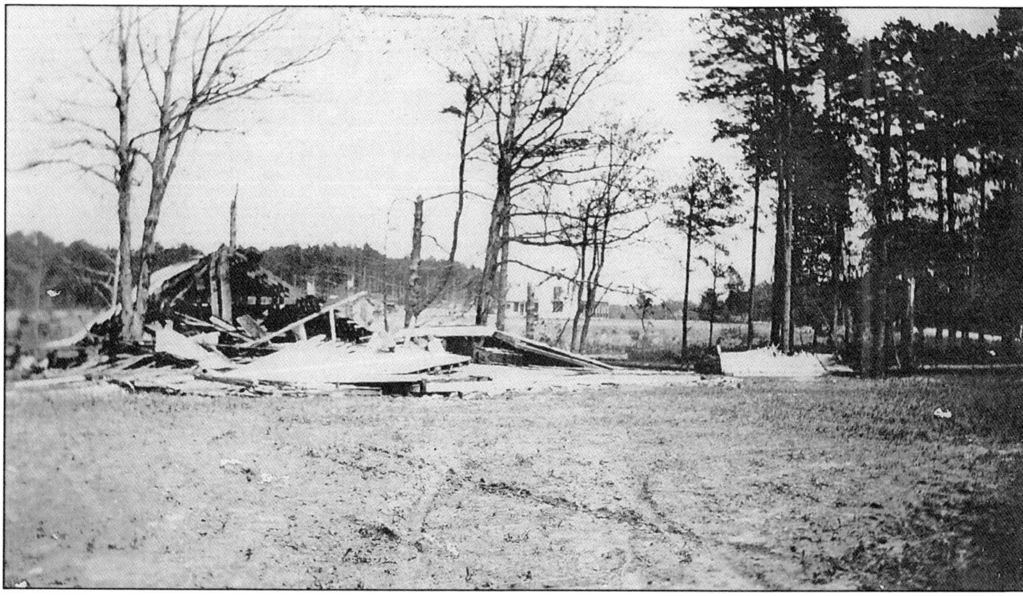

Four meteorites hit Forksville in 1924. In this postcard photograph are the results of what this card calls a "cyclone" that touched down in Bracey in April 1923; however, there are still, strangely, no recorded cyclones in Virginia so perhaps it was actually a Category 4 tornado. It was brief, and the only damage was to the *c.* 1905 Bracey Baptist Church, which was unusual. (WRH.)

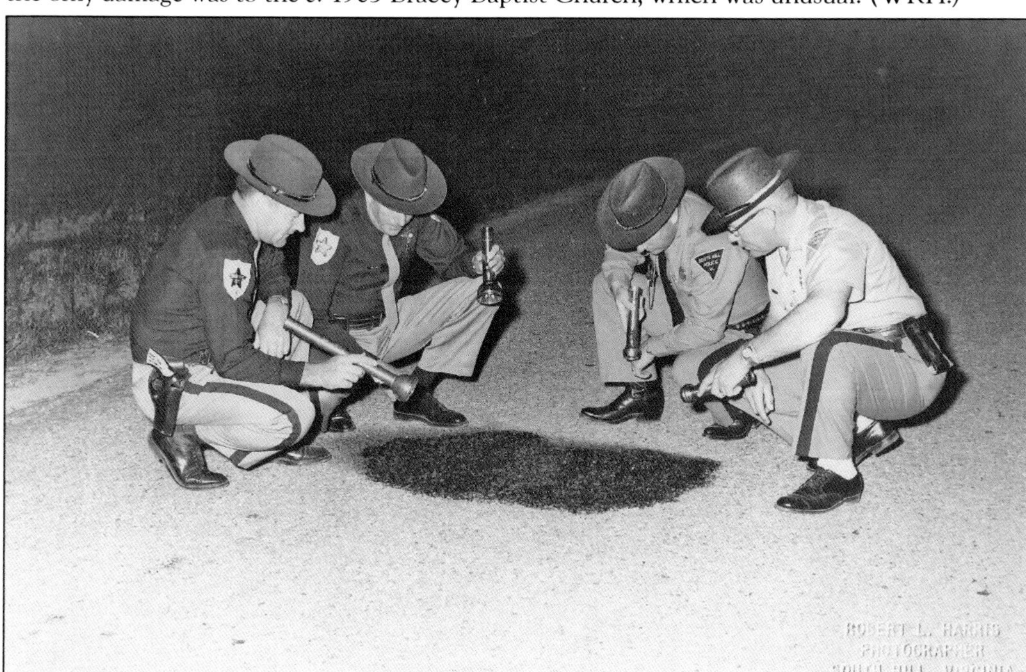

A South Hill resident later saw a spaceship, described as a 12-feet-by-15-feet (to 20 feet) metal storage tank on four legs about 3.5 feet high with a stream of white-looking fire coming from underneath. It launched straight up and out of sight. It was investigated by the U.S. government and private UFO agencies, but was not solved. In 1969, state and local police were investigating the launch site on Ferrell Street with four distinctive blast marks. (Photograph by R. L. Harris Sr.)

The *South Hill Enterprise* began operation in 1906. Frank L. Nanny Sr. was editor from 1928 to 1961 and Frank L. Nanny Jr. until 1996. Moving into larger quarters in 1952, the building burned on December 26, 1970. Pictured at right are, from left to right, Frank Nanny Jr., Harry Nanny, and fire chief Harry Mewborn. (Photograph by R. L. Harris Sr.)

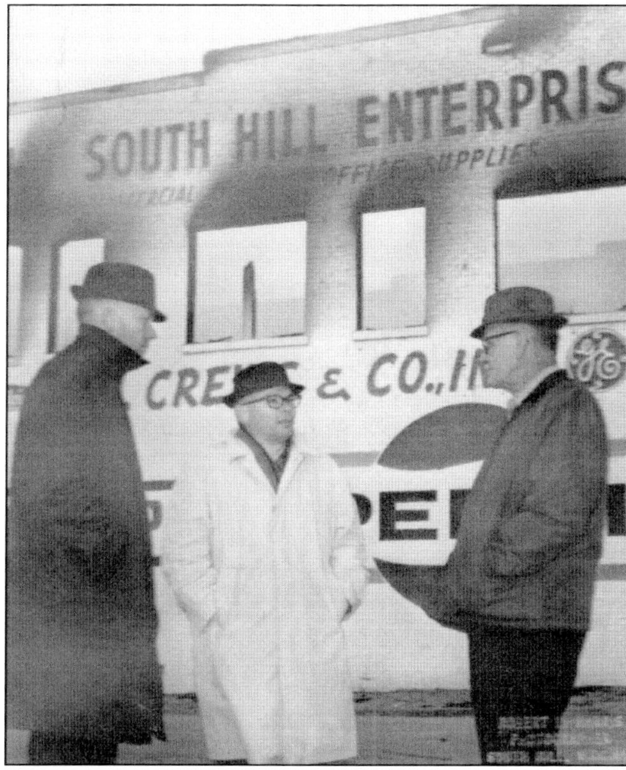

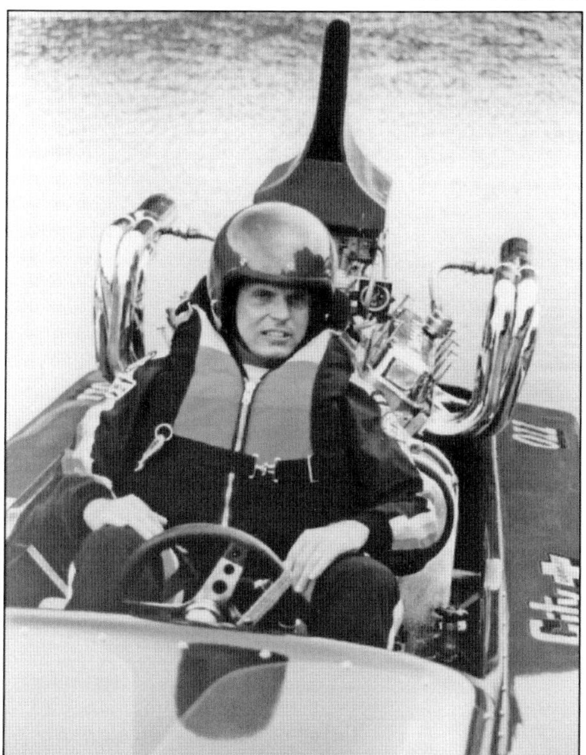

Rick Hendrick completed Park View High School and left Palmer Springs for Raleigh, North Carolina. On July 26, 1981, he set the American Drag Boat Association's record for the Unblown Gas Hydro Division at 142.63 miles per hour. His boat, the *Preparation H*, held three world titles. With driver Jimmy Wright of Richmond, another record was set in Michigan on August 9, 1981, at 211.43 miles per hour. (Hendrick Motorsports.)

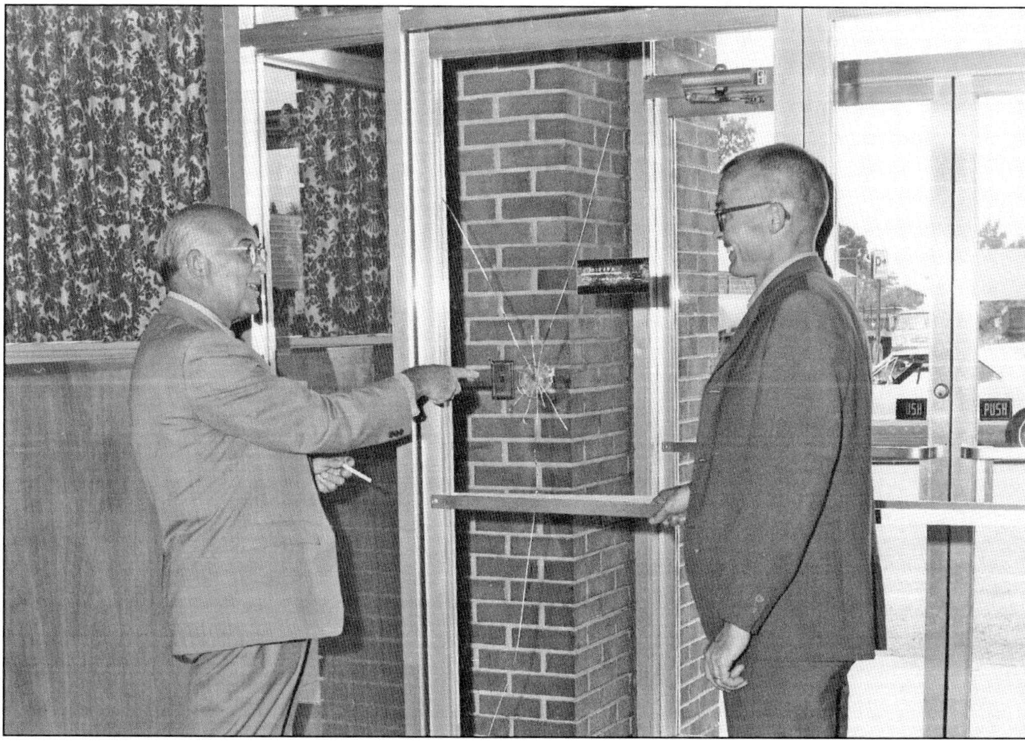

On July 21, 1972, three men robbed Citizens Bank, Inc., in South Hill. After some shots were fired they took off with a bag of money and cashier John S. Evans as a hostage. They were apprehended within 30 minutes. In this photograph is Horace Clark, executive vice president of the bank, pointing out the bullet hole to John Evans, the cashier, while holding a cigarette in his other hand. (Photograph by R. L. Harris Sr.)

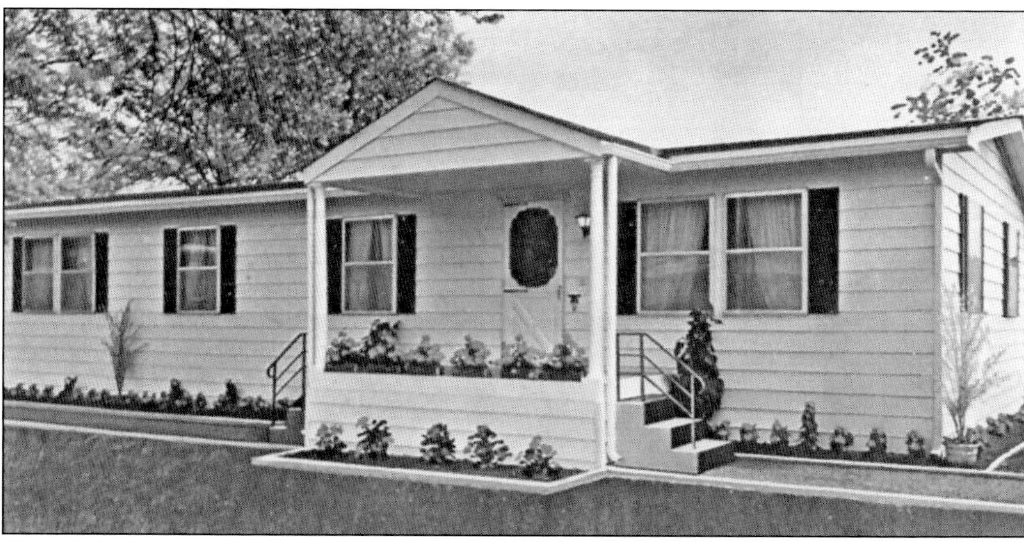

One of the largest industries in South Hill in 1958 was Magnolia Mobile Homes. They gained fame building a custom home for Pres. John F. Kennedy in 1963, Whitey Ford in 1965, and John Caknipe Jr. in 1967. As the company grew and expanded, it was sold to USCO, Inc., in 1970. It was then called a modular and marketed with 10 different floor plans. (TJS.)

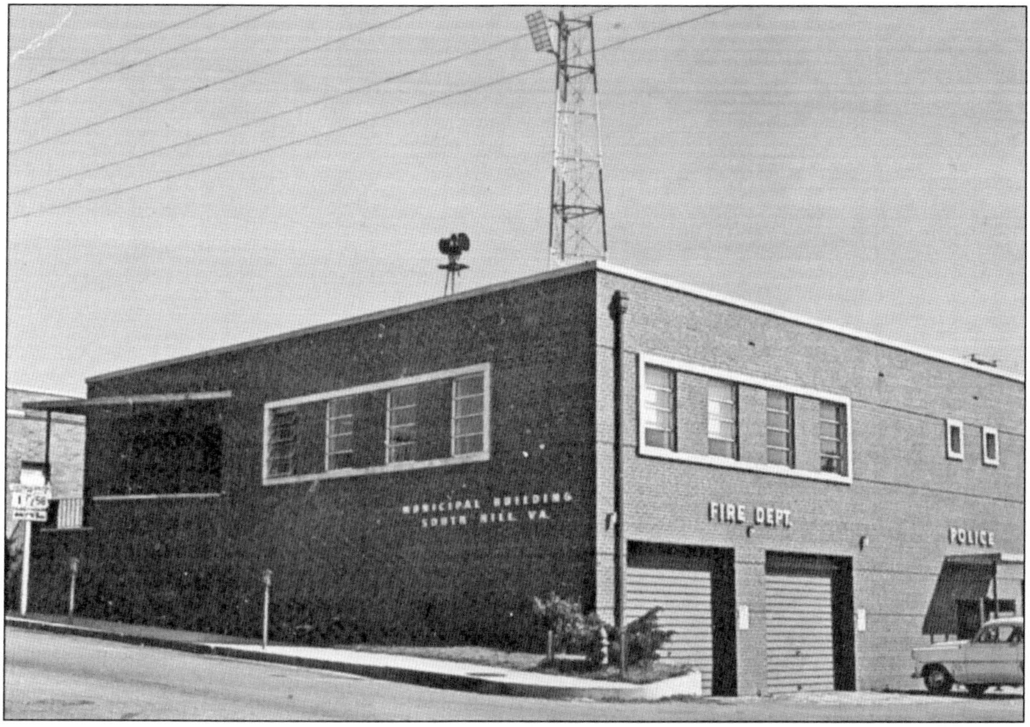

In 1952, the town of South Hill completed their new jail. This postcard is of the municipal building with the police department, fire department, jail, and town offices. In the 1960s, this building also housed a military recruiting office where many locals enlisted to serve during the Vietnam conflict. (TJS.)

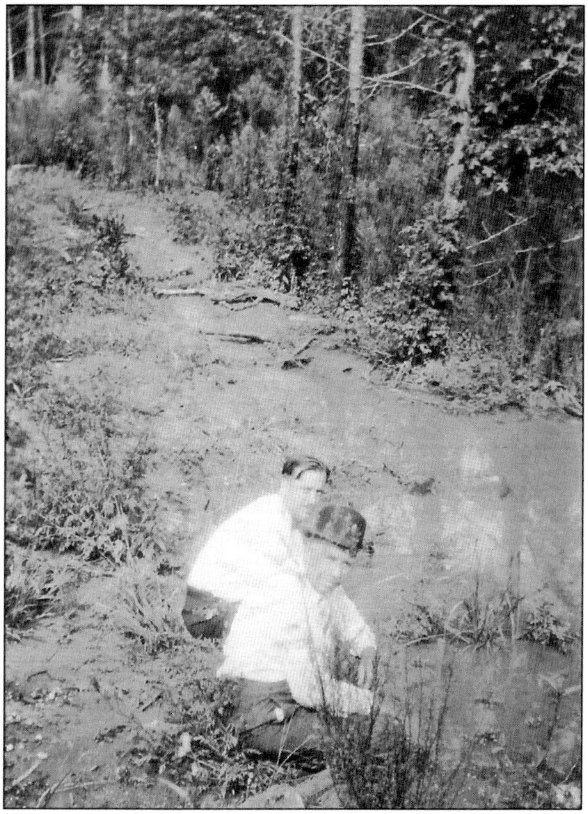

Prior to the dams and creation of the lakes, folks from all over Mecklenburg County would spend a day or afternoon fishing one of the numerous local streams. In this c. 1920 photograph, Charles R. Dunn (left) and Marshall Keeley are spending the afternoon relaxing and fishing Allen's Creek near Baskerville. (Martha Dunn Overton.)

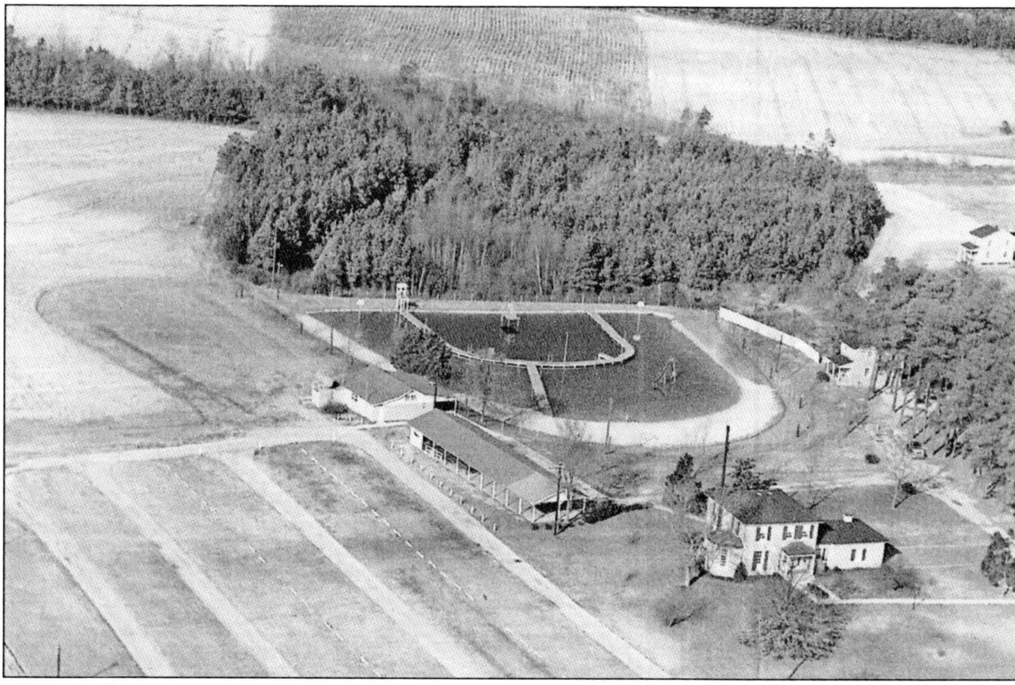

This aerial of Pine Lake taken in the 1970s shows the pavilion and clubhouse to the left of the pool. Also at left was a large parking lot, and on Fridays and Saturdays it was filled to capacity. Today the parking lot is part of the U.S. Highway 58 bypass around South Hill. (Patsy Boswell.)

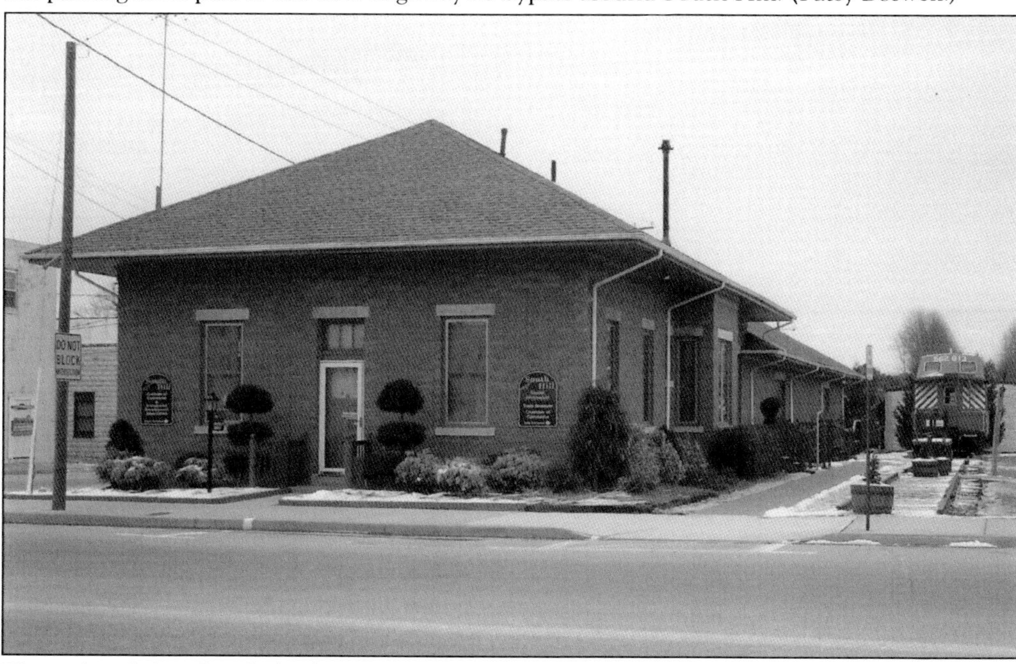

The railroad closed with the last train service around 1980. After many negotiations, the station was purchased with some rail intact, a railroad car, and some other artifacts. The railroad station now houses the South Hill Chamber of Commerce, the South Hill Model Railroad Museum, a wildlife exhibition, and the Virgina S. Evans Doll Museum. (SHM.)

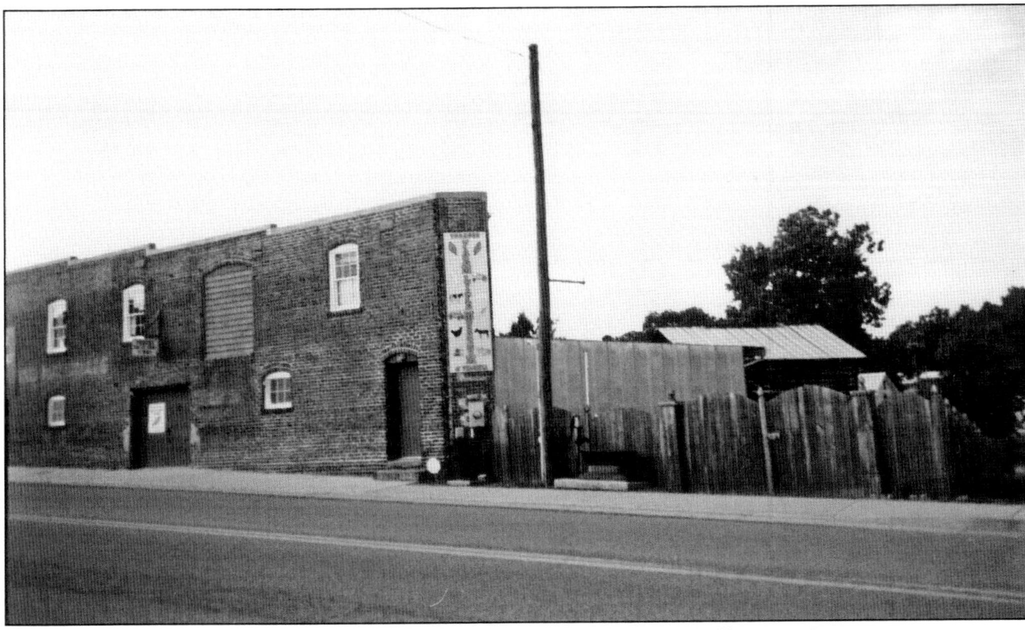

After the Harness and Tack Shop went out of business, South Hill Manufacturing constructed this triangular-shaped building. It is reported that the building had a spur railroad track that ran alongside it so the office staff could inspect and invoice the load of lumber. It has since served as the South Hill Tobacco and Family Farm Life Museum with a fully restored tobacco barn in the backyard. (SHM.)

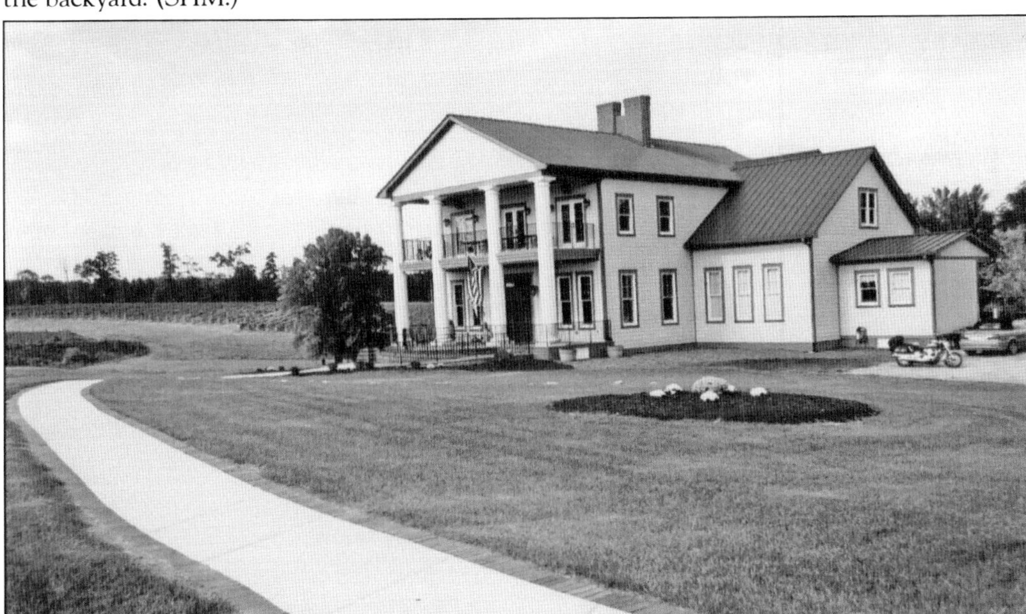

Rosemont continues to thrive today. In the hands of the fifth- and sixth-generation Rose family members, it continues to thrive as a productive farm. Instead of a truck farm, today there are vineyards of grapes and orchards of blueberries. The winery is in the basement of this building, and the family employs a winemaker from France as a consultant to teach, test, and taste the wines for the best. (Rosemont Vineyard and Winery.)